MOTHER EARTH NEWS

GUIDE TO
Vegetable
Gardening

VOYAGEUR
PRESS

contents

1
GETTING STARTED

an introduction to vegetable gardening

by Susan Sides

"I farm the soil that yields my food. I shared creation.
Kings can do no more." —Ancient Chinese Proverb

IF YOU'RE COMING to this book with some garden know-how already under your belt, then you already have a good idea of what you're in for when it comes to growing! If you've picked up this book because you're just getting into gardening, then congratulations! And welcome to the 44 percent of American families who share an addiction that we euphemistically call a hobby. Oh, you'll hear the same old rationalizations from most of us: we're gardening to save money, to keep fit, to put good food on the table, or to spend time outdoors. And those reasons might have provided motivation when we were at the same beginning gardening stage as you.

As you'll come to know, though, what makes us pull out our tools year after year is the sheer wonder of sticking that pinhead-sized little ball of a broccoli seed into the ground and—*ta-da!*—eventually harvesting something that holds up the hollandaise. Big crop, little crop—it doesn't matter really. As much fuss is made when just one fine head ripens as when we cart off bushels.

In short, it's being smack-dab in the middle of a real-life miracle that makes this pastime pretty hard to resist. Who can get enough of it? Building a cabinet or piecing a quilt just isn't quite the same. Only gardening (and having children) lets you stand so close to the miracle of life that, like the ancient Chinese proverb quoted on the facing page says, you feel as if you're sharing in creation.

Yes, welcome to gardening. None of us can ever claim to really know the territory. We're all learning as we grow. Each year's a mystery—a renewed challenge—during which you'll reap plenty of mouth-watering vegetables at the very least. What's more important, you'll occasionally have the opportunity to feel like the only person who ever saw a honeybee wake up after spending the night on a morning glory, or the only soul who's seen the wind rattle a corn leaf, making the plant appear to be scratching its own back. And like a brand-new parent, you'll be blind to the beauty of any broccoli other than your own.

GETTING STARTED

When learning to ride a bicycle, you don't read up on aerodynamics, physics, gravity, and inertia. Instead, you simply ask someone how to start, steer, and stop the thing, then hop on and give it a go. And you keep hopping on until you're pedaling vertically. The same goes for gardening. You might want to find at least one neighbor who's gardened in your area awhile and pester him or her to death (the odds are great that most gardeners won't mind at all). Then simply go get your fingernails dirty. To get you started, I offer the following basic advice. (You'll have to find the neighbor yourself.)

Soil testing is the map to any good fertilization program; it tells you how to "get there from here."

1. **Learn your climate zone:** it's on that little map you'll see in seed catalogs or some gardening books. Climate zones are bands where weather conditions (average rainfall and temperature) fall into the same range, and seed catalogs will list (by number) which ones are suitable for certain plants.
2. **Memorize your first and last frost dates:** planting times for everything from radish seeds to fruit trees depend on when frosts occur in your location.
3. **Know your soil's makeup:** have a soil test done. (See "Soil Fertilization" on page 8.)
4. **Be aware of available warm- and cool-weather crops:** some vegetables grow best in warm weather and some in cool.
5. **Look into local clubs:** check the library or chamber of commerce for a list of garden-related clubs, organic growers' organizations, and native plant societies. They are widespread, and their members will be more than willing to help you get started.

SOIL FERTILIZATION

Soil testing is the map to any good fertilization program; it tells you how to "get there from here." It's all too easy to waste money and risk nutrient imbalances by guessing at what your soil needs. Labs whose personnel are not chemically oriented will give custom-tailored recommendations in terms of compost and such natural amendments as rock powders and animal bone, and blood byproducts that are dried, ground, and bagged. These additives break down more slowly than synthetic fertilizers, are gentler to plants and soil, and are much less likely to be leached away.

Best of all, "natural" soil-testing firms speak a language you can understand. Granted, the local agricultural extension service, home kits, and many standard labs are much cheaper—but will you know what to do with all those unexplained numbers and equations?

Fall is the best time to send samples for evaluation, and you should plan to prepare for next year's garden this autumn. I guarantee the results will be quicker than in this year's unavoidable last-minute spring rush.

With clean utensils, and without touching the soil with your hands, gather samples at a depth of from 6 to 8 inches, and do so in ten to fifteen places around the garden. Mix the soil thoroughly to create a composite specimen. Secure at least a pound of dirt in a plastic bag enclosed in a small but sturdy box, and mail it off. To continue your soil journey, you'll find much more, starting on page 45.

GARDENING TOOLS

I'll bet a quart of fresh raspberries that no two sheds in America contain the exact same set of garden tools. My neighbor's traditional hoe has a deep, smooth gully worn in the handle from years of use. I, however, tended to avoid hoes until I discovered the more recently introduced stirrup kind.

Equip yourself with at least the basics, some of which you may already have. You can always add more equipment if and as the need (or, let's face it, simple covetousness) arises. For starters, round up a wheelbarrow, leaf rake, garden rake, trowel, soil-turning tool of choice (motorized tiller or garden fork), spade, hoe, and sharp knife (for harvesting, cutting twine, etc.). Add some quality hoses, a few sprinklers, and a hose attachment (such as a fan sprayer or, better yet, a watering wand) for watering by hand. You'll also need a hammer, pegs, and twine for laying out lines and patterns, plant tags, a file for keeping a sharp edge on things, buckets (plastic are often free for the asking), and an assortment of empty containers (coffee cans, milk jugs, and such).

After you've obtained the basics, anything you can imagine—from the practical to the absurd—is out there for your pleasure. I'm pretty sure I can forgo ornate brass faucet handles and copper watering cans, but don't ask me to give up my soft-spray nozzle attachment, hand pruners, or minimum-maximum thermometer.

SITE SELECTION

Think big—dream of future orchards, vine-covered walkways, and stone walls—but start small. A compact garden will leave you with enough time to get to know

your piece of earth and the plants and insects that share it with you; time to do things right.

Think weather. The placement of a garden, even within the framework of a small lot, can significantly determine how much energy you'll have to expend battling the elements. Generally speaking, hillsides are better locations than either the tops of hills (where wind can batter plants) or the bottoms (where water and cold air accumulate). A south-facing slope gets the most sun and turns its back on cold north winds. Western slopes allow frozen plants to thaw slowly, though higher overall temperatures occur there than on east-facing hillsides, which shelter heat-sensitive plants in midsummer. And even northern slopes can be put to good use as orchard sites, since lingering spring cold can keep early buds from opening too soon.

You might not know it, but there's a great little microclimate on the south side of your house or outbuilding, which offers protection against north winds and provides mass to absorb radiant heat during the day and slowly release it at night. Lakes and ponds also reflect heat and light onto edge-of-the-water plants, but sometimes they provide open pathways for winds as well.

Watch what happens to rain- and snowfall. Does the ground drain or puddle? Does snow melt quickly (a sunny spot) or linger for days (possibly too shady)? Will crops get at least 6 to 8 hours of direct sunlight each day?

Think water. Is the area in mind close to a source of reliable, easily tapped water? If not, consider what it will take (laying pipe, purchasing a pump, etc.) to bring the life-giving liquid to your crops.

All factors considered, it pays to choose a location close to your house. The farther you must go to weed the carrots or pull some greens for dinner, the greater the chance you won't. If you're lucky enough to have several small sites, plant herbs, lettuce, tomatoes—things you cook with most often—within plucking distance of the kitchen door.

The placement of a garden, even within the framework of a small lot, can significantly determine how much energy you'll have to expend battling the elements.

Last, but not least, kick the dirt around a little. Dig up a spadeful at each potential site. Handle it, squeeze it, smell it. Crumbly, loose, and sweet-smelling earth will be easier to work with than soil that feels like modeling clay or sand that sifts through open fingers.

There, that didn't take too long, did it? And now, get out the champagne, straw hat, and red-ribboned spade—it's finally time to break ground.

SITE PREPARATION

If weeds and grass now stand tall where your dreams call for corn and tomatoes, top them with a mower or swing blade, pile the cuttings near the site of your compost heap, and consider yourself fortunate to have found a good source of organic matter. Then, pull out any large rocks and clear the area of trash.

Now stand back and once again envision that garden-to-be. Try to put borders on that dream. To do so, simply ask yourself, how much time will I honestly be able (and willing) to devote to this garden?

A postage-stamp plot (so called for its tiny dimensions) is perfect for people with busy schedules. One or, at the most, two 4-by-20-foot raised beds or a single 20-by-20-foot row plot is garden enough for most folks to start with. For those who can (and will) put in 4 to 6 hours per week of garden time, four 4-by-20-foot raised beds or one 20-by-40-foot row plot can produce all the fresh vegetables needed by a family of four, and then some.

Areas that have been in sod for many years are among the toughest to prepare. So is heavy clay. In the best of all worlds, you'd be able to first turn the soil in fall and plant a winter cover crop to break up hard clods and choke out grass. If the turf has a persistent root system, remove it, roots and all, and shake the topsoil back onto the plot. Small areas can be worked by hand with a spade and fork; large plots will probably require a garden tiller or tractor (you might borrow or rent this tool, at least for the first year).

And how thoroughly should you work your soil? If you're doing the job by hand, try to break up the soil thoroughly to at least the depth of your garden fork's tines. A rake can be handy for the final shaping and pulverizing of the seed-bed. Double-digging, a technique used to prepare wide raised beds, is very popular among our staff. This involves first using a spade to remove the upper soil to about a foot in depth, then loosening the undersoil to the depth of a garden fork's tines, and finally replacing the removed soil to produce a "huffed" bed that's higher than the surrounding soil and loosened to a depth of almost 2 feet.

Previously used garden sites are, of course, relatively easy to prepare, and you should think seriously about using one, if available. Whatever the situation, as you work and shape the soil, incorporate an inch of compost (purchased, if you haven't had time to make your own yet) and the natural amendments recommended in the results of your soil test. Again, this would best be done in fall to give these slow-releasing fertilizers a chance to break down, though spring is a good second choice.

Now it's time to give yourself a pat on the back. Behind you is some of the hardest work you'll ever need to tackle in the garden.

GARDEN CULTURE

At this stage, the garden looks orderly—but somehow timid—with its small green points of life hopefully punctuating the brown of the soil. But those green dots will quickly spread, so don't blink or you'll miss something. Make sketches; take notes and photographs. Enjoy the full spring blush of colors and textures, the bounty of late summer, and the rebirth of fall (which can be much like a second spring).

Throughout the year, your care will ensure your plants a long and healthful life. Perhaps the most important job is to learn how and when to water. Plants need ample liquid, and what rain doesn't provide, you'll have to. Whenever you think things look dry, dig down a finger's depth to see how much moisture is in the root zone. Sandy soil loses moisture rapidly, while clay can be hard to drain. When you decide it's time to water, do so deeply. Shallow watering encourages shallow roots that become susceptible to drought and are unable to anchor plants.

Early mornings and late afternoons are the best times to water. You'll lose less to evaporation, and plants will have a good supply to carry them either through the night (when much of their actual growing is taking place) or through the heat of midday.

Second, give heavy-feeding crops additional nutrition by side-dressing them with compost or dosing them with manure tea or nursery-purchased fish-emulsion tea. Do this several times a season for nonfruiting plants (spinach, lettuce, cabbage, potatoes), but not after flowering for fruit bearers (tomatoes, cucumbers, squash, eggplant).

Pull weeds when they're young. It's easier on you to cart out handfuls now instead of armfuls later—and it's easier on your plants too.

Third, be on the lookout for insects and disease. Catching a problem early can mean the difference between a Band-Aid or a coffin to your crops. Actually, many insects are on your side, consuming hundreds of their damaging kin every day.

Fourth, pull weeds when they're young. It's easier on you to cart out handfuls now instead of armfuls later—and it's easier on your plants too. You can actually get even by eating any edible weeds. Many, like lamb's quarters, are delicious and vitamin packed to boot (be sure of your identification before sampling any wild edibles).

There's an old saying that your shadow is your garden's best fertilizer, so, finally, be sure to spend time there. Not just time spent working, either. Construct a simple bench, picnic table, barbecue, or sandbox—put up a hammock—anything to give people an excuse to play in the garden.

WRAPPING UP THE YEAR

There's a simple way to have a zero-maintenance crop of greenery when other gardens are only a brown memory—to have a crop that checks erosion, aerates soil, and supplies spring compost material. Sound too good to be true? As (or even just before) each vegetable crop is harvested, sow a cover crop in its place. We use winter rye mixed with hairy vetch.

Before the weather gets too cold, gather up garden tools, clean them, and rub them down with vegetable oil. Run the gasoline out of power machines, and store all tools under cover.

Bring in hoses, trellises, stakes, benches, and anything else that winter will wear hard on. Remove plant debris to the compost pile, and tidy up any trash. If you have carrots, leeks, parsnips, or other overwintering crops in the ground, mark them with visible stakes for easy location under snow.

Crowfoot, a Blackfoot warrior and orator, was a gardener, though not in our sense of the word. His plot was that which man neither planted nor tended—nature's garden—the out-of-doors. With his dying words he reflects on this garden and the lessons he learned there.

"What is life?" he questions—and answers, "It is the flash of a firefly in the night. It is the breath of a buffalo in the wintertime. It is the little shadow which runs across the grass and loses itself in the sunset."

There's no end to these little miracles that await your observation in the garden. Soon you'll be adding trees, shrubs, and small fruits, or perhaps designing an entranceway of climbing roses. Maybe you'll save your own seeds, build a small pond or a simple birdhouse, or just learn to identify praying mantis egg cases and watch as the tiny hatchlings pour out.

When you think about it, the real miracle, after all, may be not in the procession of growth in the garden but in the birth and development of a brand-new gardener.

The edible landscape in action: instead of a flowering vine, garden writer Mary-Kate Mackey planted grapevines at the corners of this pergola in her Oregon backyard retreat. It gives her outdoor dining area fresh fruit *and* a European feel.

cultivating beauty and bounty

by Rosalind Creasy

AMERICANS COVER MILLIONS of acres of valuable agricultural land around their homes with lawn, marigold and azalea beds, wisteria, and an occasional privet or maple. Yet as a landscape designer, I know most edible plants are beautiful and that homeowners could grow a meaningful amount of food in their yards—a much more noble use of the soil.

Instead of the typical landscape, we could minimize lawn areas and put in decorative borders of herbs, rainbow chard, and striking paprika peppers. Instead of the fleeting color of spring azaleas, we could grow blueberries that are decorative year-round—or pear and plum trees that put on a spring show of flowers, have decorative fruits, and yellow fall foliage. These plants aren't just pretty; they provide scrumptious fruit and can save you money.

THE FUTURE IS NOW

I'm convinced that in addition to being a viable design option, an edible landscape (if maintained using organic methods) is the most compelling landscape concept for the future. Edible landscapes offer incredible benefits:

- **Energy Savings:** Food from your yard requires no shipping, little refrigeration, and less energy to plow, plant, spray, and harvest.
- **Food Safety:** You know which chemicals (if any) you use, and huge batches of vegetables won't be combined and therefore can't contaminate each other.
- **Water Savings:** Tests show that most home gardeners use less than half the water that agricultural production needs to produce a crop. Drip irrigation saves even more. And unlike in agriculture, fields aren't flooded and huge vats of water aren't needed to cool down the harvest.
- **Money Savings:** You can grow an unbelievable amount of food in a small, beautiful space.
- **Better Nutrition:** Fully ripe, just-picked homegrown fruits and vegetables, if eaten soon after picking, have more vitamins than supermarket produce, which was usually picked under-ripe and is days or weeks old when you eat it.

DESIGNING YOUR EDIBLE LANDSCAPE

Any landscape design begins with choosing the location of the paths, patios, fences, hedges, arbors, and garden beds—establishing the "bones" of your garden. This is critically important in an edible garden because the beds are more apt to have plants with a wide array of textures, sizes, and shapes, such as frilly carrot leaves, mounding peppers, and climbing beans. Edible garden beds may be filled with young seedlings or even be empty at times. That's when paths, arbors, fences, hedges, and even a birdbath are vital for keeping things attractive.

Next, plan your style by asking some questions: Do you want a formal or informal garden? Do you prefer a theme—maybe early colonial or Spanish? How about whimsical areas with a scarecrow or whirligigs? Have you always dreamed of a bright yellow gate welcoming folks into your garden?

After you've determined the setup of the landscape, it's time to choose the plants. Herein lies the true subtlety of the landscaper's art. First, make a list of edibles you like most and that grow well in your climate, noting their cultural needs. Be aware of their size, shape, and the color of their foliage and flowers or the fruit they produce (if any). Do you crave lots of hot reds and oranges, or do you prefer a cooler scene with lavenders, grays, and shades of blue? If fragrance is important, consider the scent of apple and plum blossoms, or heady basils and lavenders.

With your list of plants in hand, create areas of interest. You could create a curved line of frilly-leafed chartreuse lettuces or a row of blueberry shrubs whose blazing fall color can lead your eye down a brick path and to your entry. Instead of the predictable row of lilacs along the driveway, imagine a mixed hedge of currants, gooseberries, and blueberries. The possibilities are limited only by your imagination.

PLANT COMBINATIONS TO INSPIRE YOU

Not everything in your landscape has to be edible. Consider these colorful combos (*inedible plants):

- A geometric design of orange tulips* underplanted with mesclun salad mix and bordered with parsley or frilly lettuces
- Red or orange cherry tomatoes growing over an arbor interplanted with blue or purple morning glories*
- Cucumbers climbing a trellis to form a backdrop for a splash of coral gladioli*
- Gold zucchini and yellow dahlias* bordered by red zinnias* and purple basil
- A bed of fernlike carrots surrounded by dwarf nasturtiums

The charming structure of designer Linda Vater's Oklahoma City vegetable garden is extremely effective. The flagstone paths, clipped boxwood hedge, scarecrow, arbor, and bench area draw you in. Long after Vater has harvested the basil, parsley, peppers, and tomatoes, this garden remains wonderfully inviting.

Who would think humble romaine lettuces could form the centerpiece of a decorative patio garden bed? To create this design, purchase an inexpensive vertical wood trellis, cut off the two legs, then paint it an inviting color, such as this soft purple. After laying it on the prepared soil, plant a single lettuce in each square. As the lettuce grows, continually harvest a few outer leaves from each plant to maintain the design. Oregano, cilantro, mustard, flax, and nonedible hens-and-chicks frame the vignette.

- A path bordered with dwarf red runner beans backed with giant red-and-white-striped peppermint zinnias*
- A wooden planter overflowing with strawberries and burgundy-leaved cannas*

GET STARTED!

As we all try to do our part to protect the planet and our own health, finding ways to grow more of our own food is a worthy goal. So how do you start your edible landscape? You could replace a few shrubs with easily grown culinary herbs and salad greens. The next step may be to add a few strawberry or rhubarb plants to your flower border. And maybe this is the time to finally take out a few hundred square feet of sunny lawn in your front yard to create a decorative edible border instead.

easy kitchen gardening

by Roger Doiron

IN ITS SIMPLEST form, a kitchen garden produces fresh fruits, vegetables, and herbs for delicious, healthy meals. A kitchen garden doesn't have to be right outside the kitchen door, but the closer it is, the better. Think about it this way: the easier it is for you to get into the garden, the more likely it is that you will get tasty things out of it. Did you forget to add the chopped dill on your boiled red-skinned potatoes? No problem—it's just steps away.

STARTING A KITCHEN GARDEN

If you have to choose between a sunny spot or a close one, pick the sunny one. The best location for a new garden is one receiving full sun (at least 6 hours of direct sunlight per day) and one where the soil drains well. If no puddles remain a few hours after a good rain, you know your site drains well.

After you've figured out where the sun shines longest and strongest, your next task will be to define your kitchen garden goals. My first recommendation for new gardeners is to start small, tuck a few successes under your belt in year one, and scale up little by little.

But what if you're really fired up about it? Even in year one, you may be able to meet a big chunk of your family's produce needs. In the case of my garden in Scarborough, Maine, we have 1,500 square feet under cultivation, which yields enough to meet nearly half of my family of five's produce needs for the year. When you do the garden math, it comes out to 300 square feet per person. More talented gardeners with more generous soils and climates are able to produce more food in less space, but maximizing production is not our only goal. We're also trying to maximize pleasure and health, both our own and that of the garden. Kitchen gardens and gardeners thrive because of positive feedback loops. If your garden harvests taste good and make you feel good, you will feel more motivated to keep on growing.

PREPARING THE GARDEN SITE

If you're starting your kitchen garden on a patch of lawn, you can build up from the ground with raised beds or plant directly in the ground. Building raised beds is a good idea if your soil is poor or doesn't drain well and you like the look of containers made from wood, stone, or corrugated metal. This approach is usually more expensive, however, and requires more initial work than planting in the ground.

Think carefully about the best garden location—the closer to your kitchen, the better.

Whether you're going with raised beds or planting directly in the ground, you'll need to decide what to do with the sod. You can remove it and compost it, which is hard work but ensures that you won't have grass and weeds coming up in your garden. If you're looking to start a small or medium-sized garden, it's possible to cut and remove sod in neat strips using nothing more than a sharp spade and some back muscle. For removing grass from a larger area, consider renting a sod cutter.

Otherwise, to avoid sod removal altogether, you can use a technique called sheet mulching or lasagna gardening whereby you smother the grass with one or more layers of organic goodness (untreated cardboard, newspaper, loam, compost, leaves, grass clippings, etc.) in such a way that the grass underneath dies and decomposes, enriching the soil with organic matter. Sheet mulching is particularly effective for kitchen gardens started in the fall, as the sod has more of a chance to break down over the winter. One variation on sheet mulching is to use instant garden beds, which are made by laying out bags of topsoil to form beds.

CHOOSING GARDEN CROPS

The most important recommendation after "start small" is "start with what you like to eat." This may go without saying, but I have seen first-year gardens that don't reflect the eating habits of their growers—a recipe for disappointment. That said, I believe in experimenting with one or two new crops per year that aren't necessarily favorites for the sake of having diversity in the garden and on our plates.

One of the easiest and most rewarding kitchen gardens is a simple salad garden. Lettuces and other greens don't require much space or maintenance, and they grow quickly. Consequently, they can produce multiple harvests in most parts of the country. If you plant a "cut-and-come-again" salad mix, you can grow five to ten different salad varieties in a single row. And if you construct a cold frame (which can be cheap and easy if you use salvaged storm windows), you can grow some hearty salad greens year-round.

When it comes to natural flavor enhancers, nothing beats culinary herbs. Every year I grow standbys such as parsley, chives, sage, basil, tarragon, mint, rosemary, and thyme, but I also make an effort to try one or two new ones. One consequence of this approach is that I end up expanding my garden a little bit each year, but that's okay, because my skills and gastronomy are expanding in equal measure, as are my sense of satisfaction and food security.

GARDEN SEEDS OR TRANSPLANTS?

When the time comes to plant your kitchen garden, you'll need to decide which plants to start from seed and which to buy as transplants. Many gardeners choose to plant all of their crops from seed for a variety of reasons, including lower costs, greater selection, and the challenge and satisfaction of seeing a plant go from seed to soup bowl. But whether you're a greenhorn or a green thumb, there's no shame in buying seedlings. Doing so increases your chances of success, especially with crops such as eggplants, peppers, and tomatoes, which require a long growing season.

MULCH, MULCH . . . AND MORE MULCH

After you've sown your seeds or planted your plants, introduce yourself to the kitchen gardener's best friend, Mr. Mulch. Just about any organic matter you can get your hands on—straw, grass clippings, pine needles, shredded leaves, dead weeds that haven't gone to seed—can be used as mulch. I bring in mulch from neighbors who would otherwise throw it away. Mulch plays three main roles: it deters weeds, helps retain moisture, and adds organic matter to the soil as it decays. I apply it to the pathways between my beds and around all of my plants.

WHEN AND HOW MUCH TO WATER YOUR GARDEN

Fruits and vegetables are made mostly of water, so you'll need to make sure your plants are getting enough to drink. This is especially important for seedlings that haven't developed a deep root structure. You'll want to water them lightly every day or two. Once the crops are maturing, they need about an inch of water per week, and more in sandy soils or hot regions. If Mother Nature isn't providing that amount of rain, you'll need to water manually or with a drip irrigation system.

GARDEN MAINTENANCE: KEEP AN EYE ON IT

Sun and rain willing, fast growers such as radishes and salad greens will begin to produce crops as early as 20 to 30 days after planting. Check on them regularly so you get to harvest them before someone else does. In my garden, those "some-ones" include everything from the tiniest of bacteria to the largest of raccoons. Various protective barriers and organic products can deter pests and diseases, and if you have trouble with rabbits, deer, or other four-legged critters, your best defense may be a garden fence.

SUCCESSION PLANTING: PLANT NOW AND LATER

Getting the most pleasure and production from your garden comes from learning the beauty of succession planting. Rather than trying to "get your garden in" during one busy weekend, space your planting out over the course of several weeks by using short rows. Every time you harvest a row or pull one out that has stopped producing, try to plant a new one. Succession plantings lead to succession harvests spread out over several months—one of the key characteristics of a kitchen garden.

As you gain new confidence and skills, you can look for ways to incorporate perennials including asparagus and rhubarb into your edible landscape. And no discussion of kitchen gardens would be complete without mentioning flowers, which should be added from the start. Flowers add beauty and color to the garden and the kitchen table. They also attract beneficial insects while, in some cases, repelling undesirable ones.

JOIN THE KITCHEN GARDEN REVOLUTION!

What started as a whisper has quickly grown into a full-throated chorus of people calling for a kitchen garden revolution. The resurgence of kitchen

You'll be wise to employ much mulch throughout the growing season.

With a kitchen garden, families can be happier and more active by growing awesome food with their own hands.

gardens couldn't come at a more relevant time in our nation's history, or in that of the planet.

Concerns about food safety are nothing to sneeze at, considering foods as seemingly benign as spinach and peanut butter have been contaminated with harmful *E. coli* bacteria in recent years. You can't bank on the nutrition of grocery store fare, either. The commercially grown foods we're eating today are significantly less nutritious than they were just 30 years ago. Breeding crops for higher yields has delivered cheaper food, but it has also diluted nutrients.

Over the next few decades, the international community will face health, food security, and environmental challenges more daunting than any civilization has ever faced. The United Nations estimates that food production would need to increase by 70 percent to feed the projected global population of 9 billion in 2050. Plus, we'll need to grow our food in an unstable climate with a greatly depleted natural resource base.

While the challenge facing poor countries is too little food production, one of the challenges in wealthy ones is too much of the wrong type. Sixty-eight percent of the American adult population is now overweight, and 28 percent of it is obese. The situation with children is even more alarming. According to the Centers for Disease Control and Prevention, one in three children will develop type 2 diabetes in their lifetime, one in two if the child is black or Hispanic.

But before you hurl yourself onto the nearest compost pile in despair, I've got some good news: the solutions to many of these problems are as close as your own backyard. What we need are millions of new people joining the movement by planting healthy kitchen gardens of their own or, in the case of existing gardeners, converting their summer veggie plots into more productive four-season gardens. You can also connect with gardeners in your area to help other people and groups (schools, clubs, companies, retirement communities, food pantries, etc.) start gardens.

A garden that is efficiently laid out and attractive to look at will become a productive food garden that is more fun to work in. It will take a few years to develop a garden as pleasant to work in as this one.

creating a permanent food garden

by Barbara Pleasant

DEVELOPING AN ORGANIC garden is a long-term proposition. Each infusion of compost or mulch that melds with soil nudges organic matter content higher, until eventually you have soil you can work with your bare hands. Do you see this process happening in your garden, along with other signs of maturity such as fewer weeds and easier overall upkeep? As the season winds down, look around and consider your garden's progress as a sustainable system. Then do what you must to enhance its efficiency in the seasons ahead.

One of the first signs of a garden's maturity is the emergence of permanent beds. They need not be raised beds, because it's the constancy, not the height, that matters. Why is permanence so important? Corridors and pathways become compacted each time you step on them, and after a while they can become so compressed that even weeds won't grow there. Cultivated space, on the other hand, becomes downright fluffy if you avoid walking on it and add organic matter regularly. Soon the only cultivation will be a simple matter of forking the soil by hand between plantings.

In some of my terraced hillside beds that haven't felt human footprints in years, when I lose my balance and fall in, I sink down 4 inches. Each such tumble squeezes out air (and squashes thousands of busy soil-dwelling microcritters). If you have a well-designed system of permanent beds, broad corridors, and narrower pathways, you can concentrate water and fertilizer onto the areas where crops are growing. To improve upon the design you already have, make rough drawings with pencil and paper, and consider how various bed configurations might help your garden work better. Here are some things to keep in mind when you're gardening for keeps.

MANAGING MAIN CORRIDORS

Depending on your garden's size, you may need only one main wide corridor that can accommodate big things such as wheelbarrows, tillers, or mowers, with secondary pathways branching off from there. A large garden may need two or three wide lanes. In addition to providing all-weather access, the main corridors serve as the garden's utility area, so it makes sense to have water, compost, and a spot for stashing tools, pots, stakes, and buckets somewhere in this space. One of the best improvements I've made was to build a sturdy worktable next to the main compost pile; both are along the edge of the garden's main corridor. The table is a natural magnet for tools and supplies, and it's the perfect spot to groom veggies before they come into the house.

Wide corridors get a lot of traffic, but like the row middles in fruit orchards, they are not too compacted to support grasses, clovers, and other low-growing plants. Letting corridors go green helps them double as habitat for ground beetles, earthworms, and other beneficial life forms (some that we can see and some that we can't). Clippings gathered from mowing the corridors can be used to mulch nearby beds.

SIZING UP GARDEN BEDS

What balance of bed and pathway dimensions gives the most efficient use of space? After experimenting with several bed sizes, agricultural researchers at the Samuel Roberts Noble Foundation research farm in Ardmore, Oklahoma, settled on 40-inch-wide beds separated by 20-inch-wide pathways as their high-efficiency choice. The Noble Foundation beds are raised, but 40 inches is also a good width for in-ground beds because you can step over or straddle them.

Symmetry is always tempting, but don't assume that your garden should consist of uniformly sized beds connected to a central corridor. As you play around with the best sizes for your permanent beds, you may find that a mix of bed sizes will work better for you in the long run.

For example, let's say you grow sweet corn, winter squash, watermelons, or other crops that need a block of space, so you will need two or more unusually wide beds. Other beds might be sized to suit trellised beans or peas, or tomatoes grown in custom-built cages. Smaller beds, on the other hand, make it easy to keep up with successive sowings of salad greens, radishes, and other come-and-go veggies.

Bed length reaches a point of diminishing returns too. If you have to keep trudging down to the end of a long row and make a turn to get to the other side, you're working too hard. This problem is easy to fix by using boards as temporary overpasses that allow you to walk across wide beds. Whenever a task requires you to step on a permanent bed, standing on a board will distribute your weight and limit compaction. When you're not using your "garden boards" as standing stations, they can come in handy for holding down fabrics or trapping slugs.

PAVING GARDEN PATHWAYS

The pathways between beds are important workspaces, and they have an uncanny talent for becoming broader as the season progresses. When working permanent beds that are not framed, you will probably need to re-dig bed edges that have turned into pathways at least once a year to undo the damage caused by compaction.

For the first year or two, you can let pathways go green and mow them, but as compaction increases over time, very few plants are likely to grow in heavily used pathways. Just like trampled footpaths in the park, repeated footfalls eventually make garden pathways unsuitable for plants. This is good! It means less mowing or hoeing, and you should be able to keep pathways clear with durable mulch, such as wood chips, which are often free from tree-trimming crews. You can place sections of wet newspaper or cardboard under wood chips or any other mulch to enhance weed deterrence, but stay away from non-biodegradable weed barriers. After organic matter accumulates on top of fabrics or plastics, weeds start pushing their roots through the stuff, and in my experience you end up with a mess of weeds and shredded plastic or geotextile fibers.

Plan a place to relax and enjoy the fruits of your labor.

These homemade hose guides make it easier to move hoses around in your garden.

Factor in appearance as you choose pathway mulches. If your vegetable garden is your favorite destination in your yard, let it look the part. There is nothing wrong with going for the well-groomed look of shredded hardwood mulch (undyed, of course). Sawdust mulch keeps its neat good looks all summer, or you can use hay, straw, or pine needles. Experiment with various pathway treatments using locally available materials until you find a plan that pleases your eyes, your feet, and your garden.

WHAT GOES WHERE IN THE GARDEN

If you divide your garden into zones based on how much and how often each area is used, you will probably find that culinary herb beds, composting spots, and the clutter-prone area near the water faucet receive the heaviest traffic. Bringing these elements together into a garden control center can streamline maintenance in a hard-working food garden.

We know better, but few of us put away all of our tools and toys at the end of a gardening session. At my house, digging forks and hand trowels became much easier to find after I marked the handles with red plastic tape or paint, and I seldom lose brightly colored gardening gloves, buckets, or trugs.

You will never again drag a hose over a newly planted seedling if your beds are protected by hose guides, which can be purely practical (pieces of 1-inch pipe placed over rebar stakes) or as whimsical as you dare (old golf clubs or croquet mallets stuck into the ground). The best hose guards rotate when a hose rubs against them, so any weatherproof cylinder that can be popped over a sturdy stake will do. To blend function with beauty, cut a pipe into 12- to 16-inch pieces, paint the pieces with metallic copper paint, and then use silicone caulk to mount large marbles (such as what you'd find at toy stores) on one end of each piece. Slip over rebar stakes that protrude about 10 inches from the ground, and you have faux copper hose guides with glass finials.

THE PERMANENT GARDEN: FINISHING TOUCHES

Framing permanent beds is always optional, but dressing up your garden's front edge looks sharp and can add to its versatility. There's no need to spend time and money to build frames from lumber. High-visibility edges can be defined with logs, recycled cedar fence rails, pieces of firewood, or rocks placed over strips of old carpeting. A friend laid a single run of concrete blocks down the side of his garden closest to the water faucet, filled the openings with good soil, and then helped his 5-year-old turn the edge into his own little garden. Pieces of terracotta chimney pipe or drainage tile can be set into the ground vertically, filled with soil, and used to grow mints that might otherwise grab way too much space.

If you maintain the outer edges of your garden with your lawnmower, a hard edging may end up complicating your life, but the opposite will happen if you edge beds with flowers and herbs. Fragrant annual sweet alyssum attracts beneficial insects, and dwarf curly parsley dazzles in perimeter plantings. If you prefer, keep a clean edge with a ribbon of grass clippings allowed to accumulate where they fall. When it comes to gardening for keeps, the simplest ideas are usually the best.

2

CREATIVE
GARDENING
TECHNIQUES

small-space gardening

by Roger Doiron

NO SPACE IS too small for growing food. Whether your garden consists of a window box in the city or an acre in the country, you can still benefit from applying the techniques of small-space gardening.

SOIL IS NO SMALL MATTER

All successful gardening endeavors, big or small, start with fertile soil. If you have a large plot, you can get away with having less-fertile soil by planting more and spacing out your crops. In a small space, however, that approach simply doesn't work. When I was preparing my front yard garden back in 2008, I remember sifting my sandy soil through my fingers and realizing I had to improve it. I added lots of organic compost along with a little lime and bonemeal, and I add more organic matter each year.

The ideal soil type for growing most crops is loam, the rich halfway point between clay and sandy soils. If you're not sure which soil type you have, hold some in the palm of your hand, wet it, and try to make a ball. If it forms a tight, hard wad, then you have lots of clay in your soil. If you can't form a ball, you have sand. If the ball forms but pretty easily breaks apart, you probably have loam. No matter which type you have, you can improve both your soil's structure and fertility by working compost into the top layer each year. Those with really limited space can take heart in knowing there are effective composting options suitable for even the smallest of spaces.

GET INTENSE

Fertile soil that retains nutrients and water is one of the keys to success with intensive planting, which is a fancy way of saying planting a lot in a little area. America's intensive-growing tradition has two fathers: John Jeavons and Mel Bartholomew. In his classic 1974 book, *How to Grow More Vegetables (and Fruits, Nuts, Berries, Grains, and Other Crops) Than You Ever Thought Possible on Less Land Than You Can Imagine*, Jeavons introduced Americans to French intensive-gardening techniques, notably deep soil preparation through double-dug beds and intensive crop-planting patterns. Seven years later, Bartholomew offered a new way to think about these patterns in a classic book of his own, *Square Foot Gardening*.

Instead of rows, Jeavons and Bartholomew suggest planting in tightly spaced geometric patterns that will allow the crops to create a "living mulch" of foliage as they mature. This living mulch performs two of the main tasks that regular old

Opposite: Don't let limited growing space stop you from creating a bountiful garden. Learn about this impressive urban garden in London at www.verticalveg.org.uk.

In square-foot gardening, you create a grid and plant crops in 1-by-1-foot squares.

dead mulch does: keeping the soil moist and suppressing weeds.

In order to create this effect, however, you need to know how much space to give each plant. Mel Bartholomew's brilliantly simple tactic is to set a 1-by-1-foot grid onto a garden space and plant crops into the grid. Large crops such as broccoli, peppers, and cabbage require a whole square, whereas small ones such as carrots and radishes can be planted sixteen to a square.

One critical lesson the square-foot gardening technique can teach newbie small-space gardeners is that they may have to put their dreams of squash, watermelons, and potatoes on hold. For some, a garden without zucchini isn't really a garden. However, if faced with the choice of having one bush summer squash plant or one tomato plant, one cabbage, one pepper, one large basil, one broccoli, four lettuces, four chards, sixteen carrots *and* sixteen onions (i.e., the number and types of crops you could get out of the same square footage required for one squash plant), you would *really* have to love zucchini bread to choose the former.

Books such as Jeavons's and Bartholomew's can be invaluable for making planting decisions like these. For those looking for a more modern tool for deciding what to plant where and in what quantity, there are some excellent online garden planners available that allow you to sketch out your garden on your computer screen and drag and drop crops onto your layout. I think the best one so far is *MOTHER*'s interactive, easy-to-use Vegetable Garden Planner, found at www.motherearthnews.com/garden-planner/vegetable-garden-planner.aspx.

One last thing to keep in mind about an intensively planted geometric layout versus a row layout is that you won't walk between your crops but rather will reach into them. So, unless you happen to have the arm span of an orangutan, your beds shouldn't be wider than 3 or 4 feet. The length depends on the space you have and the amount of food you want to grow. Bartholomew recommends building wooden boxes for your beds, but you can get the same benefits by forming and planting into boxless, level mounds.

GO VERTICAL, BABY

One cool technique for increasing your choices and your harvests in a small-space garden is vertical growing, which some people refer to as cubed-foot gardening. As you can guess, it's about understanding and fully exploiting the vertical space plants can occupy.

I've seen this technique applied—or, more accurately, misapplied—in my own garden. My family and I rented our house and garden for a year to some lovely, well-meaning tenants who were eager to scratch at the dirt and decided to plant sunflowers in the southern part of our backyard garden. The plants thrived, reaching heights up to 9 feet, but the sun-starved squash planted behind them were not nearly as happy.

The first rule of vertical growing is knowing the heights of plants and situating the tallest ones in the northern part of your garden so as not to shade out the pip-squeaks. A more advanced lesson is learning the vertical space a crop is willing to *occupy* if coaxed and supported. While sunflowers shoot skyward without any cheerleading, crops such as tomatoes, cucumbers, and even melons are willing to grow upward if trellised and shown the way. Understanding these three dimensions of gardening will allow you to harvest more from each precious square foot of soil.

DON'T SETTLE FOR A SHORT SEASON

Another way to get more out of your small space is so cool that it's ice cold: season extension. Putting season extension to work will allow you to start gardening before your neighbors have even cracked their seed catalogs and finish long after they've stopped growing for the year. If Jeavons and Bartholomew are the patriarchs of America's intensive-planting movement, Maine farmer and garden writer Eliot Coleman is the father of season extension.

Casual small-space gardeners may not be interested in reading about Coleman's experiments with portable and minimally heated greenhouses, yet they could learn a lot from his writings on cold frames, which are essentially miniature greenhouses. Unlike a typical raised-bed container garden with sides that are all the same height, the south-facing side of a cold frame is shorter so that it lets in more of the sun's warming rays. The angle may not look like much, but as the sun starts to sink deeper in the autumn sky, those few extra degrees of slope translate into extra degrees of heat that can keep plants alive—and thriving!

Plant intensively in raised beds for maximum production.

If a deck or balcony is the only space where you can grow, go crazy with containers.

Get creative by planting wherever you can! You can even turn a wheelbarrow into a mini-garden.

If you're just starting a small-space garden, work a season-extension option into your design. For example, rather than building a typical raised-bed box, you may be better off with a sloping cold frame design. Other season-extension options for small-space gardens include low tunnels and cloches.

SUCCESS IN SUCCESSION

After you have a season-extension plan in place, you'll discover that your growing season has increased by several weeks, which is critical for implementing the small-space gardener's most important technique of all: succession planting. Small-space gardening is not just a voyage in space, but also time. Just as you should avoid unproductive gaps in your planting layout, you should also avoid holes in your planting calendar. Succession planting is about turning unproductive spaces into productive ones by removing a crop that has stopped producing and replacing it with a new one.

Here the challenge isn't simply understanding how tall or wide a crop grows but how long it takes to mature. Succession planting requires that we toss the traditional notion of "getting your garden in Memorial Day weekend" onto the compost pile of outdated ideas and replace it with a new approach in which the garden is never really "in" but always in the process of being planted. When we do this, we transform gardening from an isolated activity that we try to fit into our busy lives into a holistic lifestyle that can bring health and happiness.

COMPACT VARIETIES FOR SMALL-SPACE GROWING

Variety selection is more crucial to small-space gardening than you may think. The amount of space that a particular crop occupies can vary greatly from one variety to another. If you're gardening in limited space, especially containers, you should be looking for vegetable varieties listed as "compact" or, in the case of fruit trees, "dwarf."

- **'Alibi' Cucumber.** You'll need an alibi to tell your family after you've picked this short-vine variety clean and eaten all of the cukes yourself. Matures in 50 days.

- **'Bush Delicata' Squash.** If you absolutely must plant squash in your tiny space, 'Bush Delicata' is a good choice. This open-pollinated heirloom variety only spreads about 4 to 6 feet, and you can save its seeds for the next year.

- **'Compatto' Dill.** It may not grow any taller than 20 inches, but 'Compatto' will deliver the dill taste you need for salads and garnishes.

- **'Green Tiger' Zucchini.** This stout, bushy variety produces brilliant 6- to 8-inch fruits with glossy, dark green skin and pale stripes.

- **'Mohawk' Pepper.** Picture 4- to 5-inch brightly colored bell peppers spilling over your deck railing or window box, and you're picturing 'Mohawk'.

- **'Ophelia' Eggplant.** This one is perfect for the patio. The eggplants are small— a little more than 2 ounces each—and grow in clusters like tomatoes do.

- **'Temptation' Strawberry.** Compact, vigorous growth makes 'Temptation' well suited for hanging baskets, grow bags, and short-season climates.

- **'Totem' Tomato.** Growing no taller than 2 feet high and requiring no staking, 'Totem' offers big tomato taste in a small package.

- **'Tumbling Tom' Tomato.** 'Tumbling Tom' is a heavy yielder of beautiful bright red cherry tomatoes. Perfect for hanging baskets, as the tomatoes really do tumble over the edges.

CHOOSE YOUR SMALL-SPACE ADVENTURE

Here are my top suggestions for creating a productive garden within the constraints of whatever space you have to work with:

- **No Space:** If you have a large south-facing window, you can grow herbs and salad greens in pots, containers, or a window box. You may also succeed with container-grown crops such as tomatoes and peppers depending on the amount of sun you can provide them. The key to success is picking compact varieties suited to your taste and available space.

- **Small Balcony or Patio:** In addition to the options above, a person in this category can grow crops that require more sun and vertical space. For example, try growing large pots of strawberries or trellising cucumbers. The most inspiring gardener I know from this category is Mark Ridsdill Smith, who grows more than $1,000 worth of food each year on his 9-by-6-foot balcony and five south-facing window boxes in London.

- **Small Yard:** Perhaps choose plants that go well together. For example, you could plant a salad garden (i.e., different varieties of greens and lettuce), a soup garden (i.e., carrots, onions, and celery), or a salsa garden (i.e., tomatoes, peppers, and cilantro). For people just starting out and those growing in shady conditions, I think a small salad garden consisting of a few varieties of "cut-and-come-again" lettuce varieties or mesclun mixes, one to two favorite herbs, and a compact tomato plant or two is a great introduction to the pleasures of the kitchen garden. Leafy greens such as spinach and chard also do well in small, shady plots.

vertical gardening techniques

by Barbara Pleasant

WHETHER YOUR GARDEN is large or small, you can make better use of every square inch by using vertical gardening techniques to grow upright crops. Pole beans typically produce twice as many beans as bush varieties, and the right trellis can double cucumber yields. Then there are crops such as tomatoes that need some type of support to keep them above damp ground, where diseases have a heyday. All properly supported plants are easier to pick from and monitor for pests, plus you'll get help from bug-eating birds that use trellises as hunting perches.

Gardeners have invented or adapted a variety of implements to facilitate vertical gardening. Clockwise from top left: Rigid livestock panels do double duty as a fence and support for tomatoes, plus they can be bent to create an arched entry; saplings or bamboo poles are easy to use for pole bean tipis; pea tendrils love to cling to twiggy brush; and so-called tomato cages work better to support peppers and eggplants.

HOW PLANTS CLIMB

Plants that benefit from garden trellises use a variety of methods to cling to support, including curling tendrils, twining stems, or, in the case of tomatoes, long, ropy branches that form roots in places that touch the ground.

Curling tendrils produced by peas and cucumber-family crops will twist around whatever is available, so you have plenty of versatility when supporting these crops. Tendrils cling to horizontal and vertical parts of a trellis, so netting woven from biodegradable string attached to posts often works well. Twining stems spiral around their support, growing steadily upward until they turn back on themselves—a growth habit seen in hops, pole beans, Malabar spinach, and yard long beans.

Twining stems have little use for horizontal lines, so they do best with trellises composed mostly of poles or an upright fence.

Tomatoes like to throw themselves over their support. They must be trained and tied to an upright trellis, which isn't as easy as growing them in wire cages. The larger, more robust the tomato plant, the more you need a sturdy tomato cage that provides support on all sides.

TEMPORARY OR PERMANENT?

In my experience, a truly sturdy upright garden trellis must be anchored by T-stakes or vertical 4-by-4 posts (or 3-inch-diameter saplings from the woods) sunk 18 inches deep. Installing this semipermanent garden structure takes time and muscle. In my garden, the most versatile trellises are about 8 feet wide, stand 4 to 5 feet high, and are made of woven wire fencing or a livestock panel attached to two posts. Allowing 4 inches of clearance between the bottom of the fencing and the ground makes the area easier to weed and cultivate. The advantages of such a trellis are the ready availability of the structure each spring and the option to make an attractive permanent feature in the garden.

The drawback of this or any other long-lasting vertical gardening support (like an existing fence) is that it limits rotations to peas, beans, tomatoes, and cucumber-family crops. Temporary trellises, such as bamboo tipis, give you more flexibility in terms of what you plant where, but they need to be taken down and stored in a dry place through the winter to keep them from rotting. If you gather trellis parts, bind them together with string or strips of cloth in the fall, and store them over the winter, they will go up quickly the following season.

I make a number of temporary trellises every year, often by looping cotton, hemp, or jute lines around upright stakes or posts (what I call "string" is a ball of any of these natural biodegradable materials). By using biodegradable materials, I can snip down the trellis and pull out the plants at the same time, then throw it all on the compost pile.

Most tomatoes need tall, sturdy supports; stiff wire used to reinforce concrete works well.

Some crops climb using tendrils that can cling to netting or string.

CROP-SPECIFIC SUPPORTS

The most successful garden trellises increase the leaf-to-fruit ratio of the plant by allowing more leaves access to sun. A good support should also allow you to see and reach through the vines to harvest your crop, and it must be strong enough to hold its load.

Peas of any type (snow, snap, or shell) prosper if grown on a vertical trellis made by weaving string into a grid attached to two posts, starting with the horizontal lines. The stakes should be as high as the variety is expected to grow, which can range from 2 to 6 feet. Small bare branches stuck into the ground between plants will help lead pea seedlings to their support. Long-vined pea varieties often require extra support if they become top heavy with pods. One easy fix is to add four stakes, one at each outer corner of the planting. These stakes can anchor a corral made of two or three horizontal runs of string, up to 5 feet from the ground. Pea vines that lose their moorings will cascade over the strings, where they are wonderfully easy to pick from. Or try an old idea: using grains as pea supports. Overwintered cereal rye plants thinned to about 14 inches apart work great, though you will need a tall pea to make use of rye's 5-foot height.

To make the most of any pea trellis, "stack" the base of the trellis with both a short and a tall variety, such as 'Sugar Ann' snap peas with 'Sugar Snap'. The shorter variety will grow quickly, providing a little support for its slower-growing brethren, and it will start bearing just as the taller one begins to bloom.

Pole beans, runner beans, and asparagus beans become extremely heavy at maturity. Upright trellises must be sturdy or they can be pushed askew by summer thunderstorms. There is perhaps no better use for an existing woven-wire fence than to use it to support pole beans. So-called half-runner varieties are a perfect fit for a 4- to 5-foot-tall fence. If needed for longer-vined varieties, tall stakes can easily be added to increase the fence's height. You can attach these stakes with string to create a vision in vines. When I did this with a mixture of pole beans that produced yellow, purple, and green pods, the result was delightful.

Beans take off when given a tripod or tipi-style trellis, which naturally resists toppling because it pulls downward on itself as the weight it bears increases. You should carefully consider height when planning a bean trellis. Nothing is worse than watching beans go unpicked because you can't reach them without standing on something. You can control height to some extent by avoiding long-vined varieties, but you will need to limit the height of the trellis too.

Personally, I have two favorite bean trellises: a humble 3-foot-diameter woven wire tomato cage anchored with two metal fence posts for an early planting, and the stalks of sweet corn for a late-season trellis. Pole beans eagerly scramble up withering corn, and the corn doesn't mind as long as you wait until it's at least a foot tall to plant the beans.

Cucumber varieties vary in how well they take to a trellis. Large-fruited burpless hybrids can be easily trained up an upright grid-type trellis made of string or wire. Just push the growing vines through the mesh about once a week. Smaller pickling cucumbers tend to branch more, making them more unruly to train.

Woven-wire tomato cages contain their exuberance reasonably well and make the ripe fruits easier to find.

Melons offer a unique opportunity to use diagonal, or A-framed, trellises. Melon vines prefer to stay close to the ground, but raising them up protects them from diseases and insects that travel on the ground. Look for varieties that you should harvest at "forced slip," which means the melons must be cut from the vine when ripe. Small-fruited honeydews are excellent candidates for trellis culture.

If your garden space is tight and you don't think you have room for melons, think about connecting adjoining beds with an arch or A-frame trellis for this delicious summer fruit. This trick temporarily turns a pathway into usable aboveground gardening space.

Tomatoes growing in woven- or welded-wire cages need monitoring until you get to know a variety's unique growing habits, because the same trellis that satisfies a compact 'Juliet' will be a disaster with a gangly 'Brandywine'. The top choice for homemade cages is concrete reinforcing wire, which will last for years, and the 6-by-6-inch openings make picking easy. Make the cages in slightly descending diameters so they can nest together for storage.

Among ready-made cages, three-ring welded cages are adequate only for early determinate varieties. The four- and five-ring models can handle varieties of modest to average size and vigor, but most tomatoes will spew out the top and sides, and then start leaning toward the sun. Similarly, a lanky variety such as 'Sun Gold' can be trained and tied to an upright trellis or fence, but varieties that grow into dense 6-foot bushes, such as 'Black Krim' or 'Better Boy', need support on all sides, which is best provided by a cage. Even the best tomato cages become top heavy when the plants are in full fruit, so they should be well anchored to deeply set stakes.

Tall non-vining crops such as peppers and cutting zinnias benefit from some support. This is where the small tomato cages can be helpful. Place one cage in each corner of a bed, then thread twine around and through the cages, making a support matrix for the leggy plants.

Almost any garden can benefit from vertical gardening techniques: they save space, make harvesting easier, discourage soilborne disease, maximize production, and encourage beneficial bird activity.

Other plants, such as beans, twine their stems around whatever they touch.

make an inexpensive mini-greenhouse with low tunnels

by Barbara Pleasant

AT ANY TIME of year, a visitor to my Zone 6 garden will find at least a couple of low tunnels at work. Supported by wire hoops or arches made from wire fencing, my garden tunnels are covered with row cover and/or plastic when it's cold to create mini-greenhouses. During winter, they provide protection from wind, hail, and most critters while speeding soil warm-up for summer crops. In summer, I cover the greenhouse tunnels with lightweight row cover or tulle to exclude insect pests such as flea beetles and squash vine borers, and to provide shade for heat-sensitive crops such as lettuce. The cycle begins again when I plant fall-sown onions such as 'Olympic' and 'Top Keeper' or hardy greens inside my multipurpose, portable mini-greenhouses.

This portable greenhouse, made from 1-inch electrical conduit pipe, was inspired by the book *The Four Season Farm Gardener's Cookbook*, written by our favorite "dirtly duo," Barbara Damrosch and Eliot Coleman.

ANATOMY OF A LOW TUNNEL

Any garden tunnel has three parts: the support hoops or arches; the cover; and the pins, ropes, or weights to keep the edges secure. For supports, many gardeners use hoops made from stiff 9- or 10-gauge wire, or they make their own hoops from inexpensive ½- to 1-inch-diameter poly pipe (the type used for underground water lines). Pipe hoops are more likely to stay erect if they are slipped over sturdy rebar stakes or into sleeves made from rigid metal or PVC pipe. They can also be attached to the outside of framed garden beds with metal brackets. Tunnels made using fence-wire arches will be more secure if staked down with U-shaped metal pins.

Whether made from wire, plastic pipe, or another smooth, non-snagging material, your hoops should be the right length to arch over your garden beds. For 3-foot-wide beds, hoops cut 76 to 80 inches long are best. Hoops are usually spaced 2 to 3 feet apart, so you may need a lot of them. The cheapest way to go is to buy a spool of 9- or 10-gauge wire or poly pipe and cut the hoops yourself. If that doesn't seem doable, consider hoops available online. Expect to pay $35 for twenty, or more for double-wide Super Hoops ($20 for six).

I have used a set of wire hoops for 10 years and will probably use them for 10 years more. In some instances, however, arches made from wire fencing work better than hoops. The main advantage of fencing arches in winter is their ability to withstand heavy loads of ice or snow without collapsing (as hoop-held tunnels are prone to do).

Use plastic over a wire-fencing arch to protect spring crops from frost. When the weather warms, remove the plastic and allow the arch to double as a trellis.

Several seasons back, I received a letter from a reader in Washington, DC, who was harvesting 6-inch-wide spinach leaves in February under a snow- and ice-covered tunnel supported by an arch of wire fencing covered with plastic, and I've been using fencing arches ever since. In spring, I can plant compact varieties of peas under an arch-supported mini-greenhouse, and then take off the cover and let the peas use the arch as a trellis after the weather warms. Later, I do the same thing with pickling cucumbers—first using row cover over a fencing arch to exclude insect pests, and then removing the cover to let in pollinators and allow the cukes to ramble up through the arch that's now doubling as a trellis.

Two types of fencing dominate my collection of arches: woven-wire fencing with big 6-inch openings and stiff welded wire with 2-by-4-inch openings. I use the more flexible woven wire in situations when I know I'll want to uncover the tunnel and reach in often—to weed carrots or onions, or to harvest leafy greens, for example. I choose the arches made from the smaller fencing if I need to protect newly planted beds from animals or birds. Also, you can staple the plastic to the arch and then the unit is very easy to take on and off as needed. Another option is to construct a rigid, portable mini-greenhouse by connecting electrical conduit pipe to a rectangular foundation frame. This greenhouse tunnel is light and rigid enough to pick up and move.

COVERS FOR LOW TUNNELS

Several studies have measured the temperature differences inside and outside low tunnels that are covered with various materials. During a winter in Durham,

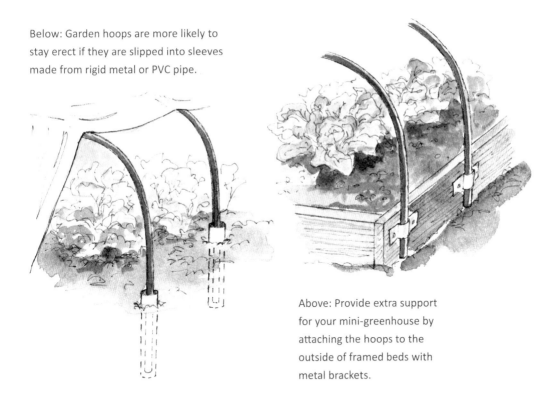

Below: Garden hoops are more likely to stay erect if they are slipped into sleeves made from rigid metal or PVC pipe.

Above: Provide extra support for your mini-greenhouse by attaching the hoops to the outside of framed beds with metal brackets.

New Hampshire, temperatures under tunnels covered with row cover and a second layer of plastic were more than 20°F warmer than outside the tunnels. Additionally, the top 1½ inches of soil inside the garden tunnels never froze, while the outside soil was completely frozen. Studies from the University of New Hampshire have shown that the combination of row cover topped with sheet plastic is the best way to overwinter onions, broccoli, kale, and other hardy crops in the chilly Northeast.

In climates with milder, sunnier winters, be careful when using sheet plastic to cover beds, with or without a layer of row cover underneath. On a sunny 65°F day, a plastic-covered mini-greenhouse can quickly heat up to 130°F or more, which can be lethal to most plants. From Zone 6 southward, plants are often safer beneath row covers than they would be tucked in with both row covers and plastic.

I like both perforated and slitted plastic row covers, which are made of thin plastic peppered with holes or long rows of vents. These covers capture daytime heat while allowing excess warmth to escape. They admit a little rain, but hail bounces off them. At night, the covers deter rabbits and deer. Easy to handle and tolerant of substantial wind, most pieces of perforated or slitted plastic get at least 3 years of use. Best used during the last 3 weeks before and 2 weeks after your last spring frost, a season-specific mini-greenhouse is the best way to capture the warmth of sunny spring days for plants that need it, such as cucumbers, melons, or early tomatoes. It's also a great way to transition veggies that have become accustomed to the filtered light beneath row covers to the open garden. Ask your local garden center about sourcing slitted or perforated plastic row covers.

When it comes to using greenhouse tunnels to exclude summer insects such as flea beetles, squash vine borers, and squash bugs, garden hoops are all you need to support lightweight row covers. It is usually best to hold even feather-weight covers above the foliage to prevent friction with the tender new plants. To save money and material, consider reusing an old sheet or curtain. You may need stakes to keep covers from sagging. To keep the stakes from punching holes in your covers, slit tennis balls and pop them over the tops of the stakes.

SECURING THE EDGES

Like many tunnelers, I used to struggle to keep my plastic in place during strong winds. I've learned that row covers and perforated plastic can be held steady with bricks, pieces of firewood, old bicycle inner tubes filled with sand or water, or sandbags. But even when I buried the edges, winds over 40 miles per hour some-times ruined tunnels, especially those made with unperforated plastic. Then a friend suggested using a second set of garden hoops over the first, on the outside of the row cover—a great technique that I still use to secure various covers over low tunnels.

But truth be told, lash lines work better than outer hoops when it comes to holding down plastic-covered tunnels. To create lash lines, diagonally cross soft nylon line (such as the kind sold for clothesline) over the hoops, threading the rope through hardware in your bed frame (or running board) on the long sides of the bed. In the permanent beds maintained at the Noble Foundation, a nonprofit agricultural institute in Oklahoma, ropes have been installed across low tunnels between pipe hoops, which are spaced about 3 feet apart. In addition to holding the plastic in place, the ropes make it easy to remove the weights from one edge, roll back the plastic for weeding, and then quickly pull it back into place.

My garden hoops and arches stay in the garden year-round, but I store covers that are not being used in a large storage bin. The less time the covers spend in the sun, the longer they will last, and it's great to have them ready and waiting when I need a tunnel fast. Not counting my spades and hoes, my tunnel-building gear is among my most valuable garden equipment.

perennial vegetables: grow more food with less work

by Vicki Mattern

SUPPOSE A NEW agricultural breakthrough promised higher yields, a longer growing season, and much less work. These claims can become real benefits for those willing to make a change to a way of gardening that more closely mimics nature.

Nature's ecosystems always include not only annual vegetables but also perennials—edible roots, shoots, leaves, flowers, and fruits that produce year after year. Besides fruit-bearing trees and shrubs, more than 100 species of perennial vegetables grow well in North America.

By growing perennials, you'll create a more diverse garden that ultimately needs less from you: you'll spend less time working and more time harvesting.

"It's as close to zero-work gardening as you can get," says Eric Toensmeier, author of *Perennial Vegetables*. "Our perennial vegetable beds planted 11 years ago still bear food, and all we do is add compost and mulch once a year."

What's more, growing perennials extends the harvest season without a greenhouse, cold frame, or other device. You can harvest Jerusalem artichokes (also called sunchokes) all winter as long as you mulch enough to keep the ground from freezing.

"Some perennial crops, such as sorrel, are up and ready to eat in March when the snow is melting," says Toensmeier, who gardens in Massachusetts. "Most of our springtime food harvest comes from perennials. By the time they're finished, the annual vegetables are coming in."

Growing perennial vegetables doesn't mean giving up tomatoes, peppers, and other annual crops. You can experience the amazing benefits of perennial edibles simply by rethinking your existing garden plan and pioneering new, unused areas of your landscape.

Layering shade-tolerant veggies under taller plants is a permaculture technique.

THREE WAYS TO INCORPORATE GARDEN PERENNIALS

Design and planning are critical parts of "perennializing" your food garden: after your new perennial edibles have put down roots, they'll be set for years to come. There are three basic design approaches:

1. **Push the Envelope:** "One method to begin perennial edible gardening is to expand the edges of an already established garden," says Bethann Weick, garden

educator at D Acres, an organic permaculture farm and educational homestead in Dorchester, New Hampshire. Perennial vegetables do well in beds devoted only to perennials because their extensive root systems grow undisturbed by digging and cultivating. However, interplanting with annuals can also be a successful strategy and one way to control erosion in your perennial garden.

To expand your garden's edges, hand-dig or till a 3- to 4-foot-wide perimeter bed on one or more sides. Or, if you're willing to wait a year to plant, follow Weick's easy sheet mulch method to prepare the site: "Cover your lawn with four layers of cardboard, and top that with a thick layer of wood chips," she says. "Place compost beneath the cardboard layers for additional fertility. Within a year, the grass will die and the mulch will become rich organic matter ready for planting." Other locally available mulch materials work equally well, Weick says. For instance, thick layers of newspaper could be topped with shredded leaves or grass clippings.

If space or conditions won't allow you to expand your garden's edges, you can experiment and create a perennial vegetable border within the bounds of your existing vegetable garden.

Asparagus is a perennial spring treat.

2. **Dive into Edible Landscaping:** If you already grow a perennial ornamental border or foundation shrubs, consider integrating some perennial vegetables, such as sea kale or sorrel. Many have attractive leaves or flowers, and they won't become so aggressive that they overtake ornamentals. If your gardening space is limited, try growing perennial vegetables—especially greens—in containers.

   Take advantage of currently unused areas of your landscape, matching the conditions to the appropriate perennial edibles.

   "One of the things I love about growing these foods is that there are different ones for different niches," says Toensmeier. "Not all require full sun and loamy soil the way most annual vegetables do. You can grow many perennial greens and herbs—such as wild leeks—on the shady north side of the house, below trees, in a wet site, or in other unused areas of your property."

3. **Pioneer a Plant Community:** If you're already growing perennial vegetables and want to take garden diversification to the next level, consider permaculture gardening. Like nature's ecosystems, this approach promotes greater partnerships between plants, soil, insects, and wildlife. In permaculture designs, edible vegetables, herbs, fruiting shrubs, and vines grow as an understory to taller fruit and nut trees. The technique is sometimes called layering.

   Weick suggests a 5-year plan for gardeners who want to begin layering their landscape with edibles. "In the first year, plant fruit trees as the outposts. That same year and over the next several years, use the sheet mulch technique to prepare planting areas beneath the trees for the understory plants," she says. Sheet mulch a 2- to 3-foot-radius area around each fruit tree the first year and gradually increase the mulched area as the trees grow. After the first year, you can begin planting the mulched area with perennial vegetables, fruiting shrubs, and vines.

The bright blooms of sunchokes are as beautiful as the plant's edible tubers are delicious.

TEN BEST PERENNIALS

The following are widely adapted perennial vegetables selected for their flavor, productivity, and versatility. All but one go to Zone 4.

1. **Ramps, or Wild Leeks (*Allium tricoccum*).** This onion relative grows wild in deciduous forests east of the Mississippi, emerging in spring. Leaves and bulbs are both edible. Grow in a shady border in moist loam, or naturalize beneath trees. Hardy to Zone 4.

2. **Groundnut (*Apios americana*).** Native to eastern North America, this nitrogen-fixing 6-foot vine bears high-protein tubers that taste like nutty-flavored potatoes. Grow the vines as Native Americans did: near a shrub (as support) in a moist site that receives full sun or partial shade. Harvest in fall. Hardy to Zone 3.

3. **Asparagus (*Asparagus officinalis*).** This familiar plant is long-lived and productive, bearing delicious green or purple shoots in spring. Asparagus thrives in full sun and moist, well-drained soil. For best production, plant male hybrids. Hardy to Zone 3.

4. **Good King Henry (*Chenopodium bonus-henricus*).** A traditional European vegetable known for its tasty shoots, leaves, and flower buds, this spinach relative grows in full sun or partial shade and moist, well-drained soil. Plant seeds in compost-enriched soil, and harvest the tender shoots in spring. Hardy to Zone 3.

5. **Sea Kale (*Crambe maritime*).** Sometimes grown as an ornamental, this coastal native bears gray-blue leaves and white flowers on 3-foot-tall plants. Cover the plants in spring and harvest the blanched, hazelnut-flavored shoots when they are about 6 inches tall. The young leaves and flowers are edible too. Plant nicked seeds in moist, well-drained soil in full sun. Hardy to Zone 4.

6. **Jerusalem Artichoke, or Sunchoke (*Helianthus tuberosus*).** Grown by Native Americans, sunchokes bear sunflowerlike blooms on 6- to 12-foot stems. The crisp, sweet tuber can be eaten raw and used like potatoes. An added bonus: sunchokes attract beneficial insects. Plant tubers in full sun and well-drained soil. Harvest in fall and winter. Hardy to Zone 2.

7. **Lovage (*Levisticum officinale*).** The young leaves and stems of this 6-foot-tall perennial are an excellent substitute for celery in springtime soups. The seeds and roots are also edible, and the umbel flowers attract beneficial insects. Lovage thrives in average garden soil, in sun or partial shade. Hardy to Zone 4.

8. **Rhubarb (*Rheum × cultorum*).** Although most people think of rhubarb for dessert, the reddish stems have a long history of use as a vegetable in soups in Asia. Caution: don't eat the leaves or roots, which are poisonous. Plant rhubarb roots in full sun and rich, well-drained soil. Harvest in spring. Hardy to Zone 1.

9. **French Sorrel (*Rumex acetosa*).** The lance-shaped leaves of sorrel add a wonderful, lemony tang to salads and soups, and they can be harvested from early spring to late fall. Look for sorrel transplants in the herbs section at your local nursery. Sorrel grows in sun or shade and average soil. Hardy to Zone 3.

10. **Crosnes, or Chinese Artichoke (*Stachys affinis*).** Also known as mintroot, this little-known mint relative sets out runners that form a dense 12-inch-high groundcover. The small white tubers are crisp and sweet, and add a great crunch to salads. Harvest the tubers annually for best plant growth (just leave a few for the following year). Grow crosnes in full sun or partial shade in well-drained soil. Hardy to Zone 5.

HAPPY RETURNS FROM PERENNIAL GARDENS

Keeping your perennial plantings going isn't much different from caring for annual crops. In fact, after they've been established, perennial vegetables practically care for themselves. "These plants have deeper root systems, so they need fewer outside resources—such as fertilizer and water—than annual crops usually need," says Toensmeier.

Giving the plants a strong start is key. Before planting, dig compost and other necessary amendments deeply into the soil, as you would for perennial flowers. Give aggressive perennials—such as Jerusalem artichokes or self-seeding garlic chives—their own bed so they won't overtake more modest growers. Be especially sure to stay on top of weeds the first year or two until your perennials have spread out above and below the ground. Mulch the beds with a generous layer of compost, wood chips, or shredded leaves early on. "You also can experiment with an edible groundcover, such as violets or wild strawberries," Toensmeier says.

With its increased diversity, your garden should have fewer insect and disease problems. For added insurance against pests, Weick interplants calendula and other flowering plants to attract beneficial insects. Otherwise, maintenance is simple. Feed perennials annually with compost or another organic fertilizer, replenish the mulch each spring, and remove any weeds that sneak in. Consider these measures a small investment, because "planting perennial edibles is planting for the future," Weick says. "Over time, you'll put in less work and harvest more food while building diversity and stewarding the land for future generations."

3

MAINTAINING
SOIL HEALTH

building fertile soil

by Doreen Howard

IT'S A FUNDAMENTAL axiom of organic gardening and farming, and once you understand what "feeding the soil" means to building fertile soil, you'll also understand why organic methods, and no-till techniques in particular, work so well.

Even though you can't see most of it, a complex soil food web lives in your garden; it's teeming with earthworms, mites, bacteria, fungi—all kinds of mostly microscopic, interdependent organisms that release mineral nutrients and create the loose soil structure crops need to thrive. Beneficial mycorrhizal fungi grow in and around plant roots, mining subsoil for nutrients and water to share with your crops. Other microorganisms prevent diseases and help plants withstand insect attacks.

Your crops actually help feed all this underground life. Ray Weil, a renowned soil scientist at the University of Maryland–College Park, says that while plants invest a "substantial amount of their photosynthesis in feeding soil microbes, the plants are obviously getting benefits back."

Think of plants, with their green chlorophyll, as little solar-powered engines that pipe a steady flow of carbohydrates out through their root hairs. Between 20 percent and 40 percent of a plant's total carbohydrate production is released into the soil through its roots. In the nutrient-rich area around the root hairs, microscopic bacteria and fungi feed and multiply. Nematodes (tiny worms) and other critters move in to feed on the bacteria; in turn, the root hairs absorb nutrients released by the concentration of microbes.

But this complex, mostly invisible soil ecosystem can be damaged easily. Chemical fertilizers, dehydrated chicken manure, or high-nitrogen blood meal can burn tender root hairs, and tilling or plowing destroys soil texture, disturbing the layered web. Leaving the soil bare shuts off the carbohydrate food supply; lack of moisture and ultraviolet rays kill some of the organisms that dwell in the surface layer. (Mother Nature almost never leaves the soil uncovered; only on farms and in gardens do we see naked soil.)

More and more farmers and gardeners are learning new ways to protect and promote the development of this amazing soil food web. They foster the natural fertility that comes from a healthy food web, and you can do the same.

First, minimize plowing, tilling, and digging. Second, use compost, grass clippings, leaves, and other organic mulches on a regular basis to promote and sustain the soil food web. Third, always keep the soil covered with live crops or, at minimum, an organic mulch. Whenever you are not growing a food crop, sow a cover crop so the carbohydrate pipeline isn't shut off.

PERMANENT GARDEN BEDS AND NO-TILL SOIL

Every time the soil is tilled, surface-layer organisms are buried, threads of beneficial fungi are broken, and earthworm tunnels are destroyed. Steve Diver, an agriculture specialist with National Sustainable Agriculture Information Service (ATTRA), says plowing can bury plant debris and topsoil up to 14 inches deep—where oxygen levels are too low for decomposition.

The buried debris then acts as a physical barrier to the movement of water upward and downward. Tilling or plowing also introduces excess oxygen that causes organic matter to decay too fast, and tilling causes plants to give off more carbon dioxide, contributing to global climate change.

"Even if you cultivate only 2 to 3 inches deep," says Weil, "more damage is done than good." Worm channels and root paths that facilitate water absorption are destroyed, and soil clumps or aggregates are broken up, leaving little air space in the top layer. Then, raindrops pound on the soil particles, pushing them even closer together, creating an impenetrable, crusty surface.

Weil says good garden soil should be about half porous space occupied by air and water. Compacted soil, created by rainfall on bare ground and the use of heavy equipment or repeated walking upon the ground, has much less space for air and water. That's a recipe for crop failure.

Weil's specialty is managing microbes on farmland, but he handles the soil food web in his home garden the same way. He makes permanent beds that are 4 feet across, so all work can be done from the sides without having to ever step on the soil.

The object is to avoid walking on the soil in the beds, or disturbing it or any plant roots in other ways. Diver says, "The roots left in the ground are food and shelter for microbes and earthworms." To incorporate compost into the soil, he suggests spreading it across the surface with a rake and covering it immediately with mulch. "The worms will move the compost into the soil."

Fertile soils should be about 50 percent air (shown in gray) and water (blue). Tiny mites, springtails, and other critters move through the spaces, feeding on organic matter.

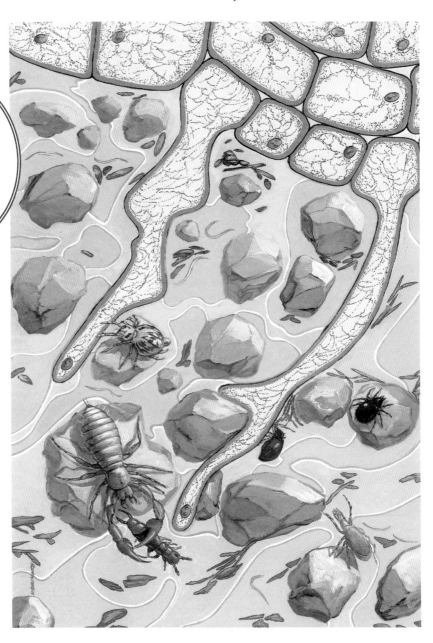

Weil advocates a no-till/cover crop approach to microbe management. "Start by applying a layer of compost and mulch if the soil is decent," he says. "The soil is not compacted if you can push a wire flag 12 inches into wet ground."

If the soil is severely compacted or poorly drained, build raised beds (see page 146). Weil likes to begin in late summer or early fall by staking out the beds and planting a cover crop of a mixture of rye and hairy vetch.

The following spring, he uses a scythe to cut the cover crop (electric or gas-powered weed trimmers work well too), cutting as close to the surface as he can and spreading the debris to an even thickness over the bed with a rake. (You also could let Mother Nature handle this job by using a less winter-hardy crop, such as oats, that will grow strongly in the fall and die in the winter in Zone 6 and north, and in much of Zone 7.)

"The best mulch will be had," Weil says, "if the cover crop is allowed to grow until it 'heads out' or flowers, and if high-residue cover crop species (such as rye) are included in the mix." However, if the cover crop residue is too thin to completely cover the soil, Weil recommends spreading a couple of inches of mulch to cover the soil well. To set out transplants, he simply makes a hole in the mulch and digs out enough soil to accommodate the rootball. The soil is replaced, and mulch is pushed around the transplant. Seeds can be planted by making a narrow part in the mulch with a rake, then drawing a small furrow with a pointed stick in which to sow the seeds. If the soil is too firm, Weil pulls an old meat hook or curved crowbar through it like a single tine on a harrow; the zone of disturbed soil need be only a couple of inches wide.

Once a permanent bed is established, feed the soil food web regularly. Elaine Ingham, president of Soil Foodweb Inc., a firm that specializes in growing plants without pesticides and inorganic fertilizer, says the best way to manage a healthy microbial ecosystem in a home garden is to routinely apply organic material, such as compost.

Ingham suggests gauging the amount needed by what has disappeared from the soil during the previous season. Generally, adding ½ to 1 inch of compost every spring will be plenty. In hot climates, where decomposition is rapid, or in regions with heavy rainfall or sandy soil, make at least two 1-inch applications, one in early spring and the second in late summer or early fall.

Routine application of compost helps keep your home garden ecosystem healthy.

MULCHING THE GARDEN IS A MUST

Beyond the obvious benefits of suppressing weeds and preventing soil crusting, mulch helps maintain the soil food web. Mulch dramatically increases the amount of rainwater that enters the soil and decreases the amount of water that runs off the surface. Runoff takes soil with it, damaging the food web. Even modest mulch or cover crop coverage (10 percent to 30 percent), Weil says, substantially improves rainfall saturation and erosion control. (In some areas, mulch may keep the soil too wet or cool, in which case you can rake some of it back to allow the soil to warm up and dry out.)

Organic mulch also feeds soil microbes. Earthworms move organic matter from the surface down to root zones where it can be used by bacteria. Many diseases are prevented or slowed by beneficial fungi living in mulch. A North

Instead of discarding autumn leaves, shred them with a lawnmower and use them to mulch beds. Other easy-to-find mulch materials include hay, grass clippings, and wheat straw.

Carolina State University study showed that only 3 percent of tomatoes mulched with composted cotton gin trash became infected with southern blight, a fungal disease, compared to 66 percent of unmulched control plants. The composted mulch was an ideal breeding ground for beneficial fungi (*Trichoderma*), which killed or prevented the blight. Numerous disease-causing bacteria and fungi are found in the soil, but a healthy, diverse soil food web nourished by mulch allows beneficial microbes to naturally control or eliminate those that cause problems.

Start with a 3- to 6-inch layer of organic matter (tell your neighbors you want their bags of clean grass clippings and leaves). As the material rots and compacts, add more to maintain the depth.

If you don't grow cover crops, mulch thickly so microbes and earthworms have cover and a food supply during the winter. Instead of discarding autumn leaves, shred them with a lawnmower and use them to mulch beds. Other easy-to-find mulch materials include hay, grass clippings, and wheat straw.

COVER CROPS FOR THE GARDEN

Cover crops are the web's best friend. They protect bare soil, add nutrients, and offer a stable environment for microbes and earthworms when ground is fallow. Cover crops help reduce the harmful effects of erosion from rain and wind, and, by moderating soil temperature, prevent heaving caused by alternate freezing and thawing. As cover crop roots decay, they leave channels for new plant roots to find.

A large garden area with a lush mix of mature cover crops. Cover crops are the web's best friend. They protect bare soil, add nutrients, and offer a stable environment for microbes and earthworms when ground is fallow.

While Weil favors a legume-grass mixture (a hairy vetch-and-rye combination) for cover crops, Diver favors clovers. "I love crimson clover because it has such a pretty flower," Diver says, "and subterranean clover because its plant residue is very effective at suppressing weeds." He says the effectiveness of oilseed radishes as a cover crop also has been studied in cold climates. The radishes endure frigid winters, send taproots deep into the soil, and manufacture glucosinolates that repel parasitic nematodes. Glucosinolates are sulfur compounds found in the Brassica family, including radishes, that act as biofumigants for the soil. Consider using a brassica cover crop if pest nematodes are a big problem in your garden. (Some nematodes attack plants while others help control soil-dwelling insect pests such as lawn grubs. This second type can be purchased and introduced to the garden.)

It's important to match cover crops to your region's seasonal growing cycles. Some covers, such as buckwheat or sorghum, thrive during hot summer months, while others, such as oats or winter rye, will grow only when temperatures are barely above freezing. And if you are going to rake, dig, or till in a cover crop, Weil cautions, do it at least 10 days before planting. "Some plant residues have short-lived allelopathic or ammonium-release effects, which could interfere with crop seed germination, as well as weed seed germination," he says.

your garden soil's pH matters

by Barbara Pleasant

To ensure that your garden crops make the most of the rich, organic soil you create, you need to understand your soil's pH. The pH describes the relative acidity or alkalinity of your soil's makeup, and it has important implications for plant health and growth. Soil pH impacts beneficial fungi and bacteria in the soil and influences whether essential minerals are available for uptake by plant roots.

WHAT IS SOIL pH?

A solution's pH is a numerical rating of its acidity or alkalinity. All pH is measured on a logarithmic scale from zero (most acidic) to 14 (most alkaline, or basic); 7.0 is neutral. The pH scale is used by chemists to measure the concentration of reactive hydrogen ions (H+) in a solution.

Most food crops prefer a pH of 6.0 to 6.5, but you can have a productive food garden as long as your pH is about 5.5 to 7.5. A difference of just 0.5 may not seem like much, but the pH scale is logarithmic, which means, for example, a pH of 7.0 is actually *ten times* less acidic than a pH of 6.0. Potatoes and most berries, which grow best in more acidic soil, are the main exceptions to the average preferred pH range.

A soil's pH results from interactions among native rocks, plants, and weather conditions over many years, and it varies with climate and physical surroundings. In moist climates that support dense forests, such as those east of the Mississippi River and along the Pacific Coast, soil tends to be acidic, with pH ratings usually between 4.0 and 5.5. The grasslands of the comparatively dry Midwest often have *slightly* acidic soil (6.0 to 6.5), while most arid regions, such as the Rocky Mountains, are dominated by alkaline soil (7.0 to 7.8). Local differences in rock can cause huge variations within these general patterns, however—for example, when weathered limestone creates alkaline patches in otherwise acidic landscapes or when elevation leads to more or less rainfall. Plus, soil is often severely disturbed during construction, and sometimes native topsoil is completely lost.

Some synthetic chemical fertilizers—mainly those high in ammonium or sulfur—can make soil more acidic, as can tillage methods that reduce soil's levels of organic matter. Acid rain caused by air pollution from coal combustion began to acidify streams and soil during the late 1800s and continues to push soil in some regions into the acidic range every time it rains. In addition to outside influences, some types of organic matter, such as peat moss and pine needles, acidify naturally during decomposition.

Alkaline soil occurs naturally in places where soil is formed from limestone or other calcium-rich minerals, and high water-evaporation rates common in arid climates aggravate the problem by loading the topsoil with accumulated salts. Many garden plants can still thrive when grown in alkaline soil that has been generously enriched with organic matter, which also improves the soil's ability to retain water. Mulches also will slow the buildup of salts in plants' root zones by reducing the amount of surface evaporation.

HOW TO TEST SOIL pH

Soil chemistry is complex, so how can we boil it down to help you in your garden? If your crops seem to be thriving, then you probably don't need to worry much about your pH. But if you find that plants just don't seem to be growing as well for you as they do for your neighbors, then the problem could be related to pH and you should probably have your soil checked with a pH test. The cost for basic soil evaluation done by a state soil-testing lab ranges from free to $25, depending on the state in which you live, and typically includes a pH test along with results for major and sometimes minor nutrients. Soil-test kits with detailed instructions are usually available at extension service offices, or you can order them by mail.

If one bed or small section of your garden goes wonky, you might try a home pH test kit rather than waiting on lab results. When a team of Missouri extension experts submitted soil samples to eighty-two soil-testing laboratories and compared the labs' results with those from do-it-yourself pH-measuring kits, the $20 LaMotte home color kit earned high accuracy ratings. Personally, I like pH color kits because they are fun to use, and a practiced eye can detect the small changes in color between shades of orange (acid) and green (neutral to alkaline) in the test results.

You may need to acidify your soil with pH-lowering sulfur to grow acid-loving blueberries.

START BY ADDING COMPOST

Raising the organic matter content of soil will usually move the pH of both acidic and alkaline soils toward the neutral range. This is because organic matter plays a buffering role, protecting soil from becoming overly acidic or alkaline. Finished compost usually has a near-neutral pH, so regular infusions of compost should be the primary method you use to improve soil with extreme pH issues. If your pH readings are only slightly acidic or slightly alkaline, compost and organic mulches may be the only amendments you need to keep your crops happy and your garden growing well.

RAISING THE pH OF ACIDIC SOIL

The standard intervention for overly acidic soil is to amend it with lime, an inexpensive soil amendment made from ground limestone that slowly raises the pH over a period of months. Products labeled "dolomitic lime" are usually preferred because they contain both calcium and magnesium. But if you have dense soil and a soil test indicates excess magnesium (which can tie up nitrogen), you should use low-magnesium, calcium-rich powdered crab or oyster shells as your liming material. Read and follow the label, because products differ in application rates, which, in turn, vary with soil type. You can't apply a correct amount of lime unless you know your soil's pH first, and if you apply too much, it will be extremely difficult to correct. Err on the cautious side by applying too little lime at first.

After the pH of acidic soil is raised above 6.0 using organic amendments and dolomitic lime, I've found it can be maintained with a light yearly application of alkaline woodstove ashes. In addition to containing enough calcium and magnesium to have a liming effect, wood ashes contain an array of micronutrients too. The key is to use them *sparingly*, in small, dispersed amounts, and to never add wood ashes or lime to soil with a pH higher than 6.5. One quart of wood ashes (1 pound) is about right for 50 square feet of cultivated space. When you have a lot of ashes to spread, apply no more than 20 pounds of ashes per 1,000 square feet of garden bed.

If you are not using acidic chemical fertilizers, a normally acidic soil may not require liming again for several years, if ever. Then again, if your soil is porous sand in a high-rainfall area, pH testing may show a need for liming every other year. Just be careful to never apply lime unless a pH test shows it is needed, and never use it where you are growing plants that prefer acidic soil conditions, such as blueberries and azaleas.

LOWERING THE pH OF ALKALINE SOIL

If you have exceptionally alkaline, or high-pH soil, you can often tame it by adding organic matter and powdered sulfur. However, sulfur may do little good in alkaline soil that is rich in free lime, also known as calcium carbonate. You can test for free lime by covering a soil sample with vinegar; if it bubbles, you have free lime and should consider gardening in beds filled with non-native soil.

Extension experts in places where alkaline soil predominates emphasize that most plants will grow well in organically improved soil with a pH as high as 7.5, and improving soil quality with organic matter—rather than lowering the pH—should be your primary goal. Alkaline soil can be stubborn about releasing its valuable phosphorus to plants, so amend it every chance you get with composted manure, which has been found to solve several problems associated with high pH levels. The humic acids in both composted manure and vermicompost help make phosphorus available to plants grown in alkaline soil, as does the presence of rotted plant tissues from both regular compost and cover crops. Acidic mulches, such as pine needles, can help lower soil pH slightly, but other mulches, such as bark or wood chips, have little effect on soil pH.

In my own garden, which has dark, fluffy soil that has been nurtured organically for years, soil pH tests show a near-neutral pH. My newer beds that have tight clay, on the other hand, test acidic. Monitoring the soil pH helps me gauge how well I'm improving the soil and maximizing the soil's microbial activity.

grow cover crops for the best garden soil

by Harvey Ussery

CONSIDER COVER CROPS your *most important* crops, because the requirements for abundant food crops—building soil fertility, improving soil texture, suppressing weeds, and inhibiting disease and crop-damaging insects—can be best met by the abundant use of cover crops season after season.

Cover crops at work: cowpeas (center bed) will add nitrogen to this garden's soil, and Dutch white clover (right bed) will make a great living mulch for interplanted food crops.

FIVE BENEFITS OF COVER CROPS

1. **Soil Fertility**: A vast array of soil organisms decompose once-living plants into nutrients easily taken up by plant roots, and add to your soil's humus content (the final residues of organic matter in your soil, which assist nutrient uptake, improve texture, and hold moisture). I grow organic matter in place using cover crops because, in many ways, a living cover crop is even better than adding manure and compost for fertility.

The area of most intense biological activity ultimately the definition of soil fertility—is the rhizosphere, the zone immediately around plant roots. Plants release nutrients through their roots to feed their buddies in the soil—beneficial microbes and mycorrhizal fungi—which increase access to water and convert soil nutrients into forms more readily utilized by plants. If the intense bioactivity in the rhizosphere is the key to fertility, imagine the contribution of closely planted cover crops with vastly more root mass than more widely spaced food crops.

2. **Soil Texture:** Mycorrhizal fungi (beneficial fungi that grow in association with plant roots) produce glomalin, a substance that glues microscopic clay and organic matter particles into aggregate clumps, stabilizing the soil and making it nice and crumbly. This crumbly texture is more porous to oxygen and water. Bacteria encouraged by cover crops produce polysaccharides, which also act as soil glues.

    Grass and grain cover crops with fine, dense root masses loosen soil texture as they decompose. Others, such as sweet clovers and sorghum-sudangrass hybrids, grow deep, aggressive taproots that break up soil compaction.

3. **Erosion Prevention:** A cover crop's tight canopy protects the soil from the drying and scouring effects of wind and the forceful impact of heavy rain. The loosened soil structure achieved by cover cropping allows rapid absorption of rain and prevents runoff.

4. **Soil Moisture:** Organic matter added by cover crops acts like a sponge in the soil, absorbing rainwater and holding it for gradual release to plant roots. Thus, gardens that have been home to regular use of cover crops become more resistant to drought.

5. **Protection from Weeds, Diseases, and Insect Damage:** Garden beds frequently planted with cover crops will have fewer problems with weeds. Cover crops suppress weeds, outcompeting them for water and nutrients and shading them under a tight canopy, sometimes releasing chemical compounds that inhibit germination of weed seeds (a phenomenon called allelopathy). Plus, the roots of cover crops release nutrients that feed beneficial microbes in the soil. These microbes then suppress pathogens that cause root diseases. Some cover crop plants, such as rape, rye, and sorghum-sudangrass hybrids, inhibit root knot nematodes, which can be disastrous to beets, carrots, and other root crops in some regions.

    You can cut cover crops and use them as mulches to boost populations of beneficial ground-dwelling species, such as rove beetles and spiders. Other cover crops can provide a wonderful habitat for the pollinators that help keep your food garden thriving. Cover crops that flower, for example, provide important food sources for honeybees and butterflies.

Above right: Field peas are a popular leguminous cover crop. Above left: Common vetch, a winter annual legume that flowers from April to July, performs well as a self-seeding cover crop.

COVER CROP SPECIES

Depending on your climate, gardening goals, and the time of year, you'll have a variety of cover crop options. Cover crop species vary widely in their tolerance of cold, heat, soil moisture extremes, and soil types. It's often good practice to plant a mix of different species.

The most important division among species is between legumes and non-legumes. Legumes such as cowpeas, vetches, and clovers serve as hosts to rhizobia, bacterial alchemists that live in plant roots and convert nitrogen from the atmosphere into nitrogen compounds that help plants grow. Some of this "fixed" nitrogen remains attached to legume roots in nodules—like beads on a string—and becomes available to other plants after the legume dies.

Non-legumes include all other cover crops. grasses such as small grains, various millets, annual and perennial rye, and sorghum-sudangrass hybrids; crucifers such as mustards, rape, and forage radish; and buckwheat.

COVER CROPPING STRATEGIES

The most important strategy of all is *do it now!* When I complete a food crop harvest in fall, that same day I plant an overwinter cover crop. If I harvest a spring crop such as lettuce from a bed that I won't be planting again until fall, I sow a fast-growing interim cover crop that does well in summer heat, such as buckwheat or cowpeas. The best time to plant a cover crop is anytime a bed is not covered by a food crop or mulch.

The easiest way to incorporate more cover cropping is the half-and-half strategy: I dedicate every other garden bed to cover crops for an entire year. I may grow several fast-growing covers, such as cowpeas and buckwheat, in succession, or a cover such as sweet clover, which takes a full year to yield all its benefits. In the following year, the beds previously in cover crops now grow food crops, and vice versa. This strategy allows you to grow mulches in place. Using a scythe or sickle, you can cut cover crops that produce a lot of biomass—hairy vetch, rye, and sorghum-sudangrass hybrids—and lay them out as mulches in an adjacent bed that's planted with food crops. Most cover crops cut when in their vegetative growth stage will regrow to produce even more mulch. If you can't give half of your garden space to cover crops, how about one bed out of three? Or four? Or even ten?

Some cold-hardy cover crops grow well through fall frosts, then die if the ground freezes solid—this is known as winterkilling, and you can use it to your advantage. When I remove the top growth from asparagus beds in late September, I plant a mix of winter peas and oats. They create a knee-high tangle of green by the time the ground freezes, and they both reliably winterkill here in northern Virginia, leaving a thick weed-suppressing mulch come spring. Plus, the leguminous peas fix nitrogen in the soil for the heavy-feeding asparagus.

It's possible to grow both a food crop and a cover crop in the same bed at the same time. Under tall-growing crops with a small footprint, such as tomatoes or pole beans, plant an undersown cover crop such as low-growing Dutch white clover or perennial ryegrass. If such a cover has already been established, leave it in place as a living mulch and open up holes for large transplants such as tomatoes or broccoli, or open up rows for beans.

Shade-tolerant species—annual ryegrass, cereal rye, hairy vetch, and some clovers—can be sown as overseeded cover crops into existing crops such as corn or brassicas up to several weeks before harvest. The cover crops will grow slowly under the existing canopy, then come on strong when the food crop has been removed.

Try frost-seeding a cover crop into overwintered grains. In late winter, broadcast the seeds—small round ones, such as clovers, work best—into the grain beds.

Flowering cover crops such as red clover will attract butterflies.

Winter freezes and thaws will work the seeds into the soil, where they will germinate in spring rains. The grain could mature into a food crop for feeding your pigs or chickens while serving as a nurse crop to establish the clover, which will grow rapidly after you harvest the grain.

Some species work as reseeding cover crops. Subclovers (cool-season legumes) will die back in winter, but the seeds they leave behind will remain dormant through much of the next growing season, then sprout in the fall to establish a new cover.

Permanent cover crops are appropriate in orchards, vineyards, and border areas never planted with food crops. Keeping these areas in mixed flowering species—perennials, such as clovers, or annuals that reseed themselves, such as crucifers—protects the soil, supports pollinators, and encourages insect diversity. Encouraging lots of different kinds of insects is the key to preventing crop damage, as the bug-munching insects will help you control the crop-munching insects. In high-traffic areas, covers that can take a good deal of wear are in order, such as annual ryegrass and white clovers.

PLANTING COVER CROPS

Plant cover crops with as much care as you plant food crops. Make a furrow for larger or more vigorous seeds such as cowpeas or sorghum-sudangrass, sow thickly, and then cover with soil. For smaller seeds, such as clovers, crucifers, and small grains, scatter, rake in, and tamp the bed with the back of a garden rake to ensure good soil contact. To speed germination, apply a light mulch and water occasionally. Seeds of vigorous covers, such as annual ryegrass, oats, and hairy vetch, will germinate if left on the surface, especially if broadcast just before a soaking rain.

You can plant a food crop as soon as the cover crop is killed unless there could be a temporary problem of allelopathy or nitrogen tie-up. In such cases, wait about 3 weeks or so before planting.

KILLING A COVER CROP

It's better to avoid deep mechanical tillage, which disrupts soil life and breaks down soil structure. Tall, heavy stands of cover crops, such as rye and hairy vetch, are a nightmare to till in with a power tiller in any case. So what's the best way to kill a cover crop so decomposer organisms can break it down to feed your soil?

Remember that a cover crop in the vegetative stage (i.e., not flowering) usually regrows after being cut. Most cover crops in the reproductive stage (i.e., flowering), however, will die if cut. A complete no-till strategy that works for most covers is to cut the cover just above soil line after it has flowered and transplant crops such as tomatoes, peppers, or broccoli through the severed tops, leaving the cut tops and cover crop stubs as a mulch. For small areas, use a hand sickle for the cutting. Or, use a heavy field hoe to chop cover crop plants just below the soil surface to kill them without disturbing the soil deeper down. Another option is to loosen the soil with a broadfork and pull the cover plants out by the roots, again laying them on a bed as mulch. As your soil becomes more friable, the broadfork may not be necessary.

POTENTIAL DISADVANTAGES

Thirsty rye may deplete available soil moisture enough to inhibit the following crop in a dry season. A few crops—small grains such as rye and sorghum-sudangrass hybrids—may temporarily release chemicals that will inhibit the growth and germination of other plants. Though these allelopathic effects help with weed control, they can suppress germination and growth of food crops that follow, especially small-seeded ones, such as lettuce, spinach, and onions. Just wait a few weeks after killing a cover crop to plant your food crop and you won't run into problems.

Cover crops susceptible to diseases, herbaceous insects, or nematodes could serve as vectors if grown beside or followed by food crops with the same susceptibilities. If you allow cover crops to mature their seeds before being killed, they can later volunteer as weeds in following crops. However, the more diverse our gardening practices and the more complex our rotations, the less likely we will encounter such problems. And the more we learn about cover crop species, the more we discover management solutions to problems that could occur. For example, if rye has been allowed to mature, the high carbon content of its residues, both roots and top mass, can temporarily tie up nitrogen in the soil and inhibit growth of the following crop. But if you grow the rye in a mix with a compatible legume, nitrogen fixed by the legume will minimize nitrogen tie-up.

Begin experimenting with cover crop species in your garden today, and you'll soon see that the enormous advantages far outweigh any problems that may crop up. Ultimately, cover crops will lead to healthier soil and bigger, better harvests.

One method of making biochar: pile up woody debris in a shallow pit in a garden bed, burn the brush until the smoke thins, damp down the fire with a 1-inch soil covering, let the brush smolder until it is charred, and then put the fire out. The leftover charcoal will improve soil by improving nutrient availability and retention.

making biochar to improve soil

by Barbara Pleasant

I, TOO, HAVE committed one of the great sins of gardening: I've let weeds go to seed. One year when I was cleaning up in fall, I faced down a ton of seed-bearing foxtail, burdock, and crabgrass. Sure, I could compost it hot to steam the weed seeds to death, but instead I decided to try something different. I dug a ditch, added the weeds and lots of woody prunings, and burned it, thus making biochar. It was my new way to improve soil—except the technique is at least 3,000 years old.

What's biochar? Basically it's organic matter that is burned slowly, with a restricted flow of oxygen, and then the fire is stopped when the material reaches the charcoal stage. Unlike tiny tidbits of ash, coarse lumps of charcoal are full of crevices and holes, which help them serve as life rafts to soil microorganisms. The carbon compounds in charcoal form loose chemical bonds with soluble plant nutrients so they are not as readily washed away by rain and irrigation. Biochar alone added to poor soil has little benefit to plants, but when used in combination with compost and organic fertilizers, it can dramatically improve plant growth while helping retain nutrients in the soil.

AMAZONIAN DARK EARTHS

The idea of biochar comes from the Amazonian rainforests of Brazil, where a civilization thrived for 2,000 years, from about 500 B.C. until Spanish and Portuguese explorers introduced devastating European diseases in the mid-1500s. Using only their hands, sticks, and stone axes, Amazonian tribes grew cassava, corn, and numerous tree fruits in soil made rich with compost, mulch, and smoldered plant matter.

Amazingly, these "dark earths" persist today as a testament to an ancient soil-building method you can use in your garden. Scientists disagree on whether the soils were created on purpose, in order to grow more food, or if they were an accidental byproduct of the biochar and compost generated in day-to-day village life along the banks of the earth's biggest river. However they came to be, there is no doubt that Amazonian dark earths (often called *terra preta*) hold plant nutrients, including nitrogen, phosphorous, calcium, and magnesium, much more efficiently than unimproved soil does. Even after 500 years of tropical temperatures and rainfall that averages 80 inches a year, the dark earths remain remarkably fertile.

Scientists around the world are working in labs and field trial plots to better understand how biochar works, and to unravel the many mysteries of *terra preta*. At Cornell University in Ithaca, New York, microbiologists have discovered bacteria in *terra preta* soils that are similar to strains that are active in hot compost piles. Overall populations of fungi and bacteria are high in *terra preta* soils too, but the presence of abundant carbon makes the microorganisms live and reproduce at a slowed pace. The result is a reduction in the turnover rate of organic matter in the soil, so composts and other soil-enriching forms of organic matter last longer.

In field trials with corn, rice, and many other crops, biochar has increased productivity by making nutrients already present in the soil better available to plants. Results are especially dramatic when biochar is added to good soil that contains ample minerals and plant nutrients. Research continues, but at this point it appears that biochar gives both organic matter and microorganisms in organically enriched soil enhanced staying power. Digging in nuggets of biochar—or adding them to compost as it is set aside to cure—can slow the leaching away of nutrients and help organically enriched soil retain nutrients for decades rather than for a couple of seasons.

FINDING FREE BIOCHAR

Biochar's soil-building talents may change the way you clean your woodstove. In addition to gathering ashes (and keeping them in a dry metal can until you're ready to use them as a phosphorus-rich soil amendment, applied in light dustings), make a habit of gathering the charred remains of logs. Take them to your garden, give them a good smack with the back of a shovel, and you have biochar.

If you live close to a campground, you may have access to an unlimited supply of garden-worthy biochar from the remains of partially burned campfires. The small fires burned in chimneys often produce biochar too, so you may need to look no further than your neighbor's deck for a steady supply.

Charcoal briquettes used in grilling are probably not a good choice. Those designed to light fast often include paraffin or other hydrocarbon solvents that have no place in an organic garden. Plain charred weeds, wood, or cowpies are better materials for this promising soil-building technique based on ancient gardening wisdom.

HOW TO MAKE BIOCHAR

To make biochar right in your gardens, start by digging a trench in a bed. (Use a fork to loosen the soil in the bottom of the trench and you'll get the added benefits of this "double-digging" technique.) Then pile brush into the trench and light it. You want to have a fire that starts out hot but is quickly slowed down by reducing the oxygen supply. The best way to tell what's going on in a biochar fire is to watch the smoke. The white smoke produced early on is mostly water vapor. As the smoke turns yellow, resins and sugars in the material are being burned. When the smoke thins and turns grayish blue, dampen down the fire by covering it with about an inch of soil to reduce the air supply, and leave it to smolder. Then, after the organic matter has smoldered into charcoal chunks, use water to put out the fire. Another option would be to make charcoal from wood scraps in metal barrels.

I'm part of the Smokey-the-Bear generation raised on phrases like "learn not to burn," so it took me a while to warm up to the idea of using semi-open burning as a soil-building technique. Unrestrained open burning releases 95 percent or more of the carbon in the wood, weeds, or whatever else goes up in smoke. However, low-temperature controlled burning to create biochar, called pyrolysis, retains much more carbon (about 50 percent) in the initial burning phase. Carbon release is cut even more when the biochar becomes part of the soil, where it may reduce the production of greenhouse gases including methane and nitrous oxide. This charcoal releases its carbon 10 to 100 times slower than rotting organic matter. As long as it is done correctly, controlled charring of weeds, pruned limbs, and other hard-to-compost forms of organic matter, and then using the biochar as a soil or compost amendment, can result in a zero-emission carbon cycling system.

Burning responsibly requires simple common sense. Check with your local fire department to make sure you have any necessary permits, wait as long as you must to get damp, windless weather, and monitor the fire until it's dead.

THE BIGGER PICTURE

If global warming is to be slowed, we must find ways to reduce the loss of carbon into the atmosphere. In the dark earths of the Amazon, and in million-year-old charcoal deposits beneath the Pacific Ocean, charcoal has proven its ability to bring carbon release almost to a standstill. If each of one million farmers around the globe incorporated biochar into 160 acres of land, the amount of carbon locked away in the earth's soil would increase five-fold.

But there's more. What if you generate energy by burning a renewable bio-mass crop (such as wood, corn, peanut hulls, bamboo, willow, or whatever) while also producing biochar that is then stashed away by using it as a soil amendment? The carbon recovery numbers in such a system make it the only biomass model found thus far that can produce energy without a net release of carbon. Research teams around the world are scrambling to work out the details of these elegantly Earth-based systems.

Much remains to be known about how biochar systems should tick, but some may be as simple as on-farm setups that transform manure and other wastes into nuggets of black carbon that help fertilizer go farther while holding carbon in the soil.

As gardeners, it is up to us to find ways to adapt this knowledge to the needs of our land. To make the most of my bonfire of weeds, I staged the burn in a trench dug in my garden and then used the excavated soil to smother the fire. A layer of biochar now rests buried in the soil. Hundreds of years from now, it will still be holding carbon while energizing the soil food web. This simple melding of soil and fire, first discovered by ancient people in the Amazon, may be a "new" key to feeding ourselves while restoring the health of our planet.

Homemade liquid fertilizers made from free, natural ingredients such as grass clippings, seaweed, chicken manure, and human urine can give your plants the quick boost of nutrients they need to grow stronger and be more productive.

free homemade liquid fertilizers

by Barbara Pleasant

MANY ORGANIC GARDENERS keep a bottle of liquid fish fertilizer on hand to feed young seedlings, plants growing in containers, and any garden crop that needs a nutrient boost. But liquid fish-based fertilizers are often pricey, plus we're supporting an unsustainable fishing industry by buying them. So what's a good alternative?

MOTHER EARTH NEWS commissioned Will Brinton—who holds a doctorate in environmental science and is president of Woods End Laboratories in Mount Vernon, Maine—to develop some water-based homemade fertilizer recipes using free, natural ingredients such as grass clippings, seaweed, chicken manure, and human urine.

WHY AND WHEN TO USE LIQUIDS

Liquid fertilizers are faster acting than seed meals and other solid organic products, so liquids are your best choice for several purposes. As soon as seedlings have used up the nutrients provided by the sprouted seeds, they benefit from small amounts of fertilizer. This is especially true if you're using a soil-less seed-starting mix (such as a peat-based mix), which helps prevent damping-off but provides a scant supply of nutrients. Seedlings don't need much in the way of nutrients, but if they noticeably darken in color after you feed them with a liquid fertilizer, that's evidence they had a need that has been satisfied. Liquid fertilizers are also essential to success with container-grown plants, which depend entirely on their growers for moisture and nutrients. Container-grown plants do best with frequent light feedings of liquid fertilizers, which are immediately distributed throughout the constricted growing area of the containers.

Out in the garden, liquid fertilizers can be invaluable if you're growing cold-tolerant crops that start growing when soil temperatures are low, for example overwintered spinach or strawberries coaxed into early growth beneath row covers. Nitrogen held in the soil is difficult for plants to take up until soil temperatures rise above 50°F or so, meaning plants can experience a slow start because of a temporary nutrient deficit in late winter and early spring. The more you push the spring season by using cloches and row covers to grow early crops of lettuce, broccoli, or cabbage in cold soil, the more it will be worth your time to use liquid fertilizers to provide a boost until the soil warms up.

Water-soluble homemade fertilizers are short acting but should be applied no more than every 2 weeks, usually as a thorough soaking. Because they are short acting, liquid fertilizers are easier to regulate compared with longer-acting dry organic fertilizers, though 1 like using both. With an abundant supply of liquid fertilizer to use as backup, you can use a light hand when mixing solid organic fertilizer into the soil prior to planting.

Remember: if you mix too much nitrogen-rich fertilizer into the soil, you can't take it back. As soil temperatures rise, more and more nitrogen will be released, and you can end up with monstrous plants that don't produce well. In comparison, you can apply your short-acting liquid fertilizers just when plants need them—sweet corn in full silk, peppers loaded with green fruits—with little risk of overdoing it. Late in the season, liquid fertilizers are ideal for rejuvenating long-living plants such as chard and tomatoes, which will often make a dramatic comeback if given a couple of drenchings.

MAKING YOUR OWN

To explore the art of making fertilizer tea, Brinton began by trying various ways

HOMEMADE FERTILIZER TEA RECIPES

Add the amount of dry ingredients shown below to a 5-gallon bucket, then add water to fill, and steep for three days. Strain or decant the tea and dilute as shown below. To make fertilizer tea from urine, simply dilute urine in 20 parts water and it's ready to use. Water plants with these solutions no more than once every two weeks.

TYPE	AMOUNT	DILUTE
Dried chicken manure with wood shavings	⅓ bucket	1:1
Seaweed	⅓ bucket	none
Fresh grass clippings	⅔ bucket	1:1
Urine		1:20

to mix and steep grass clippings, seaweed, and dried chicken manure (roughly 33 percent manure mixed with 66 percent wood shavings). The best procedure he found was to mix materials with water at the ratios shown in the pictured chart (above) and allow the teas to sit for 3 days at room temperature, giving them a good shake or stir once a day.

"By the third day, most of the soluble nutrients will have oozed out into the water solution," Brinton says. Stopping at 3 days also prevents fermentation, which you want to avoid. Fermented materials will smell bad, and their pH can change rapidly, so it's important to stick with 3-day mixtures and then use them within a day or two. Brinton also studied human urine, which is much more concentrated than grass, manure, or seaweed teas, and doesn't need to be steeped.

The lab analyzed the four extracts for nutrient and salt content. Salts are present in most fertilizers, but an excess of salts can damage soil and plant roots. Brinton found that chloride and sodium salts were so high in urine that it needed to be diluted with water at a 1:20 ratio before being used on plants. In comparison, the seaweed extract could be used straight, and the grass clipping and chicken manure extracts needed only a 1:1 dilution with water to become plant-worthy.

As a general guideline, most vegetables use the three major plant nutrients—nitrogen (N), phosphorus (P), and potassium (K)—in a ratio of roughly 3-1-2: 3 parts nitrogen, 1 part phosphorus, and 2 parts potassium. This means that an N-P-K ratio of 3-1-2 is more "balanced" in meeting plants' needs than 1-1-1, the ratio many gardeners assume is best. Because liquid fertilizers are a short-term, supplemental nutrient supply secondary to the riches released by organic matter and microbes, they don't need to be precisely balanced. The teas made from grass clippings and urine come closest to providing the optimum 3-1-2 ratio.

Nitrogen helps plants grow new stems and leaves. Phosphorus is essential for vigorous rooting, and is usually in good supply in organically enriched soils. Potassium is the "buzz" nutrient that energizes plants' pumping mechanisms, orchestrating the opening and closing of leaf stomata and regulating water

New seedlings will benefit from a biweekly drink of liquid fertilizer.

distribution among cells. The grass clipping and poultry manure teas are rich in potassium, which should make for sturdy plants with strong stems when used to feed young seedlings. Blending some grass or manure tea with a little nitrogen-rich urine would give you a fertilizer to promote strong growth in established plants. I like to add a few handfuls of stinging nettles, comfrey, lamb's quarters, or other available weeds to various mixtures, which probably helps raise the micronutrient content of my homemade concoctions in addition to providing plenty of potassium.

On the practical end of liquid-fertilizer making, you may need to use a colander to remove some of the grass clippings before you can pour off the extract. If you haven't completely used a batch of fertilizer within 2 or 3 days, pour it out beneath perennials or dump it into your composter.

It's important to relieve drought stress before doling out liquid fertilizer. Watering before you fertilize helps protect plants from taking up too many salts. Also keep in mind that continuous evaporation in containers favors the buildup of salts. By midsummer, a patio pot planted with petunias or herbs that are regularly fed with any liquid fertilizer may show a white crust of accumulated salts inside the rim. Several thorough drenchings with water will wash these away, making it safe to continue feeding the plants with liquid fertilizers.

There is no doubt human urine can be a valuable fertilizer for garden plants. The average adult produces about 1½ quarts of urine per day. Diluted 1:20 with water, this would make 7.5 gallons of high-nitrogen liquid fertilizer, so a family of four could produce a season's worth of high-nitrogen fertilizer for an average garden. As Brinton suggests, when we think of N-P-K, we should also think N-Pee-OK!

Maybe it's all the diapers I've changed, but I don't like minding pails of pee. In winter at my house, we have a bucket of sawdust stationed on the deck to help us capture this valuable resource, and we keep a designated bale of hay out in the garden for urine deposits. If you do the same, you can use the urine-enriched sawdust and the hay from "pee bales" as nutrient-rich mulches in your garden.

Whatever materials and methods you choose, you'll be pleasantly surprised by the simplicity of making your own no-cost liquid fertilizers.

maintain healthy soil with crop rotation

by Barbara Pleasant

ONE OF THE rules of good organic gardening is to rotate plant families from one season to the next, as best you can, so related crops are not planted in the same spot more often than every 3 years or so. The purpose of crop rotation is to help maintain the balance of nutrients, organic matter, and microorganisms necessary for healthy soil. Of these three, the invisible world of soil-dwelling microcreatures is the one that most benefits from crop rotations.

Take potatoes, for example. In the course of a season, the fungi that cause scabby skin patches may proliferate, along with root-killing *Verticillium* fungi (which also damage tomatoes and eggplant) and tiny nematodes that injure potatoes. If you plant potatoes again in the same place, these pathogens will be ready and waiting to sabotage the crop. Rotating the space to another unrelated crop deprives the potato pathogens of the host plant they require. Most pests and diseases can damage plants of the same botanical family but cannot hurt unrelated crops (see "Rotate Your Families: The Nine Main Groups," on page 71).

What if you don't follow a crop rotation plan? Field trials in Connecticut and Europe indicate that your potato production will quickly fall by 40 percent, mostly due to disease. According to a 7-year study from Ontario, you could expect similar declines if you planted tomatoes in the same place over and over again. Compared to eight different rotations with other vegetables or cover crops, continuous tomatoes consistently produced the lowest yields. Snap beans that are not rotated will turn into paltry producers too. In a study from Cornell University, snap bean production doubled when beans were planted after corn rather than after snap beans.

In addition to interrupting disease cycles, rotating crops prevents the depletion of nutrients. For example, tomatoes need plenty of calcium the same way beans and beets crave manganese. But the exact benefits of effective rotations vary with crop sequence. Broad-leafed greens are great for suppressing weeds, and the deep roots of sweet corn do a good job of penetrating compacted subsoil. Nitrogen-fixing legumes often take no more nitrogen from the soil than they replace, and their presence stimulates the growth of beneficial soil microorganisms. But in some situations, the "rotation effect" defies easy explanation. For example, we don't know precisely why potatoes tend to grow well when planted after sweet corn, but they do.

The subject of crop rotation can get complicated so fast that it's no wonder we are tempted to cheat. What if your garden is like mine—a collection of a dozen permanent beds that are planted with 20-plus different crops in the course of a growing season? Not using rotations would be unwise. When researchers at Pennsylvania State University tracked early blight of tomatoes grown in the same place for 4 years, early-season infection rates (measured when 5 percent of fruits turned red) went from 3 percent in the first year to 74 percent in the third. When they tried the same monoculture maneuver with cantaloupes, symptoms of alternaria blight appeared earlier and earlier with each passing season.

QUESTIONING THE RULES

Some organic gardeners point out that crop rotation guidelines developed for farmers don't really fit home gardens. On farms, crop residue is either plowed under or left on the surface to decay, which means the soil receives large infusions of a single type of plant material. Gardeners are more likely to pull up and compost spent crops, and to dig in compost or other soil amendments between plantings, which replenishes nutrients and invigorates the soil food web in an extremely diversified way. Biodegradable mulches introduce more considerations: if you heavily mulch your potatoes with straw, shredded leaves, grass clippings, or all three, certainly it makes sense to factor those forms of organic matter into your rotation plans.

But don't think that just because you pull up plants you are interrupting the food supply of soilborne plant pathogens to the point that you can ignore rotations. When I pull up beans, for example, only a small tangle of roots comes up with the plants; the bulk of the root system stays behind in the soil. If I plant beans in that row again within 2 years, the plants will be at risk for micronutrient

In addition to interrupting disease cycles, rotating crops prevents the depletion of nutrients. For example, tomatoes need plenty of calcium the same way beans and beets crave manganese.

deficiency and several major bean diseases. Using a 3-year crop rotation radically reduces the chances that my beans will be bothered by root rot, white mold, and several serious blights. This is an excellent reward for taking on the task of devising a workable rotation plan in which new plantings are helped along by the bed's previous tenants.

THE EIGHT-CROP ROTATION

The eight-crop rotation plan developed by small-scale commercial farmer Eliot Coleman incorporates decades of farm and garden research, and it's a great place to start planning rotations for your garden. In order, Coleman's plants unfold like this: (1) tomatoes (2) peas (3) cabbage (4) sweet corn (5) potatoes (6) squash (7) root crops (8) beans. If you grow only these eight crops in eight rows or beds, you now have your rotation plan. Simply line up your crops in the right order, and shift them one space over every year.

But it's not likely to be this simple for your garden, so you will need a customized plan that relocates the main plant families from one season to the next. (Families are crops that are closely related and therefore prone to many of the same pests and diseases.) The nine plant families grown in vegetable gardens are summarized in "Rotate Your Families: The Nine Main Groups" at right, but expect to need more space for some families than others. For example, you may need a lot of space for tomato-family crops (tomatoes, peppers, eggplant, potatoes) and only a little for spinach, chard, or beets, and you may not be able to grow space-hungry sweet corn at all. Begin planning your rotations by making a list of your must-have crops and how much space is required by each one. Then sort them into the plant families.

You will also need to identify crop sequences that work well in your garden within the same growing season. For example, many gardeners have garlic in the ground from fall to midsummer, after which the area can be planted with a second crop. In my Zone 6 garden, I can grow shell beans after garlic if I hustle, which gives me a garlic/bean sequence. In a cooler climate, you might have a garlic/lettuce sequence.

Other sequences that work well for me include a snap pea/carrot sequence, an onion/leafy green sequence, and a broccoli/bush bean sequence. Add any crop sequences you often use (or want to try) to your list.

ROTATION PLANNING

You will need two sheets of paper, scissors, and a pen or pencil. On one sheet, make a rough drawing of your garden, noting the sizes of beds or rows. Write down, to the best of your knowledge, where various crops grew last year. If you take photographs of your garden at different times during the season, it's much easier to recall where you planted what.

Cut another piece of paper into smaller pieces that fit the rows or beds in your garden drawing, and copy the crops, the plant family they belong to, and crop sequences from your list onto these "crop markers." In my garden, I end up with markers for ten crops or crop sequences to rotate within my twelve

You can simplify your rotations by sorting your crops into these major plant families:

- **Onion family:** onions, garlic, leeks, and shallots

- **Carrot family**: carrots, celery, parsley, and parsnips

- **Sunflower family:** lettuce, sunflowers, Belgian endive, curly endive, chicory, escarole, frisee, and radicchio

- **Cabbage family:** cabbage, broccoli, brussels sprouts, kale, bok choy, as well as rutabagas and kohlrabi

- **Spinach family:** spinach, beets, and chard

- **Cucumber family:** cucumbers, melons, squash, and gourds

- **Pea family:** peas and beans

- **Grass family:** corn, wheat, oats, and rye

- **Tomato family:** tomatoes, peppers, eggplant, and potatoes

You can plan your crop rotations by using a paper template to simulate your crops and growing areas. Ample research shows that crop rotation supports healthy soil and results in better harvests for potatoes, tomatoes, beans, and many other crops.

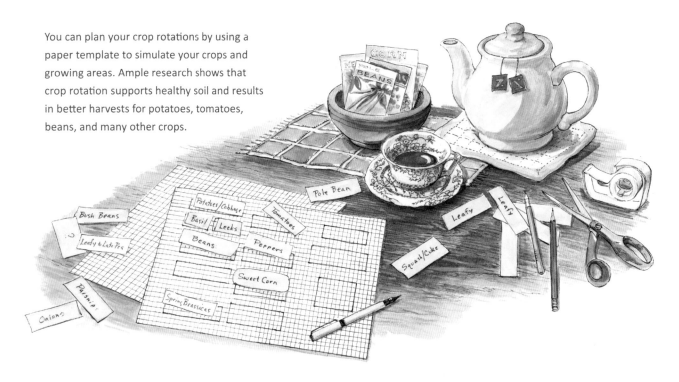

permanent beds. It's good to have a couple of beds for trial plantings and irresistible whims.

Back at the drawing board, spend some time puzzling through your plans by moving the labeled crop/plant family markers about on your garden drawing. Your goal (which may take a few seasons to implement) will be to have your plantings move in a logical order and direction, whether it's left to right, front to rear, circular, or whatever you decide. Expect to improvise and innovate. For example, I am now growing more peas and beans to stretch out years between onion and garlic plantings, which are priority crops in my garden. When in doubt about a rotation, I slip in a crop of beans or leafy greens.

If you feel frustrated, play with your drawing and markers for a while, and then pack them up for a few days of thinking time. When you go back to the task, you will probably have an easier time finding at least a few effective rotations waiting to be put into action. After a few years of fine-tuning, the payoff for this level of garden planning can be huge—a long-term rotation plan that runs itself and benefits every crop you grow.

4

MAKING
AND USING
COMPOST

home composting made easy

by Barbara Pleasant

MANY PEOPLE START composting for practical reasons. Home composting your leaves, grass clippings, garden waste, and food scraps reduces the amount of garbage you generate. Plus, compost is essential for a great garden, and starting your own pile ensures a free, regular supply. But I think there's an even better reason to compost: it's fascinating. In fact, once you understand the basics of how the process works, composting can be one of the most interesting and enjoyable aspects of keeping a garden.

Composting mimics and intensifies nature's recycling plan. A compost pile starts out as a diverse pile of kitchen and garden "waste." Left alone, any of these materials would eventually decompose. But when a variety of materials are mixed together and kept moist and aerated, the process accelerates. Compost matures into what soil scientists call active organic matter: a dark, crumbly soil amendment that's rich with beneficial fungi, bacteria, and earthworms, as well as the enzymes and acids these life forms release as they multiply.

Adding compost to garden soil increases its water-holding capacity, invigorates the soil food web, and provides a buffet of plant nutrients. Compost also contains substances that enhance plants' ability to respond to challenges from insects and diseases.

Starting a new compost pile can be a fast, easy project. But new composters sometimes feel frustrated as they struggle to learn more about how the process works—an understandable problem since there is a wealth of information available about composting and no one absolutely "right" way to do it. As we take a close look at nine basic composting facts, it's obvious that the world of composting is seldom black and white—or shall we say brown and green? At the same time, composting is much easier than what you might have heard.

NINE BASIC COMPOSTING FACTS

1. **Balancing ingredients is optional.** To help compost decompose rapidly, a balance of "two parts brown to one part green" is often preached as composting gospel, but in truth, keeping a balanced ratio is simply an option. (Dry materials such as leaves, pine needles, and dead plants are usually considered "browns," whereas wetter materials such as grass clippings and kitchen waste are considered "greens.") It's not that balancing browns and greens is wrong; it simply makes home composting more complicated than it needs to be. You can pile up all your organic material without worrying at all about greens and browns, and it will still mature into compost.

    Precise balancing of materials is crucial in commercial composting operations, though, for example, the composting of city sewage, manure from animal feedlots, or byproducts from food manufacturing plants. But the needs and objectives of a gardener are far different from those of a dog food manufacturer with a waste disposal problem. The goal of industrial composting is to neutralize the pollution potential of various materials. The goal of home composting is to support nature's self-regenerating power in ways that work harmoniously with the needs and opportunities of a person's backyard.

2. **Good compost can be either hot or cold.** Most people who carefully manage their compost piles for a balance of ingredients are trying to produce hot compost, which heats up, or "cooks," as the materials decompose. Hot compost is the fastest type of compost to produce, but it's not necessarily better than compost that rots slowly without heating up.

    High temperatures in the compost heap are generated by bacteria as they work high-nitrogen materials, so hot compost that's protected from leaching

It's not that balancing browns and greens is wrong; it simply makes home composting more complicated than it needs to be. You can pile up all your organic material without worrying at all about greens and browns, and it will still mature into compost.

may be a superior source of this essential nutrient. But there's a tradeoff: intensively worked hot compost that's produced in only 3 to 4 weeks ranks pretty low in terms of microbial diversity.

If you want the best compost, you want cured compost. This is mature compost that is set aside in a covered place where it can age for at least a couple of months. Microorganisms continue to work as the compost cures, including a special group of bacteria that produce compounds thought to prime plants to do a superior job of defending themselves from pests and diseases.

I often use the last weeks of mild fall weather to finish off a really nice batch of compost, which I sift through ½-inch mesh plastic hardware cloth and put into plastic bags or storage bins to cure. In spring, I have the perfect base for making potting soil for the next season's plants.

3. **Small or large—any size pile will work just fine.** Compost manuals frequently promise that if you build a nicely balanced heap of well-moistened materials at least 3 feet high and wide, it will heat up and start cooking within days.

You can be absolutely sure that your compost will eventually rot, but super-sizing a heap offers little insurance that it will get off to a smoking start. You can save yourself a lot of trouble by simply piling stuff together until the heap is big enough to merit some attention. Then, one day when you're in a composting mood, pick up a digging fork and spend some time setting the heap to rights by mixing the materials in the pile and adding water to keep it moist.

4. **Turning compost is optional.** Many books warn that heaps will not get enough oxygen unless they are turned. This may be true of a heap that's kept too wet, but most compost heaps aerate themselves as they shrink. Better reasons to turn compost include achieving a good mix of materials, discovering dry pockets in need of moisture, and satisfying your curiosity as to what's happening in your heap. And as the composting process advances and the materials become more fragile, turning and mixing breaks them into smaller pieces, which helps push almost-done compost to full maturity.

5. **You can gauge the moisture level of your compost pile by its fragrance.** When you dig around in a heap and don't smell the desired earthy fragrance, lack of moisture is usually the reason. Dryness is a big challenge in the fall, when most gardeners make new compost piles from leaves. Shredding the leaves before composting them will help them break down faster, but they'll need time and an amazing amount of water before they start breaking down.

To make it easier to keep these piles wet, I arrange a soaker hose in a figure-eight pattern, with about 4 inches of mower-shredded leaves and weathered hay between each layer of hose. I've found that hay vastly improves a leaf heap's ability to retain water, and until the weather gets too cold to use it, there is no easier way to moisten the inside of a dry heap than by using a soaker hose.

Unpleasant odors in compost can be caused by the materials themselves (for example, broccoli stems or rotten oranges), but even smelly things won't stink if they are buried a few inches deep. However, enclosed compost can go stinky if it's too wet, which is easily fixed by adding dry material or simply letting it dry out. If you're using a plastic bin or tumbler, do pay close attention to water, because it's easy to add too much.

6. **Compost need not be a secret.** A compost bin or pile is only ugly if you make it that way, so there's no need to hide compost in a remote corner. Carrying stuff across the yard to a hidden heap is a waste of time and energy. Locate compost as close as possible to where the materials are generated and/or where the finished compost will be used. Visually speaking, using a black or dark green enclosure will help a compost heap blend in to a shady background. Or, you can use painted posts or fencing to make your setup more colorful and visually attractive.

My yard includes four areas of working gardens, so I always have at least four heaps going—each within pitching distance from the garden beds. Those heaps will be turned three or four times, so I plan ahead for them to "walk" toward their final resting place with each turning. For example, a 5-foot-diameter heap that starts out 15 feet from a garden plot will arrive at its destination after its fourth turning (the math allows for shrinkage). It's a slow trip that starts in November and ends in June, but that's how it is when you're composting slow-rotting oak leaves.

Many books warn that heaps will not get enough oxygen unless they are turned. This may be true of a heap that's kept too wet, but most compost heaps aerate themselves as they shrink.

Carrying stuff across the yard to a hidden heap is a waste of time and energy. Locate compost as close as possible to where the materials are generated and/or where the finished compost will be used.

7. **You can compost diseased or weedy plants.** Many experts recommend keeping seed-bearing weeds and diseased plants out of the compost heap so as not to reintroduce them into your garden. This makes sense, but what are you supposed to do with the stuff? I suggest giving these bad boys their own heap. Later on, after mildewed squash vines and seed-bearing crabgrass clippings have been given a few months to shrink to a more manageable size, you can cook the half-done compost to kill diseases and weed seeds.

For this job, I use a solar cooker made from a 20-inch cardboard box lined with aluminum foil (be sure to search for "eye safety" and read the precautions for shielding your retinas from superintense light). When I have compost from diseased and weedy plants, I take a 3-gallon heavy plastic pot filled with the damp compost, enclose it in a clear plastic bag, and place it in the cooker in direct sun. You can use an oven thermometer to find out how hot your cooker is. Two hours at 140°F kills most weed seeds and soilborne pathogens.

8. **You can safely compost livestock manure**. This biologically active material is a terrific soil amendment, and composting livestock manure makes it safe to use in the garden. You should use caution with animal manures because many do contain diarrhea-inducing *E. coli* bacteria, but making and using manure-enriched compost won't make you sick unless you're careless or impatient.

The *E. coli* present in most types of animal manure is slowly eliminated by more competitive microorganisms as compost matures. Using fresh uncomposted manure near growing food plants is risky, as is consuming unwashed vegetables that grow within mud-splashing range of recently manured soil. But if you *allow the compost to mature* before applying it to your garden and *always wash your produce* before you eat it, you need not worry about this problem.

Many folks think that "teas" brewed from compost do good things when sprayed on plants, but nature's version of compost tea—rainwater filtered through composting mulch—is much simpler and safer. Any tiny traces of *E. coli* are quarantined in the soil, where they meet their destiny with death. In contrast, brewing manure-based compost and spraying it on your food just doesn't seem like a good idea.

9. **There are good uses for immature compost.** Beyond composting in aboveground heaps and containers, you can make compost in excavated holes or pile up stuff in layered beds and then plant right into the compost-in-progress. Peas, beans, potatoes, and squash are especially well suited to growing in compost-filled trenches. In my garden, I use edible legumes as the first plants in new garden space, which may or may not get dug up before I layer up half-done compost with soil and whatever else I can find—grass clippings, weathered sawdust, or horse manure from a friend's barn. Some people call this lasagna compost. If you top off the layers with burlap or some other water-permeable cloth, you can call it Interbay compost, named after the innovative gardeners at Interbay Community Garden in Seattle, who reuse burlap coffee bags to cover layered compost. I call it comforter compost because it's such a good way to tuck in soil for winter, or begin the healing process for soil that's been neglected or abused.

As for squash and potatoes, they have taught me that they are perfectly happy growing in compost, so I keep them in mind as I create new heaps in the fall. In my tight mountain clay, these crops do especially well in "dugout" beds that are filled with layers of soil and raw compostables. Even if the compost is not completely rotted by spring, potatoes and squash can't tell the difference.

Every gardener wants to make great compost, and experience is the best teacher. Just know this: you cannot fail, because compost knows what to do. As eloquently noted by longtime *MOTHER EARTH NEWS* reader Wayne Morris of Bloomingdale, New York, "The beauty of compost is that it only needs to be as much of an art or science as we wish it to be. It's like walking. You can train for a marathon or you can simply put one foot in front of the other, and eventually you will get where you need to be." Trust the composting process, follow nature's lead, and things will grow up great in the end.

Every gardener wants to make great compost, and experience is the best teacher. Just know this: you cannot fail, because compost knows what to do.

vermicompost

by Barbara Pleasant

Vermicompost, or compost made mostly by earthworms, is seven times richer in plant nutrients compared to compost created mostly by fungi and bacteria, and recent studies suggest that small amounts mixed into soil suppress diseases, slugs, and insects. Numerous studies have shown that when only 10 percent of the volume of potting soil used to grow seedlings is vermicompost, a huge range of plants simply grow better—from carrots to tomatoes to zinnias. It's easy to entice earthworms to work their magic right in your garden, or you can make vermicompost in enclosed bins, or both! In addition to improving soil fertility chemically with their castings (a mixture of manure and slime emitted through the worms' skin), earthworms improve soil physically by opening airways and drainage holes as they travel.

Notice that I did not tell you to buy worms. That's because we're recommending "catch-and-release" worm composting, which makes use of the earthworms present in your own yard. These species have already demonstrated their satisfaction with your unique climate and soil, though few (or none) of them are likely to be red wrigglers (*Eisenia fetida*), the species used in commercial vermicomposting systems. That's okay. Common red worms (*Lumbricus rubellus*) and other species plucked from compost bins or soil (or rescued after flooding rains) usually make well-behaved captives, and you can usually coax larger night crawlers (*L. terrestris*) to colonize any spot by piling on plenty of mulch.

Indeed, when it comes to using earthworms to build soil fertility, Clive Edwards, Ohio State University entomologist and author of *Earthworm Ecology*—the academic bible on earthworms—thinks night crawlers deserve top priority. "The best thing is to obtain some *L. terrestris* and inoculate your garden with them. They are the most important species in promoting soil fertility," he says.

Night crawlers are widely available as fishing worms, but before you buy any, try these simple setups to give resident night crawlers a helping hand.

- Maintain permanent pathways that are mowed or mulched so there is always a layer of decomposing litter at the surface. Night crawlers build semipermanent burrows where they stockpile food gathered at night. Providing safe year-round habitat is essential to keeping populations high.
- Use the spaces between widely spaced squash or melons as night crawler condos. Place wet newspapers or cardboard over the surface (they love the

shelter), sprinkle raw oatmeal over the newspapers (they love the food), and top with 2 inches of coarse, moist compost. Repeat the layers and top off with grass clippings, straw, or another attractive mulch. If you build it, they will come.

- Conduct composting projects in your garden, especially slow heaps that will basically sit there until they are done. Night crawlers often build deep, elaborate burrows beneath piles of slow compost.
- Try straw bale beds or simply let a pile of old hay rot atop an infertile spot. The biggest, most energetic night crawlers I've ever seen grew into giants beneath a bale of decomposing hay.

RAISING AND RELEASING YOUR CAPTIVES

Night crawlers need to burrow like birds need to fly, so they are only marginally happy when reared in bins. Yet common red worms or field worms (*Aporrectodea* species, which can be gray, pink, or even green) do fine in bins as long as you provide them with a pleasing habitat (see "Sweet Summer Setups" on page 82). When I transfer worms from my garden to the all-you-can-eat buffet conditions in a bin, they transform the mixture of bedding and food into finished worm compost in 4 to 5 months. The fresh compost also includes hundreds (or thousands) of cocoons, so as I use it in my garden, I simultaneously distribute a new generation of ready-to-hatch earthworms.

With few exceptions, the earthworms that inhabit North American gardens are exotic species introduced from Europe (the natives were wiped out in the last ice age), and Edwards points out that there are no guarantees that they will prosper in a particular space. "Available organic matter is the key to building up earthworm populations, but it may take several years because their time from cocoon to maturity is 4 to 12 months," he says.

Working with worms that have already shown their satisfaction with your climate and soil by simply being there simplifies this challenge, but even happily

Below left: In summer you should have no trouble recruiting willing worm workers from your own garden. Just poke around beneath mulches, compost piles, or clumps of grassy weeds (a favorite earthworm hangout). Below right: Earthworm castings are rich in plant nutrients and growth-enhancing humic acids, which the worms distribute as they move through moist soil.

HOW TO HERD WORMS

You can call a dog or shoo a cat, but the best way to move earthworms is to herd them with light. To harvest vermicompost from a bin, gently pile a cone of material from your worm bin on a flat surface in bright light and wait about an hour. The worms will form a dense mass in the core of the cone.

Occasionally earthworms decide to leave a bin that's become too crowded or damp. You can wick out excess moisture with cigars made of tightly rolled dry newspaper (which can then be torn into new bedding). Until you can set things right, prevent runaways by removing the bin's cover and keeping a light on at night.

Tillers are murder on earthworms, but even gentle hand cultivation causes casualties. A week or so before cultivating a bed that's well populated with earthworms, set up a haven nearby such as a compost pile, mulched pathway, or a cache of buried food scraps. Meanwhile, allow the place you plan to dig to become dry. Many worms will migrate to the better habitat, escaping a tragically premature end.

naturalized earthworms will not stick around unless the soil is moist and rich in organic matter. Digging in compost between plantings coupled with heavy mulching does the trick in most climates, though many worms do head for deeper digs as the weather heats up in summer. Dotting the garden with piles of moist organic matter that are shaded by tall plants is an easy way to keep earthworms up in the root zone in hot weather.

SWEET SUMMER SETUPS

Earthworm castings are rich in plant nutrients and growth-enhancing humic acids, which the worms distribute as they move through moist soil. I like to keep a worm bin going indoors in winter, but in the summer it's simpler to make worm compost outdoors. Here are three simple setups:

1. When container plants expire, dump the used potting soil in a large bucket until you have a couple of gallons. Add a dozen or so earthworms collected from your garden or compost pile, sprinkle the surface with cornmeal or oatmeal, then cover with 1 inch of grass clippings. Keep the bucket in a moist, shady spot protected from rain for a month. The reconditioned potting soil (with worms removed, see "How to Herd Worms," at left) will contain enough worm castings to fertilize several needy containers.

2. In a plastic storage bin perforated with ventilation holes, toss together equal parts wet newspaper or cardboard strips, soil, and compost until the mixture is 10 inches deep. Bury a pint or so of grain-based food waste such as old bread, flour, rice, or cooked pasta just below the surface, and add two hundred or more worms. Snap on the cover, and place the bin in a shady place (placing the bin in a hole will help maintain optimum temperature and moisture). In fall, use the contents of the bin to top-dress carrots and beets—two crops that respond dramatically to vermicompost.

3. To encourage earthworms to congregate in one place, dig a hole about 16 inches deep and equally wide, and refill it with veggie and fruit trimmings from your kitchen and garden, topped with 2 inches of soil. Cover with boards or an old tarp and forget about it for a month or two. Dig up your buried treasure in the fall, and transfer some of the worms to an indoor bin. Move the rest to spots in your garden near compost piles, grassy pathways, or deeply mulched beds. They will know what to do!

Whichever worm projects you decide to try, in summer you should have no trouble recruiting willing worm workers from your own garden. Just poke around beneath mulches, compost piles, or clumps of grassy weeds (a favorite earthworm hangout). After you have collected a few dozen earthworms, give them a job. You'll be doing your part to fulfill the earthworms' destinies, because every last one of them was born to spend its life turning decaying organic matter into rich, fertile soil.

5
LATE WINTER/
EARLY SPRING

starting seeds indoors

by Barbara Pleasant

I BEGAN GROWING my own vegetable seedlings more than 30 years ago, and I still remember my sad first attempts. Many seedlings keeled over and died, and some seeds never germinated at all. Experience has taught me how to prevent these problems, and every year I deepen my garden's diversity, save money, and share favorite varieties with friends by starting seeds indoors. Thousands of superior crop varieties are rarely available as seedlings in garden centers, and the same goes for wonderful culinary crops such as red celery and seed-sown shallots. If your gardening goal is to fill your table and pantry with an array of homegrown organic food, then starting plants from seed can help you achieve that goal. Starting seeds indoors under controlled conditions, with no aggravation from weeds or weather, allows you to get a prompt start on the season, whether you are sowing onions in late winter, squash in summer, or lettuce in early fall. And where growing seasons are short, some crops require an indoor head start to later reach maturity.

THE GERMINATION PROCESS

All seeds contain specialized cells that mobilize and grow when the germination process is triggered by moisture, temperature, and sometimes light. Moisture and stored nutrients energize the embryo, which contains the latent structures for a plant's root, stem, and leaves. Most vegetable seeds that germinate quickly (such as cabbage and tomatoes) enter their dormant state with mature, fully formed embryos. The carrot family is at a disadvantage, however, because most Umbelliferae seeds (think parsley, fennel, and dill) need time for their underdeveloped ovaries to grow before they can sprout. Other slow sprouters—spinach, for example—have compounds that inhibit germination in their seed coats. These compounds have to break down in the soil before the root and sprout can burst forth into the world.

Oxygen is vital to the germination process. Until seedlings have leaves to enable them to use solar energy, they rely on the food reserves in the seed combined with oxygen found in the soil to grow new cells. This is why you should always use a light-textured potting medium to start seeds, and why overwatering can cause seeds to rot instead of grow.

Appreciating the hard work that seeds must do during the germination process will likely enhance your seed-starting experience. You can watch time-lapse videos online of fast-growing bean seeds germinating, but watching them in person is even more amazing. The seeds that impress me most are squash. By the time the seedling leaves shed the seed coat, the little plant is already supported by a small mountain of roots.

Order seeds in winter to be ahead of the game for spring seed-starting.

SEED-STARTING MIXTURES

From the day they germinate, vegetable seedlings face challenges from fungi and bacteria in water, soil, and air. The fewer troublemakers they face, the better they can grow, which is why using fresh seed-starting mix each winter is so crucial. Quality seed-starting mixes are formulated to discourage common soilborne pathogens that cause seedlings to rot, and to help seedlings retain both water and air with ease.

You can make your own seed-starting mix by using either peat moss or coir as a base, and then blend it with compost that has been heated to 150°F to kill any pathogens and weed seeds. Small amounts of vermicompost can be a beneficial addition when added to a seed-starting mix, but use no more than 10 percent by volume.

As a 2005 study from North Carolina State University revealed, it's not the precise mixture but what's on top of the soil that counts most. Differences almost disappeared between commercial organic seed-starting mixtures and various homemade mixtures after all of the seeds were covered with vermiculite instead of a planting medium.

Made from two naturally occurring minerals, vermiculite has unmatched natural talents in seed-starting mixtures: it can absorb and retain several times its own weight in moisture while still holding some oxygen. (Regulations that require regular inspection of processing facilities have addressed concerns about possible asbestos contamination in vermiculite. The Organic Materials Review Institute has approved the use of the Therm-O-Rock brand.)

SORTING THROUGH SEEDLING CONTAINERS

Over the years, I have tried at least half a dozen systems for starting seeds indoors, including a special container divided into cells that fits inside a tray with a translucent dome to retain moisture, and other bells and whistles (capillary

Create seed-starting pots on the cheap by forming cylinders out of newspaper.

mats, water sensors) that eventually ended up in a garage sale because they were more trouble than they were worth. I still use parts of these systems, but in recent years, small paper cups with holes punched in the bottom have become my containers of choice, especially because they disappear into my compost after use. The same can be said for planting cups rolled from newspaper and for cardboard planting "boxes" made by refolding and stapling discarded food boxes.

I've used fancy seed-starting setups I would never use again, and I blame peat pellets for several of my early failures. I have also had seedlings grown in peat pots go into shock when the roots hit the walls of the pot, which never happens in plastic, paper, or slick cardboard containers. Egg cartons are too small to use for seed-starting unless you're working with tiny seeds. Seedlings will grow well in a container that holds 3 to 4 ounces of seed-starting mix, which is ⅓ to ½ cup. Be sure to punch drainage holes in the bottoms of containers that don't have holes.

For trays to hold seedling containers, I am moving toward old-fashioned wood flats made from scrap pieces of cedar lumber. The shallow open boxes with ¼-inch gaps between the bottom slats look nice indoors under lights; outdoors they don't blow around in the wind the way plastic trays tend to do. You will also need watertight liners for your flats, because watering from both the top and the bottom is beneficial for young seedlings. You can use plastic flats without drainage holes, shallow plastic pans such as new cat litter pans, or even seldom-used large casserole dishes or serving trays. Using sturdy trays makes a collection of seedlings easy to move, water, and fertilize.

If you don't have scrap wood or if you plan to keep your seedlings in a room where you can't get the floor wet, you may want to use plastic flats instead of wooden ones. To protect your floor, you can set your containers in flats without any drainage holes. This makes watering the entire flat of containers easier because you just pour water into the flat. If you use this approach, be sure to pour out any excess water after the containers have absorbed as much as they can.

Whatever containers you use, fill them to the top with moist seed-starting mix, and then tap the soil down with your finger to eliminate air pockets (it took me three seasons to learn this trick). Add more mix up to within ¼ inch from the top. Plant seeds at the depth suggested on the seed packet, and sprinkle the seeds gently and generously with water. When using fresh seed packed for the current season, sow no more than three seeds per container—two is even better. With large seeds, such as squash seeds, plant only one seed per container.

If you have clear plastic domes (sometimes sold with seed-starting flats), use them to retain moisture until the seeds germinate. If you are domeless, cover your flats loosely with plastic wrap, or enclose them in translucent plastic bags. Remove the coverings at the first sign of germination, and then shift your focus to giving the seedlings bright light.

PROVIDING WARMTH AND LIGHT

Let's get back to our botany lesson and to why my first seedlings keeled over. As seedlings break through to the soil surface, they are quickly running out of fuel from the seed and need a new energy source: light. If they don't get enough light,

You could buy a handy seed-starting station—or why not save big bucks and create something like this on your own?

they are more susceptible to attack by fungi. Window light is usually too weak and directional; veggies need intense overhead light—you need to have a fluorescent light fixture to grow your seedlings.

One popular way to make a light shelf on the cheap is to use a heavy-duty wire shelving unit (the big-box-store price is $65 for a four-shelf unit) and hang shop lights from the undersides of the shelves with wire. For lighting, 4-foot-wide fixtures with at least two standard fluorescent tubes are your best choice. Standard tubes are fine for seed-starting; you do not need to pay extra for special "grow lights." Fluorescent fixtures don't heat up the way incandescent lights do, but they still give off some heat. The light units I use have metal hoods that are flat on top so I can set newly planted trays there.

Warm room temperatures that rise above 75°F for several hours a day will trigger germination in just about any vegetable or herb seed, and seeds will benefit from temperatures that vary by about 10°F during the day. This happens naturally if you're using warmth from a fluorescent light that you turn off at night.

You can also rig up bottom heat using an ordinary heating pad placed under a seedling tray. (Special mats for seed-starting sound great, but in my experience the mats die before they earn back their substantial purchase price.)

After seeds have germinated, keep them under lights for 12 to 14 hours a day, and adjust the height of the lights (or the trays) to keep your seedlings very close to them. *This is important—keep the seedlings so that they almost touch the light tubes.* In late winter, you can grow salad greens to an edible size this way.

WATCHING THE WONDER

A seedling's first set of leaves is followed by a lull in the action as the seedling switches its power source, develops its first true leaf (or two), and grows a flurry of new roots. Crowded seedlings can be separated and repotted when the first true leaf appears, with tiny seedlings such as celery going into small containers and larger ones such as cabbage moving to 4-inch pots. For this step, remove the outer tines from a plastic fork and use it to gently float the babes into roomier digs, handling them only by their seedling leaves. After I move seedlings to

MAKE YOUR OWN POTTING SOIL

by Barbara Pleasant

If you have soil and compost, you've got the basic ingredients for making your own potting soil. In place of peat moss, perlite, and vermiculite (the three leading ingredients in bagged potting soil), you can simply combine your best soil with cured compost, leaf mold (rotted leaves), rotted sawdust (from untreated wood), or a long list of other organic ingredients. Prepare some small batches, mix it with store-bought stuff to stretch your supply, and gradually make the transition to what potting soil should be—a simple, nurturing medium for growing healthy plants or starting seeds.

GIVING UP EXOTIC PLANTING INGREDIENTS

At least half of any homemade potting soil is homemade compost, but most commercial potting soils are based on some combination of peat moss, perlite, and vermiculite all of which contribute to land degradation and pollution as they are mined, processed, packaged, and shipped.

For most of us, the best peat alternatives are leaf mold, rotted sawdust, or a mixture of both. A 4-by-5-foot pile of chopped leaves will take about 2 years to decompose into leaf mold. In areas where organic rice or other grain hulls are available, composting them will create a light material for fluffing up potting soil. Rotted sawdust, leaf mold, or the abundance of organic matter in garden waste compost also can compensate for the absence of vermiculite, a mined mineral with as many environmental issues as peat moss.

The main contributions of perlite ore to potting soil—lightening texture and improving drainage—often can be matched by clean sand. When you want a light mix, a handful of sand per quart will do the trick (you don't need much). As a hedge against slow drainage in the bottoms of seedling flats or containers, use a thin layer of rotted leaves, sawdust, or sand.

ADDING FERTILIZER TO THE POTTING MIX

Of the numerous recipes for organic potting mixes collected and published by the National Sustainable Agriculture Information Service, many include blood meal (for nitrogen), bonemeal (for phosphorus), and small amounts of kelp meal, greensand, or various rock-based minerals for minor nutrients. Think before you act, especially if you are substituting nutrient-rich compost for nutrient-poor peat, perlite, or vermiculite. Give real potting soil a chance, wait and see, and let experience be your teacher. Should plants grow slowly or show other signs of nutrient stress, it's easy enough to feed them with a mix-with-water organic fertilizer. Add organic fertilizer in small amounts until your potting soil is giving you the results you want.

Until 30 years ago, most gardeners made their own potting soil by combining their best garden soil with rotted manure from the barn or buckets of leaf mold hauled home from damp stream banks, topped off with a dusting of wood ashes. Contrast and compare: North American gardeners now spend more than $500 million each year on potting mixes and specialty soils. How many of those dollars do you want to come from your wallet?

slightly larger containers, I immediately return them to the position under the lights where they were before. This way, the seedlings must recover from only one stress at a time. At their next watering, I like to give transplanted seedlings a flash dunk in a pail of lukewarm water to eliminate hidden air pockets. If the potting medium settles, you can sprinkle more dry mix around the base of the seedling to help keep it upright.

Any nutrients present in the seed-starting mix will be gone after about 3 weeks, so your seedlings will need supplemental feeding. After years of using fish emulsion/kelp products, last year I made my own liquid fertilizers and saw excellent results. I doubled the dilution rate of fertilizer to water for young seedlings, which need only small amounts of nutrients because they are such little plants. As for how to deliver both water and organic fertilizer to young seedlings, you will make little mess using a squirt bottle (dishwashing liquid bottles are great) to water and feed from the top and the bottom. Using room temperature water or water/fertilizer mix, dribble in enough water to lightly dampen the surface if it's dry and wait a minute or two to see if water flows through the containers and pools around the bottom. Add more water to the pan, holding your seedlings until the water is ¼ inch deep. Wait 30 minutes, and pour off any liquid that has not been absorbed. The dryness of your indoor air will influence how often you need to water your seedlings, which prefer constant, light moisture around their roots and dry conditions at the surface. Dry containers feel light when you pick them up, so daily weight checks are the best way to find out whether your seedlings need water.

From the beginning, keep a written record of your sowing dates. As the season progresses, go back and add comments when you nail the perfect planting windows for your favorite vegetables and varieties. This information will be invaluable as you expand your garden.

all about growing blueberries

by Barbara Pleasant

LONG-LIVED AND DEPENDABLE, blueberries are among the easiest fruits to grow organically. Different species are native to various regions of North America, but you can grow some type of blueberry bush almost anywhere. The limiting factor is soil acidity: except for saskatoons, blueberries require acidic soil with a pH below 5.0. Blueberries can also be grown in containers filled with an acidic bark-based planting mix.

Start growing blueberries and you'll be rewarded with delicious, healthy berries, as well as stunning red and orange fall foliage.

TYPES OF BLUEBERRIES TO TRY

Lowbush blueberries are native to colder parts of North America. The compact bushes can be grown as an edible hedge or groundcover, even in partial shade, and they bear delicious berries that hold on the plants for a long time.

Northern highbush blueberries grow wild in the eastern mountains of the United States. Cultivated strains grow into 6-foot-tall bushes that bear for many years, with bright red or orange fall foliage.

Southern highbush blueberries are low-chill versions of northern highbush blueberries, making them a good choice in Zones 7 to 10.

Rabbiteye blueberries are descended from southeastern native plants. Tolerant of heat and humidity, rabbiteyes are the best to grow where winters are mild.

Saskatoons are the top choice for cold climates. The hardiest varieties can survive to -60°F. Related to roses, the almond-scented fruits easily pass for true blueberries. Saskatoons prefer a near-neutral soil pH between 6.0 and 7.0.

WHEN TO PLANT BLUEBERRIES

Late winter or early spring, during the 6 weeks prior to your last spring frost, is the best time for planting blueberries. Young container-grown plants may be set out later but need time to grow roots before hot weather. Blueberries are only marginally self-fertile, so you'll need to grow at least three plants of compatible varieties.

HOW TO PLANT BLUEBERRIES

Choose a sunny, well-drained site that has an acidic pH for growing blueberry bushes. Young blueberry plants need an abundance of organic matter in the soil's shallowest layers. Most soils should be amended with 4 inches of acidic organic matter such as rotted sawdust or leaf compost. Preparing the site in fall will help the organic matter settle into the soil, which will enhance transplant survival

BLUEBERRIES AT A GLANCE

In addition to choosing a type of blueberry that suits your climate, plan to grow at least three plants of different yet compatible varieties. Local nurseries may offer ensembles of compatible varieties within the same species group.

TYPE	DESCRIPTION	VARIETIES
Blueberry, lowbush *Vaccinium angustifolium*	Hardy to −25°F, these are great native shrubs for open woods with acidic soil. Not as productive as other types, but great if used as an edible ground cover along woodland paths.	Wild plants transplant easily in early spring. Named varieties such as 'Top Hat' are good for containers in cold climates. Tasty 'Brunswick' and 'Burgundy' provide outstanding fall color.
Blueberry, northern highbush *V. corymbosum*	Best adapted to acidic soils in Zones 5 to 7, but some varieties can survive temperatures as low as −20°F. Long-lived, 5- to 6-foot upright bushes bear heavy crops with little maintenance and few pest problems.	Taste-test locally adapted varieties at a pick-your-own farm, and choose three that ripen over a long period. Organically enriched acidic soil brings out the best flavor in 'Blue Moon', 'Jersey', and other high-yielding varieties.
Blueberry, southern highbush *V. corymbosum* hybrids	Fruits resemble those of other highbush varieties, but plants require little chilling, from 150 to 800 chilling hours. Good blueberries for Florida, Southern California, and other climates with mild winters.	Can be grown in containers by pairing compatible varieties such as 'Misty', 'Emerald', and 'Jewel'. Check with your local extension service for variety recommendations, or visit local pick-your-own farms.
Blueberry, rabbiteye *V. ashei*	Hardy to about 0°F, these are the best blueberries for the South. Immature berries are often pink, like a rabbit's eye. Easy to grow in fertile, acidic soil in Zones 7 and 8.	'Tifblue', 'Woodard', and 'Brightwell' are top varieties for flavor, vigor, and productivity. 'Powderblue' matures late and is quite ornamental, turning yellow-orange in fall.
Saskatoon *Amelanchier alnifolia*	Hardy across the northern United States and southern Canada, saskatoons aren't true blueberries, so they don't need extremely acidic soil. Depending on variety, saskatoons grow into spreading bushes or small trees. They make great landscape plants.	Varieties with superior flavor and productivity include 'Martin', 'Northline', and 'Pembina'. Fruits from ornamental varieties are often weak compared with saskatoons grown for their fruit.

Find blueberry bushes for your garden using our Seed and Plant Finder at *www.MotherEarthNews.com/Custom-Seed-Search*, which lets you search through the offerings of hundreds of mail-order catalogs.

in spring. If your soil's natural pH ranges between 5.5 and 6.0, you can further acidify it by top-dressing with soil sulfur twice a year. In areas with soil pH levels above 6.0, grow blueberries in large containers filled with a wood chip– or bark-based planting mixture.

Spacing recommendations for growing blueberries range from 12 inches between plants for lowbush blueberries to 12 feet between saskatoons. Allow 4 feet between highbush blueberry plants and 6 feet between rabbiteyes. Set plants at the same depth they grew in their pots. Water thoroughly, and mulch the soil's surface with at least 2 inches of acidic mulch such as wood chips. Cut back to ground level all but the two most vigorous upright shoots.

PRUNING BLUEBERRY BUSHES

Learning how to grow blueberries involves employing proper pruning technique and balancing new growth with old. Pruning is essential to keep production high, plants at a manageable height, and berry size large. Healthy highbush blueberries and rabbiteyes should produce at least one new cane each year, but there may be more. In late winter, count the number of new canes and cut off an equal number of old ones at ground level. Cut back the tips of the new canes to encourage branching, and snip out dead branches and low limbs that would touch the ground if fruit-laden. If you don't see any new canes, step up fertilization and check the soil pH.

HARVESTING AND STORING BLUEBERRIES

Blueberries taste best if they stay on the plant for a few days after they turn blue. Pick blueberries at least twice a week while they are ripe. Choose a mix of early- and late-maturing varieties to have fresh blueberries for more than a month. Freeze freshly picked blueberries without washing them or adding sugar.

PEST AND DISEASE PREVENTION TIPS

Blueberries have few serious pest or disease problems. Birds can harvest more than their share; tulle netting works well to deter them. Most other problems can be solved by adjusting your soil's acidity.

IN THE KITCHEN

Blueberries are among the healthiest foods you can eat, thanks to their high concentrations of antioxidants, which help guard against cancer and heart disease. A good source of dietary fiber and potassium along with vitamins A and C, blueberries are at their nutritional peak when eaten straight off the bush.

Almond and cinnamon each make excellent flavor partners for blueberries in cakes and muffins. Try adding chopped apples to blueberry pie to give the filling better structure. Frozen blueberries make delicious snacks, or you can use them in smoothies or in baking. Fresh or frozen blueberries can be made into low-sugar preserves, which can be canned in a water bath canner.

All types of blueberries make excellent pie, full of antioxidants and brimming with flavor.

TIPS FOR GROWING BLUEBERRIES

- Pick off flowers that form on blueberry bushes their first year. (This allows plants to put all of their energy into getting a strong start.)

- Water new blueberry plantings during dry spells, and renew mulch as needed to maintain a 2-inch-deep layer.

- After plants are established, fertilize them in spring with a light application of a balanced organic fertilizer, or use an organic fertilizer labeled for acid-loving azaleas or hollies. Fertilize blueberries in late summer to help plants set plenty of flower buds.

- Give blueberries watering priority during droughts. Blueberry bushes have extensive surface roots, so watch the wetting pattern of your watering equipment to ensure a thorough soaking to 6 inches deep.

all about growing strawberries

by Barbara Pleasant

THE FIRST FRUITS of the summer, homegrown strawberries are a thousand times tastier than the hard, flavorless supermarket options. Strawberries are cold hardy and adaptable, making them one of the easiest berries to grow. Growing strawberries in containers is a quick small-space solution, and they thrive in raised beds.

A bed of 25 strawberry plants can produce 30 pounds of tangy, delightful berries each year!

TYPES TO OF STRAWBERRIES TO TRY

Strawberry types vary in their growth habits and fruiting times. For prolonged productivity and unique flavors, consider growing several types.

June-bearing strawberries produce their crop over 3 weeks from late spring to early summer. Because of their earliness, high quality, and concentrated fruit set, June-bearers are the best for preserving.

Everbearing strawberries, also called day-neutral strawberries, produce a heavy set of berries in early summer followed by several more lighter flushes in late summer and fall. They need cool night temperatures (below 65°F) for good fruit set. These are excellent strawberries for large containers or raised beds, where you can give them attentive watering and regular feeding.

Alpine strawberries bear dime-sized, intensely flavored berries that may be red, yellow, or white, depending on the variety. Many varieties do not produce runners but do rebloom and set fruit intermittently all summer. Because of their small size, alpine strawberries are easiest to pick if grown in raised beds or roomy planters.

Musk strawberries produce small fruits with a pungent aroma and complex flavor. Berries tend to be precious and few; improve fruit set by adding male plants every couple of years. The unusually tall, vigorous plants form a dense groundcover that can choke out weeds. Musk strawberries are too rowdy for containers.

WHEN TO PLANT STRAWBERRIES

Growing strawberries requires sun and acidic soil with a pH between 5.5 and 6.5. Plant strawberries as early as 6 weeks before your last frost. Use row covers to protect new plantings from extreme cold and wind. You can also set out plants in fall, which is a common practice where winters are mild.

HOW TO PLANT STRAWBERRIES

Choose a sunny, fertile site free of perennial weeds. A strawberry patch will produce well for 3 to 4 years, so enrich the site with plenty of organic matter. Raised beds or planters are ideal for most types of strawberries, plus they make the berries easier to pick.

A few varieties can be grown from seed, but most gardeners save 1 to 2 years' growing time by setting out individual container-grown plants or dormant bare-root plants sold in bunches. Transplant individual plants to the same depth they grew in their containers. Spread out bundled plants and trim off any dead leaves and roots. Find the central crown and transplant so the base of the crown rests at the soil line and the roots are spread out. Mulch between all strawberry plants with pine needles, chopped leaves, or another mulch that supports acidic soil conditions.

Space requirements vary by strawberry type and variety. Those that produce a lot of vigorous runners should be planted 18 inches apart (they will fill in most of the vacant space by late summer). Plant alpine strawberries that do not produce runners—such as 'Mignonette'—12 inches apart in beds or 8 inches apart in containers.

Strawberries marry well with lots of different flavors, including cream cheese and a freshly toasted bagel.

TYPES OF STRAWBERRIES

TYPE	DESCRIPTION	VARIETIES
June-bearing strawberries (*Fragaria* x *ananassa*)	Easy to grow in many climates. Hardiest varieties survive winter temperatures to −30°F. Plants produce many runners. Grow as groundcover or as matted row.	'Earliglow' 'Honeoye' 'Jewel' 'Sparkle'
Everbearing strawberries (*F.* x *ananassa*)	Bloom and set fruit all season provided nights are cool. Ideal for growing in containers or raised beds. Not as hardy as June-bearers, but some varieties can survive temperatures of −15°F.	'Albion' 'Evie 2' 'Mara Des Bois' 'Seascape'
Alpine strawberries (*F. vesca*)	Small fruits with big flavor, best picked ripe and eaten fresh. Many varieties do not produce runners, making them easy to manage in containers or raised beds. Most varieties hardy to −20°F. Can be grown from seed.	'Alexandria' 'Mignonette' 'Rugen'
Musk strawberries (*F. moschata*)	Tall, vigorous plants best handled as groundcover. Presence of male plants improves productivity of these small, aromatic, intensely flavored fruits. Hardy to at least −10°F.	'Capron' 'Profumata di Tortona' 'Rosea'

TIPS FOR GROWING STRAWBERRIES

- Following spring planting, pick off flowers that form on June-bearing varieties their first season. With everbearing varieties (especially alpines), pinching off the first flowers can lead to better production of later-ripening, more intensely flavored fruits. With vigorous varieties, pinch off about half of the runners to help the mother plants concentrate on the following year's crop.

- If you don't need more plants, removing all runners from everbearing varieties will increase the production of big juicy berries.

- Renovate beds of June-bearing strawberries in summer, after the fruiting season has ended. Pull weeds, and thin plants to 6 inches apart. Mow or cut back old leaves 4 inches from the ground, and distribute a light application of a balanced organic fertilizer between the plants. Top the renovated bed with ½ inch of weed-free compost or fertile garden soil. Handled this way, a planting of 25 June-bearing strawberry plants grown in a 30-square-foot bed will produce about 25 quarts (close to 30 pounds) of strawberries annually for 3 to 4 years.

- Most strawberries produce runners, which can be trained to take root in promising places. Lift and move wanderers in late summer or first thing in spring. Varieties that do not produce runners can be divided and replanted, preferably in early spring.

HARVESTING AND STORING STRAWBERRIES

Expect some flavor variation each season. Cool, wet springs lead to soft, watery berries, while plenty of warm sun brings about firmer, sweeter fruits.

Pick strawberries with a short stub of green stem attached. Harvest in the cool of the morning and refrigerate right away. Wait until just before eating or preserving strawberries to wash them under cool running water and remove their green caps. Preserve berries within 3 days for optimal flavor and color.

PEST AND DISEASE PREVENTION TIPS

Slugs and snails chew round holes in fruits at night and hide in mulch during the day. Control them by handpicking, temporarily pulling back mulch, and capturing them in traps. Prevent theft from birds by covering your patch with netting as the first berries ripen.

Strawberries can be weakened by a number of leaf-spot diseases, which can be interrupted by mowing or cutting off the foliage in midsummer.

Older plantings often develop root-rot issues. Start a new bed in a fresh site every 4 to 5 years.

IN THE KITCHEN

A generous handful of fresh strawberries will provide your daily quota of vitamin C, along with manganese and a dozen other nutrients. Good flavor pairs include almond, mint, oranges, sharp cheeses, or chocolate. Strawberries marry well with rhubarb in tarts, pies, and even wine. Freeze imperfect fruits and use them in smoothies or muffins and other quick breads.

You can freeze strawberries whole by placing dry berries on a cookie sheet until hard and then transferring them to a freezer-safe container. Strawberry jams or preserves can be processed in a water bath canner. Dried strawberry slices and strawberry leather are easy to make in a dehydrator.

all about growing raspberries

by Barbara Pleasant

Dᴇʟɪᴄɪᴏᴜs, ɴᴜᴛʀɪᴛɪᴏᴜs, ᴀɴᴅ easy to grow, raspberries are a valuable addition to any food garden. The most cold-tolerant varieties can survive Zone 3 winters, and fall-bearing raspberries can be grown in warm climates that have limited winter chilling. All types of raspberries—including summer reds, golden raspberries, and super-nutritious black raspberries—make excellent boundary plantings in Zones 4 to 7.

Add nutrition and color to your garden by growing raspberries. All types of raspberry bushes, from red and golden to purple and black varieties, are easy to grow.

TYPES OF RASPBERRIES TO TRY

Summer red raspberries bear clusters of plump berries in early to midsummer on canes that grew the season before (called floricanes).

Everbearing red raspberries produce berries from midsummer to fall on the new season's growth (called primocanes). Bud-bearing canes that survive winter also bear light crops in late spring.

Black raspberries (also called blackcaps) grow wild in many areas east of the Rockies and are widely cultivated in the Pacific Northwest. Black raspberries are packed with nutrition and unique wild berry flavor.

Golden raspberries produce berries in shades of yellow to amber that often have unusually sweet flavor. Most golden raspberries produce best if encouraged to fruit on new growth, like everbearing red raspberries.

Purple raspberries combine the productivity of red raspberries with the flavor and vigorous growth habit of black raspberries. Heavy crops ripen in early summer.

WHEN TO PLANT RASPBERRIES

In spring, set out dormant bare-root plants 4 to 6 weeks before your last frost. Raspberry plants grown in containers should be planted after danger of frost has passed through early summer. Set plants 1 inch deeper than they grew in their nursery containers.

HOW TO PLANT RASPBERRIES

Raspberries need some afternoon shade if grown in hot climates, but in most regions, full sun is key to growing raspberries with rich, sweet flavor. Raspberries can produce for many years if grown in fertile, weed-free soil that drains well and has a pH of about 6.0. Before planting, dig out all perennial weeds and amend the soil with at least 2 inches of mature compost or other high-quality organic matter. Use a digging fork to loosen dense subsoil to improve drainage.

If your soil is acidic, use light applications of lime or wood ash to raise the pH. (Take care, though, as a pH above 7.0 can render raspberries unable to take up iron and manganese.)

Red and golden raspberries have a bushy growth habit and grow well on a garden fence or trellis. Black and purple raspberries need more space and are best grown as a thicket with a mowed perimeter.

RASPBERRIES AT A GLANCE

Growing raspberries that ripen at different times is an easy way to stretch your raspberry season.

TYPE	DESCRIPTION	RECOMMENDED VARIETIES	
Summer red raspberries (*Rubus idaeus*)	Canes that grow one year (floricanes) bear heavy crops the following summer. The best type for freezing or canning, summer reds can be grown on a modest trellis.	'Boyne' 'Latham'	'Nova' 'Taylor'
Everbearing red raspberries (*R. idaeus*)	New canes that grow in spring (primocanes) bear good crops in late summer and fall. Bud-bearing branches that survive winter produce berries in spring. Requires little or no trellising. Can be grown in extreme climates.	'Autumn Bliss' 'Heritage'	'Polana' 'Caroline'
Black raspberries (*R. occidentalis*)	One-year-old canes produce heavy crops in their second summer. Not as productive as summer reds, but more flavorful and nutritious. Wild plants respond well to cultivation.	'Blackhawk' 'Haut' 'Jewel'	'Mac Black' 'Munger'
Golden raspberries (*R. idaeus*)	Sweet flavor and excellent bird resistance have made golden raspberries popular companions for everbearing reds. Best grown as primocanes with emphasis on the fall crop.	'Anne' 'Fall Gold' 'Honey Queen'	
Purple raspberries (*R. spp.*)	Cross between red and black raspberries. Fruits ripen in early summer—after black raspberries—with heavy crops of dark, juicy berries possible. Prune and propagate like black raspberries.	'Brandywine' 'Estate' 'Royalty'	

Find raspberry bushes for your garden with the help of our Seed and Plant Finder at *www.MotherEarthNews.com/Custom-Seed-Search*. The Finder lets you efficiently search through the offerings of hundreds of mail-order seed and plant catalogs.

The flavor of red raspberries pairs marvelously with chocolate.

PRUNING RASPBERRIES

In late summer, pinch back new cane tips at 4 to 5 feet to stimulate the growth of heavy-bearing lateral branches. This type of pruning is especially effective for pushing summer red raspberries and black and purple raspberries to develop more buds. You can tip-prune everbearing raspberries in midsummer to encourage a heavier fall crop, but doing so isn't necessary.

When a raspberry cane finishes producing fruit, it naturally dies. To keep a clean patch with good air and sun penetration, remove old canes by clipping them off at the ground and pulling them out from the top. Frequently with everbearing raspberries, the tip end of a cane will fruit in fall, and buds farther down the stem that survive winter will bear a summer crop. Prune off the spent tip, but harvest the summer crop before removing the cane.

HARVESTING AND STORING RASPBERRIES

Raspberries are ripe when they show good color and come off easily when picked. Daily harvesting is best because hot sun can scald ripe berries and prolonged rains can cause them to rot.

Harvest raspberries into shallow containers, no more than three berries deep. Refrigerate picked berries immediately. Wait until you are preparing to eat or freeze raspberries to rinse them clean with cool water. To freeze, pat the rinsed berries dry with a clean towel and arrange them in a shallow pan covered with waxed paper. Place in the freezer for an hour, then transfer the frozen berries to freezer-safe containers. You can use fresh or frozen raspberries to make jams, syrups, or batches of raspberry lemonade or homemade wine.

PROPAGATING RASPBERRIES

Raspberries produce new growth from shallow buds near the main crown. Black and purple raspberries also propagate themselves by "planting" the tips of their arching canes in the ground 6 feet or more from the parent plant. In early spring, you can dig up these rooted stem tips if you want to propagate your

- A dense thicket of raspberry bushes 8 to 10 feet wide can serve as a living fence to deter deer. Prickly raspberries can also help protect young trees from deer damage.

- If hot weather strikes just as your raspberries are ripening, cover the plants with old sheets or shade cloth during the day to prevent sunscald.

own raspberries. Propagate or share only healthy plants. Viruses can seriously weaken raspberries, so it's best to start with plants from sources that offer certified virus-free stock.

PEST AND DISEASE PREVENTION TIPS

You can prevent many problems by growing raspberries in a sunny site with fertile soil, and by keeping your plants constantly mulched with organic material. A mulch of straw, weathered sawdust, grass clippings, or wood chips will suppress weeds and help maintain soil moisture. In late winter, top-dress established raspberries with a balanced organic fertilizer before renewing the surface mulch.

Raspberries can fall prey to root rot caused by *Verticillium* wilt, so avoid growing raspberries where tomatoes, potatoes, or other susceptible plants were recently grown.

If individual raspberry canes wilt, the problem is usually due to feeding by cane borer larvae. Cut back wilted canes to 6 inches below the damage to prevent further injury.

Black raspberries are a favorite food of many species of birds. Birds rarely bother yellow raspberries, but red raspberries sometimes require protection. Use tulle netting to protect your crop, which can also help protect plants from an invasion of Japanese beetles.

IN THE KITCHEN

Tangy raspberries pair well with other fruits and make a marvelous match for chocolate. Fresh or frozen raspberries add moisture to cornbread and muffins, and make a delightful topping for ice cream or cakes. Home winemakers value black and purple raspberries for the complexity they bring to apple or pear wine. A handful of any type of raspberry will add color and flavor to homebrewed teas. Raspberry leaves can be included in teas too.

One cup of fresh red raspberries contains half of an adult's daily quota of vitamin C along with an abundance of antioxidants, including ellagic acid, which may help defend the body from cancer.

all about growing grapes

by Barbara Pleasant

LONG-LIVED GRAPES CAN be grown in most climates, provided you choose appropriate varieties for your region. Cold-hardy varieties bred in Minnesota can survive temperatures to -30°F, while disease-resistant muscadine grapes excel in warm climates with limited winter chilling. Growing grapes organically is easier in the arid West than it is in the humid East, where disease prevention is a higher priority.

Growing grapes organically can be done with all types of grape varieties, including table grapes, muscadine, labrusca, and wine grapes.

TYPES OF GRAPES TO TRY

Seedless table grapes produce juicy, thin-skinned berries great for eating fresh, drying as raisins, or making into juice.

Labrusca grapes have wild North American grapes in their pedigree, which gives them a bold flavor ideal for juice and jelly. Labrusca grapes have good tolerance of cold winter temperatures.

Muscadine grapes are best grown in warm, humid climates and produce sweet berries with a robust, musky flavor excellent for eating fresh or in juice, jelly, or wine.

White wine grapes—which were created by crossing European and North American grapes—can be grown organically in hospitable sites. White wine grapes mature earlier than darker ones, so they are the best choice where summers are short. Some varieties, such as 'Traminette', need only 110 days from bloom to harvest.

Red wine grapes take between 105 and 140 days after blossoming to ripen, so choose early-maturing varieties in cold climates. Red wine grapes can produce yields in excess of 30 pounds per plant.

WHEN TO PLANT GRAPES

In spring, set out purchased plants 4 to 6 weeks before your last frost, when the plants are emerging from dormancy. Grape varieties grown in containers can be planted up until early summer.

HOW TO PLANT GRAPES

Growing grapes in full sun helps develop sweet, full-flavored fruits. Plants can produce fruit for decades if grown in deep, fertile soil that drains well. Before planting, dig out all perennial weeds and amend the soil with at least 2 inches

GRAPES AT A GLANCE

The grape varieties listed here are widely adapted and often recommended for organic gardeners because of their vigor and/or disease resistance. The grapes' color and USDA cold-hardiness zone number are included in parentheses.

TYPE	DESCRIPTION	VARIETIES	
Seedless table grapes	Choose early- and late-maturing varieties to extend the harvest season. Excellent on rectangular arbors where different colors of table grapes can be grown together.	'Canadice' (red, 4) 'Himrod' (white, 4)	'Mars' (blue, 5) 'Reliance' (red, 4)
Labrusca grapes	The rich flavor of these seedy grapes can be traced to wild North American species. Most produce downward-facing shoots, so they need a high trellis or can be grown on an arbor.	'Concord' (blue, 4) 'Delaware' (red, 4)	'Niagara' (white, 5) 'Ontario' (white, 5)
Muscadine grapes	Improved native Southern species resist diseases and require minimal winter chilling. Most newer varieties are self-fertile. Muscadine grapes do well with an overhead, X-shaped trellis.	'Carlos' (bronze, 7) 'Nesbitt' (black, 7)	'Noble' (black, 7) 'Summit' (bronze, 7)
White wine grapes	Newer hybrids have high productive potential even if grown in short-season areas. Upward-facing shoots require a two-tiered trellis and close management.	'Cayuga White' (5) 'LaCrosse' (3)	'Louise Swenson' (3) 'Traminette' (5)
Red wine grapes	Newer hybrids have high productive potential if grown where summers allow complete ripening. Varieties with upward-facing shoots require a two-tiered trellis. Vines tend to be vigorous.	'Chambourcin' (6) 'Cynthiana' (4)	'DeChaunac' (4) 'Frontenac' (3)

For more articles on growing grapes in your region, plus recipes for homemade jelly, juice and wine, go to www.MotherEarthNews.com/Grapes.

of mature compost or other high-quality organic matter. If your soil tends to be acidic, use light applications of lime or wood ashes to raise the pH levels to between 5.6 and 6.2.

Most grapes should be planted 7 to 9 feet apart, with a durable trellis installed at planting time. After planting grapes, water them thoroughly and mulch the area beneath the plants with 2 to 4 inches of wood chips or another organic mulch.

PRUNING AND TRELLISING GRAPES

Matching your trellis design and pruning practices to the natural growth habit of your chosen grapes will go a long way toward preventing disease and maximizing productivity. In general, 'Concord' grapes and other labrusca varieties produce downward-facing branches from long canes that form a cascade of foliage, so they do best on a high trellis or an arbor. Similarly, muscadine grapes are easiest to manage on an overhead rectangular trellis, sometimes called an X trellis. With these vigorous fruits, pruning should be geared toward preserving two to four 6-foot canes while trimming out excess growth.

Most table and wine grapes produce upward-facing shoots, so a two-tiered trellis that supports the branches as they gain height is best. Trellises of tightly woven wire are preferable because they do a good job of supporting the vines when they become heavy with fruit. Pruning of table and wine grapes should be aggressive—remove all old growth except for selected fruiting spurs. If you're growing table grapes on an arbor, you can prune a little less if you want to get a thick cover of foliage.

Prune grapes in late winter, before the buds begin to swell. The first year after planting, concentrate on helping your young plants grow straight, sturdy trunks. The training of side branches will begin in the second year, with buds ready to bear fruit 3 years after planting. Each grape variety you grow will respond differently to various pruning practices, so be prepared to fine-tune your methods.

HARVESTING AND STORING GRAPES

Grapes are ripe when they taste sweet. Early-maturing white or red varieties may be ready to pick a month before later-maturing blue or black grapes. Allow grapes to stay on the vine until the berries show a whitish bloom on their skins, but bring them in should a period of wet weather be in the forecast. Ripe grapes often crack after heavy rains.

Keep clusters of unwashed grapes in the refrigerator, stored in plastic bags to help retain humidity. Fresh or frozen grapes can be made into juice, jelly, or wine. Seedless grapes are easiest to dry into raisins.

PROPAGATING GRAPES

Grapes can be easily propagated by rooting 6-inch stem cuttings taken in late winter or early spring. When stuck 3 inches deep into an outdoor propagation bed or containers of moist potting soil, most of the cuttings will root within two months and be ready to set out the same growing season. Grapes should always be propagated from cuttings because they do not grow true from seed.

Seedless table grapes are perfect for snacking, can be added to salads or chutneys, or can be dried for raisins.

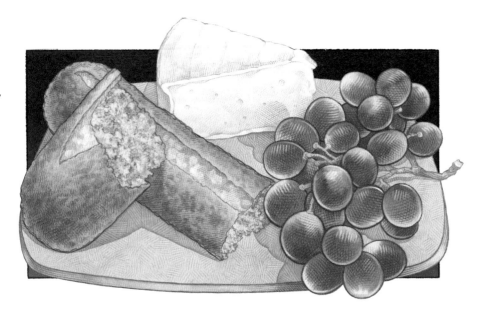

PEST AND DISEASE PREVENTION TIPS

All grape diseases can be prevented in part with attentive trellising, pruning, and mulching. In all areas, powdery mildew (evidenced by whitish patches on leaves) can weaken plants and reduce grape flavor. Preventive sprays with a solution of 1 part milk to 6 parts water can minimize this problem.

Rare in the West, the fungal disease known as black rot is a constant threat to eastern grapes. Plants often need regular sprays with organic copper-based fungicides, even if the variety is disease tolerant. Microbial fungicides based on *Bacillus subtilis* (such as Serenade) can also offer significant protection.

In the Sun Belt, gardeners should choose varieties with resistance to Pierce's Disease, common in warm-climate soils. Good choices include 'Black Spanish', 'Blanc du Bois', and 'Victoria Red'.

Grape leaves are among the favorite foods of Japanese beetles, and the fruits are a beloved snack of many wild birds. Early-season handpicking of beetles is essential to good control, and tulle netting can help protect plants from hungry birds.

IN THE KITCHEN

Seedless table grapes are perfect for snacking, can be added to salads or chutneys, or can be dried for raisins. All types of grapes give up their juice when barely heated to a simmer before being crushed and drained. Refrigerate grape juice for at least 24 hours to allow it to clear, then pour off the juice and discard the tartaric acid crystals at the bottom of the container. Grape juice can be canned, frozen, or made into jelly or wine.

Grapes provide fiber, potassium, and a smattering of vitamins and minerals, but their real nutritional punch comes from phenols and antioxidants, which are most abundant in dark-colored grapes. The antioxidants in dark purple grape juice can improve brain function, and both juice and wine made from dark grapes are good for your heart.

all about growing asparagus

by Barbara Pleasant

GARDENERS HAVE BEEN growing asparagus (*Asparagus officinalis*) for more than 2,000 years, and this sweet, slender veggie's staying power is no surprise: a well-maintained asparagus bed will start bearing 1 year after planting and will stay productive for 10 to 15 years.

Plant once, harvest for years: growing asparagus in a well-maintained bed can provide you with sweet, slender veggies for up to 15 years. In addition, its vibrant, ferny foliage makes an excellent ornamental. Shown here, from right to left, are 'Jersey Giant', 'Purple Passion', and fronds of a mature asparagus plant.

TIPS FOR GROWING ASPARAGUS

- **Get Psyched for Your Spears:** Prepare your bed when you order your asparagus crowns so you can plant them as soon as they arrive.

- **Choose Male Plants:** Most hybrid asparagus varieties are able to produce seven or more spears per mature plant because they are male plants that don't expend energy producing seeds. However, if you're growing open-pollinated or hybrid varieties that do include seed-producing female plants, dig out female plants to limit reseeding (while both male and female asparagus plants produce flowers, only the female plants will develop berries about a month after blossom). Asparagus seedlings are difficult to pull and may become bothersome weeds in some climates.

- **Tuck Them In:** Freezing temperatures ruin asparagus spears, so harvest yours before any harsh spring weather. During the first weeks of the harvest season, covering beds with row cover tunnels held aloft with hoops can help limit damage from the cold.

- **An Edible Aesthetic:** Ferny fronds of asparagus are a beautiful addition to edible landscaping beds, and asparagus stems make great filler material in flower arrangements.

A hardy perennial adapted in Zones 3 to 8, asparagus grows best in well-drained soil with a near-neutral pH between 6.5 and 7.5. The edible part of the asparagus plant is the young stem shoot, which emerges as soil temperatures rise above 50°F in spring.

TYPES OF ASPARAGUS TO TRY

Because asparagus stays productive for so long, it's important to plant the best variety available for your area. In cold climates, 'Guelph Millennium' and other varieties that emerge late often escape damage from spring freezes. In warm climates, early, heat-tolerant varieties such as 'Apollo' and 'UC-157' produce well before the weather turns hot. Gardeners in Zones 4 to 6 have a wider selection of varieties, including 'Jersey Giant', 'Jersey Knight', and other hybrids bred in New Jersey for improved disease resistance and better productivity.

WHEN TO PLANT ASPARAGUS

Plant asparagus crowns (dormant roots of 1-year-old plants) in spring at about the same time you would plant potatoes, but don't rush to plant them if your soil is still cold. A few varieties, such as open-pollinated 'Purple Passion' and hybrid 'Sweet Purple', can be grown from seed. Start seeds indoors in spring and set out the seedlings when they are 12 to 14 weeks old, just after your last spring frost. Start with asparagus crowns, however, to eliminate the year of tedious weeding that comes with starting from seed.

HOW TO PLANT ASPARAGUS

Choose a site with fertile soil that's clear of perennial weeds and grasses. A single row of asparagus plants set 15 inches apart will fill in to form a 24-inch-wide bed, or you can grow a double row in a 36-inch-wide bed. Locate asparagus along the back or side of your garden, as 5-foot-tall asparagus fronds will shade any nearby plants. A bed of 25 mature plants will produce about 10 pounds of asparagus per year.

Asparagus craves phosphorus, which is usually abundant in composted manure and in compost made from kitchen waste. Add a 2-inch layer of rich, weed-free compost to your soil before planting. Dig a trench 4 inches deep and 10 inches wide in the amended soil and arrange the crowns in the bottom, about 15 inches apart. Refill the trench without stepping on the bed.

Controlling weeds during the first two seasons will require rigorous weeding by hand. Pull out weeds early and often, and mulch with hay, grass clippings, or another organic material to suppress weeds and maintain moisture. Weeds will become less of an issue as the plants fill in.

In early winter, after several hard freezes have damaged your asparagus fronds, cut them off and compost them to interrupt the life cycles of insects and diseases. Fertilize the bed with a 1-inch layer of rich, weed-free compost or manure topped with 3 inches of straw, rotted sawdust, or another weed-free mulch. Clean spears will push up through the mulch in spring. Fertilize your asparagus again in early summer after you've stopped harvesting spears. You can top-dress with a balanced organic fertilizer, or scatter another inch of rich, weed-free compost over the decomposing mulch.

HARVESTING AND STORING ASPARAGUS

The exact dates of your spring picking season can vary by 2 weeks or more because of variations in soil temperature from year to year. Snap off spears longer than 4 inches at the soil line as soon as they appear in spring. As long as a new planting grew vigorously its first season (and your growing season is not extremely short), you can harvest spears for 2 weeks after your planting is a year old.

The next season, harvest all spears that appear for the first 4 weeks of active growth. In your third season, you can harvest asparagus for 6 weeks, and by the fourth year the plants will be strong enough to tolerate a full 8-week harvest season.

Promptly refrigerate your harvested asparagus. You can pickle, dry, or blanch and then freeze bumper crops.

PEST AND DISEASE PREVENTION TIPS

Two species of asparagus beetles damage spears and fronds throughout North America: the common asparagus beetle (black, white, and red-orange) and the spotted asparagus beetle (red-orange with black spots), which are both about ⅓ inch long.

Asparagus beetles overwinter in plant debris, so removing fronds in winter will reduce their numbers. Ladybug and several small wasps are major asparagus beetle predators.

Handpick adult asparagus beetles early in the morning when it's too cool for them to fly. Asparagus beetle eggs look like stubby brown hairs. Wipe them off spears with a damp cloth. After they've begun feeding on fronds, asparagus beetle larvae (soft, gray slug-like creatures with black heads) are unable to crawl back up plants if swept off with a broom. Many gardeners allow their poultry to clean up the asparagus bed for 3 to 5 days at the end of the harvest season to rid the plot of overwintering adults.

Asparagus beetles overwinter in plant debris, so removing fronds in winter will reduce their numbers.

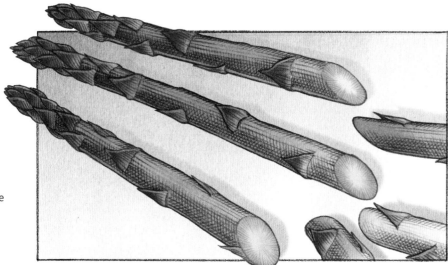

Asparagus is an excellent source of folacin, a B vitamin that helps keep the circulatory system strong, and it's a good source of potassium and vitamin C.

If you have an asparagus beetle problem but don't have poultry, set aside a section of your asparagus to serve as a spring trap crop. Don't cut the spears in spring within the plot, but patrol often to collect as many asparagus beetles as you can. In late summer, cut the fronds 2 inches from the ground and compost them. In 3 weeks or so, you can harvest a fall crop of spears from your trap crop plot.

IN THE KITCHEN

Delicate spears of asparagus are welcome at every meal. For breakfast, asparagus pairs beautifully with bacon, eggs, ham, or melon. Layer lightly steamed spears onto lunch sandwiches, or incorporate them into pasta salads, quiches, or bread puddings. Asparagus risotto can round out dinner, or you can serve asparagus roasted, braised, or grilled as a side dish.

Asparagus cooks quickly. Toss spears with olive oil, salt, and pepper, and then grill for just 2 to 3 minutes. You can make roasted asparagus by cooking oiled and seasoned spears in an open pan in an oven at 450°F for 8 to 10 minutes.

Asparagus is an excellent source of folacin, a B vitamin that helps keep the circulatory system strong, and it's a good source of potassium and vitamin C. Claims that asparagus fights cancer are based on its high level of glutathione, a potent antioxidant. Light cooking (such as steaming) for 8 to 10 minutes increases the bioavailability of asparagus' healthful compounds.

garden with cold frames to grow more food

by Barbara Pleasant

GARDENING GURU ELIOT Coleman asserts that "the basic cold frame is the most dependable, least exploited aid for the four-season harvest." We couldn't agree more. Last winter, my humble box built of 2-by-4s topped with an old shower door added a month to the front end of salad season, but the best part was being able to sow some of my spring seeds directly into the frame. This made more space available under lights indoors for tomatoes and other crops that don't like chilly conditions, and eliminated the hassle and setbacks involved with hardening off seedlings and then transplanting them. Best of all, seedlings get a nice head start in real sun so they never get stretched out and leggy as they often do when started indoors. (Indoor grow lights are vastly less intense than real sunlight.)

What can you sow in a cold frame? In spring, you get a boost with virtually any crop by sowing into frames. The list of "Top Twelve Winter Cold Frame Crops" (see page 111) can get you started, and as days get longer and warmer in spring you can try your hand at framing up peas, bulb onions, potatoes, or even tomatoes. When a cold frame is no longer needed for a crop that is up and growing, simply move it to a new location and plant more seeds.

Traditionally, gardeners have used cold frames to harden off seedlings started indoors, and you should have a frame suited to this purpose. But one cold frame is not enough. In addition to direct-seeding some vegetables right where they are to grow, you can use a cold frame to winter-sow onions, cabbage, or other hardy crops that are easily lifted and transplanted into rows.

A cold frame can be a wood box with a recycled window (or shower door) top, a hay bale enclosure covered with plastic, or you might build one with bricks or concrete blocks and top it with translucent corrugated fiberglass. Your frames need not be all alike, though having two of the same size makes it possible to stack them for added height. I like frames I can move around by myself without straining, so size and weight are important considerations. If you live north of Zone 6, you may want to create frames that are large enough to accommodate black water-filled containers for solar heat storage, and insulate the sides by

Get a jump-start on your spring garden by using cold frames to sprout seeds in a warm, protected enclosure and shelter tender seedlings from wind and frost.

adding a snug berm of soil or mulch. In climates with chronic winter cloud cover, you can maximize available light by painting the interior walls of your frames bright white, or by covering them with heavy-duty aluminum foil.

HOW COLD FRAMES WORK

Cold frames shelter plants from ice, snow, and treacherous winter winds, and heat up the soil whenever the sun shines. The soil inside a frame will warm up much faster than open ground, and because seeds of many hardy vegetables can germinate in the 50°F range, a 3-day spell of mild weather often coaxes them to life. Weed seeds will germinate alongside the seeds you plant, but you will see far fewer weeds if you cover the soil's surface with a 1-inch-deep blanket of potting soil (purchased or homemade). Be prepared to add water as needed to keep the soil from drying out.

After seeds have begun to grow inside the frames, the plants are surprisingly cold tolerant. I have watched lettuce seedlings sail through 10°F nights when the frame was covered with a thick polyester-filled blanket, and framed-up spinach never sulks no matter how cold it gets. Yet these and other winter-sown vegetables will complain if a frame is allowed to overheat, so it's crucial that frames be opened to vent out excess heat. When in doubt, it is always better to vent than to risk frying your plants. If you can't be around to open and close your frame and a warm sunny day is in the forecast, covering the top of a closed frame with a light-blocking blanket for a few days is your safest strategy. If blustery winds threaten to sabotage your venting plan, place a board over the box, between the frame and the top, to keep it from slamming shut. Or use hooks and eyes to fasten the open top to posts sunk into the ground alongside the frame.

CLIMATE-CONTROLLED FRAMES

Any cold frame will harness solar energy for your plants' benefit, and there are several low-tech ways to help your frames retain solar warmth. Black antifreeze containers, milk jugs, or kitty-litter jugs painted flat black can be filled with water and tucked into the corners. Or you can cover the spaces between plants with flat stones painted black or "solar pillows"—used freezer bags painted black and filled with water.

Historically, gardeners have used the warmth generated by rotting manure to turn cold frames into hot beds. To make a hot bed, dig a hole inside your frame at least 12 inches deep and fill it with fresh horse manure mixed with straw and topped with 6 inches of soil. As the manure decomposes, it releases heat into the frame.

But you don't have to have fresh manure to build a hot bed—or at least a warm one. For example, let's say you want to winter-sow broccoli, spinach, or another crop that needs abundant nutrients. If you dig out a bed and refill it halfway with compost mixed with the cheapest dry dog food you can find (a sure-fire compost activator) and then top it with 6 inches of soil, the compost will generate enough heat to keep the little plants from freezing and thawing quickly—if they freeze at all. In spring, when the plants' roots find the buried treasure deep in the bed, you may be looking at the biggest, best plants you have ever grown.

Another option is to use the warmth generated by rotting hay to heat your cold frame from the sides. If you have plenty of space available and you plan to mulch with hay or straw this season anyway, go ahead and get four bales and arrange them in a semicircle on ready-to-plant ground, with the open side facing south. Plant the middle, and then top the bales with a wide sheet of plastic stapled to two 2-by-4s; one board will lie atop the back bales, and the other will anchor the plastic to the ground in front. You can make a bigger hay bale haven by arranging seven or eight bales in a square and topping the enclosure with an old window, glass door, or piece of sheet vinyl or corrugated fiberglass. Or, make your bales go twice as far by breaking them in half and encircling your planting with half bales set side-by-side with their cut sides out. Allow the broken bales to get nice and damp before you plant, and then cover the bed and bales with a large piece of plastic sheeting. As the wet hay decomposes, much of the heat it releases will stay inside the bed.

TOP TWELVE WINTER COLD FRAME CROPS

These twelve vegetables are easy to grow when sown in cold frames in late winter.

- Arugula
- Broccoli
- Beets
- Cabbage
- Chard
- Chinese cabbage
- Green onion
- Kale
- Lettuce
- Mustard
- Radish
- Spinach

MINI–COLD FRAMES: MILK JUG SEED STARTERS

This simple technique was developed for seeds that need to spend a winter outside before they will germinate, but it's also a great method to start garden seeds in late winter if you don't have indoor lights or a cold frame.

1. Cut a gallon milk jug (or other large plastic container) in half horizontally, leaving one edge intact to use as a hinge. Discard the cap.

2. Punch several drainage holes in the bottom.

3. Fill the bottom with 3 inches of potting soil, moisten well, and plant your seeds.

4. Fold down the top cover, and secure the cut seam with duct tape. Enclose the planted jug in a large clear or opaque plastic bag (such as a produce bag) held together at the top with a twist tie.

5. Place in a sunny, protected spot outdoors.

6. One week before transplanting, harden off seedlings by removing the bag and tape, and propping the jug open with clothespins.

To prepare a hot bed, warm bed, or solar-charged cold frame when the soil is frozen, simply place a closed frame over the spot for several days. Daytime heating will thaw the soil inside an inch or two at a time.

Various types of cold frames are multiplying like rabbits in my garden. With the help of the frames, spring now comes to my garden at least 6 weeks ahead of schedule.

ANATOMY OF A COLD FRAME

Site Surface: Frames work best if the top is angled slightly toward the winter sun. You can either cut slanted sides or, as an alternative, mound soil as needed to make the back edge of the frame sit slightly higher than the front.

Frame: Scrap wood or untreated 2-by-4 or 2-by-6 pine boards are fine, or you can upgrade to rot-resistant cedar, redwood, or locust, or composite plastic lumber. Other options include logs, baled hay or straw, bricks, or concrete blocks.

Corners: If you only have a handsaw, a hammer, and a screwdriver, you can build a sturdy box from 2-by-4s, a few screws, and four steel corner brackets. Brackets come in different forms—some for inside the box and some for outside. The simplest (and cheapest) ones screw into the top of a frame that's already been banged together with 3-inch box nails.

Covers: The best materials for topping cold frames are tempered glass patio doors or shower doors, which often are discarded when homes and apartments are remodeled. Heavy enough to resist strong winds, shatter-resistant tempered glass doors are better scavenger hunt treasures than standard storm windows or paned windows, which can be a safety hazard. Look in thrift stores (Habitat for Humanity often sells donated doors), or call people in home remodeling or salvage businesses. Look for doors that still have plenty of hardware attached, and leave the hardware intact as you scrub down your prize. Later, after you've built a frame, the existing hardware may prove handy as part of a nifty hinge or a ready-made handle. Tempered glass doors come in all sorts of weird sizes, so it's best to secure a top first and then tailor the frame to match its dimensions.

Use thick blankets, quilts, or bedspreads to bring winter-sown frames through winter storms or to block sun when you can't be around to vent the frames. Snow makes a good insulating cover too.

all about growing potatoes

 by Barbara Pleasant

POTATOES VARY IN size, shape, color, texture, and time to maturity. Maturation time is the most important variable, because potato tubers grow best when soil temperatures range between 60 and 70°F. Try to get your crop harvested before hot summer temperatures arrive.

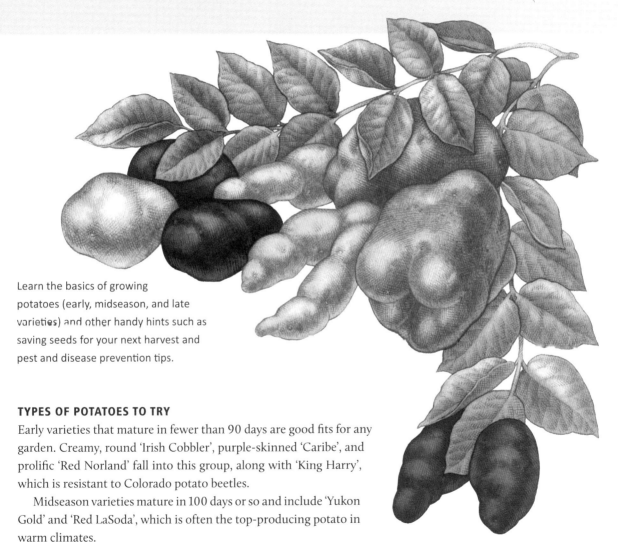

Learn the basics of growing potatoes (early, midseason, and late varieties) and other handy hints such as saving seeds for your next harvest and pest and disease prevention tips.

TYPES OF POTATOES TO TRY

Early varieties that mature in fewer than 90 days are good fits for any garden. Creamy, round 'Irish Cobbler', purple-skinned 'Caribe', and prolific 'Red Norland' fall into this group, along with 'King Harry', which is resistant to Colorado potato beetles.

Midseason varieties mature in 100 days or so and include 'Yukon Gold' and 'Red LaSoda', which is often the top-producing potato in warm climates.

Late varieties need 110 days or more of growing time, but they typically produce a heavy set of tubers that keep well in storage. 'Butte' is an all-purpose brown-skinned potato that performs well when grown in the Midwest; 'Katahdin' and 'Kennebec' rule in the Northeast.

Elongated fingerling potatoes vary in their maturation times and come in a range of colors and sizes. None are very early, but late-maturing fingerlings will size up earlier if you pre-sprout the seed potatoes before you plant them.

WHEN TO PLANT POTATOES

In climates with short springs and hot summers, plant the early and midseason varieties 3 to 4 weeks before your last spring frost date.

In climates with long springs and hot summers, plant early and midseason varieties 3 to 4 weeks before your last spring frost date; plant late-maturing varieties in early summer so they will mature in the cooler fall.

In climates with cool summers, plant early, midseason, and late varieties 2 to 3 weeks before your last spring frost date.

HOW TO PLANT POTATOES

Prepare the planting bed by loosening the soil to at least 10 inches deep. Potatoes adapt well to acidic soils with a pH below 6.0, which is lower than what is preferred by many other vegetable crops. Thoroughly mix in a layer of compost or rotted leaves along with a half ration of alfalfa meal, soybean meal, or another high-nitrogen organic fertilizer (follow label directions). Do not use manure, because it is correlated with an increase in rough patches on spud skins.

PEST AND DISEASE PREVENTION FOR POTATOES

PROBLEM	DESCRIPTION	CONTROLS
Colorado potato beetle (*Leptinotarsa decemlineata*)	Yellow- and black-striped beetles lay orange eggs on leaf undersides. Brick red larvae eat leaves and flowers.	Resistant varieties ('King Harry'), row covers, straw mulch, crop rotation, handpicking, spinosad.
Slugs and snails	Soft-bodied mollusks, with or without shells, chew holes in leaves at night or during rainy weather.	No evening watering, handpicking, trapping, encouraging ground beetles and other natural predators with enhanced habitats, practice delayed or reduced mulching.
Flea beetles (*Epitrix cucumeris*)	Tiny black beetles chew numerous small round holes in leaves. Second generation may tunnel into tubers.	Tolerate light damage, or use spinosad to control serious infestations.
Scab (*Streptomyces species*)	Soilborne bacteria cause corky patches to form on potato skins. Affected potatoes are good to eat, but less than beautiful.	Rotate with nonrelated crops, maintain constant soil moisture, use resistant varieties, do not use any kind of manure.
Early blight (*Alternaria solani*)	Widespread fungal disease causes brown spots to form on leaves. Encouraged by wet weather and the presence of mature, failing plants.	Maintain wide spacing and use drip irrigation to keep leaves dry. Harvest plants before the disease becomes severe.
Late blight (*Phytophthora infestans*)	Devastating fungal disease encouraged by mild, wet weather; causes leaves to wilt and turn brown within a few days.	Resistant varieties, early planting, wide spacing to help keep leaves dry.

TIPS FOR GROWING POTATOES

- Buy interesting-looking potatoes if you see them in stores. If you love the way they taste, save a couple and use them as seed potatoes in the spring. In rural areas, farm supply stores sell seed potatoes of varieties known to produce well under local conditions.

- Get an earlier crop by pre-sprouting your seed potatoes indoors. Pre-sprouted seed pieces will mature up to a month ahead of seed pieces bearing dormant eyes. Five weeks or so before planting, spread out your seed potatoes in a single layer in a warm, well-lit room, and wait for them to sprout from the eyes. Pre-sprouted potatoes are fragile, so be careful when handling them. Large sprouts that break off the parent potato often will grow when planted in moist soil.

- Fertilize in halves, with half of the fertilizer mixed into the soil before planting and the rest used if needed as a sidedressing when the plants are 12 inches tall, just before piling on mulch or hilling up soil around stems (to prevent sunburned spuds). See "How to Plant Potatoes" at left.

- Use old blankets to protect newly emerged potatoes if late frosts are forecast. Once the blankets are removed, the stems will pop back up within a day. (If nipped back by frost, potatoes will regrow from secondary buds.)

- Mulch plants heavily with weathered leaves or straw to keep the soil moist and protect tubers from sunlight. In slug-prone seasons, hill up loose soil over the bases of the plants instead of mulching.

- After harvesting the potatoes in the early stages of summer, plant the vacated space with beans or squash or with a cover crop of buckwheat.

Two days before planting, cut the seed potatoes into pieces so that each piece has two to three buds (or "eyes"). Cutting the seed potatoes and letting the cut pieces dry for about 2 days reduces the risk of rotting. Work carefully if the eyes have already grown into sprouts. Allow the cut pieces to dry in a well-ventilated room. Plant the pieces 12 inches apart in 4-inch-deep furrows; cover the seed pieces with 2 inches of soil. Fill in the furrows after the first sprouts emerge.

HARVESTING AND STORING POTATOES

Potato plants die back as they finish making their crop. Begin digging when the foliage starts to yellow and wither. Gently knock off dirt and allow the tubers to dry indoors, covered with dry towels, for a day or two. Take care to protect the tubers from sunlight at all times to prevent greening, which may result in bitterness. Store the most perfect tubers in a cool, 50 to 60°F place to be used as seed potatoes. Eat the less-than-perfect potatoes first, but keep in mind that they won't store forever. For longer storage, potato slices can be blanched and dried. A pressure canner must be used to can potatoes.

PROPAGATING POTATOES

Occasionally potatoes produce true seeds, but they are easiest to propagate by replanting the actual potatoes. If you are a new gardener, start with certified disease-free seed potatoes. Resist the urge to eat all of your perfect medium-sized potatoes—save several pounds; they will be great for planting the following year. Most experienced gardeners experiment with varieties and eventually assemble a collection of favorites. About 6 pounds of seed potatoes are needed to plant 50 feet of row—yield will vary from 75 to 125 pounds.

Dry beans and peas are a healthy staple crop that can be stored long into winter. With a huge variety of colorful pods and seed shapes and colors, it's almost impossible to grow every kind of bean and pea variety available. Pictured here is the 'Good Mother Stallard' dry bean.

all about growing dry beans and peas

by Barbara Pleasant

DRY BEANS AND peas provide as much protein per serving as well-known protein powerhouses such as eggs and cottage cheese, with the added benefits of fiber and an array of minerals. You could eat the dry seeds from any green bean or pea, but certain bean and pea varieties grown for their higher yields of flavorful, nutrient-dense seeds are a better use of garden space. When growing dry beans and peas in most climates, plant after your spring crops so they mature in dry fall weather. Legume flowers attract beneficial insects, and because of legume plants' ability to obtain much of their nitrogen through partnerships with soil-dwelling bacteria, beans and peas remove fewer nutrients from the soil compared with most other crops.

TYPES OF DRY BEANS AND PEAS TO TRY

Choosing varieties that suit your climate is key to growing dry beans and peas. Note that all dry bean and pea varieties can be harvested and cooked fresh as the seeds approach ripeness, or you can leave them to mature into their dry easy-to-store form.

Soup peas (*Pisum sativum*) are a cool-weather crop cultivated like green shell peas, but starchy soup peas are smooth rather than wrinkled. These frost-tolerant peas should be planted quite early, in cool spring weather. Bush-type varieties such as 'Gold Harvest' form self-supporting blocks when grown in wide beds, but 'Blue Pod Capucijners' and other tall varieties will need a sturdy trellis. Soup peas grow best in cool northern climates, in slightly acidic to neutral soil with a pH from 5.5 to 7.0.

Traditional dry beans (*Phaseolus vulgaris*) look and grow like green snap beans, but the pods quickly become too tough and stringy to eat. Bush-type New England heirlooms, including 'Kenearly Yellow Eye' and 'Jacob's Cattle', tolerate cool soil conditions, so they are the best beans to grow where summers are short and cool. In warmer areas, bushy black-and-white 'Yin Yang' (also known as 'Calypso') beans are as dependable as they are pretty. 'Dwarf Horticultural' beans can be sown after spring crops in areas with long summers. These and other true dry beans grow best in near-neutral soil with a pH between 6.5 and 7.0.

Many gardeners prefer to grow pole-type dry beans, which are grown up trellises or sown among knee-high sweet corn or sunflowers. Heirloom long-vined varieties—including intricately marked brown-and-white 'Hidatsa Shield' and maroon-and-white 'Good Mother Stallard'—will eagerly scramble over drying corn in many climates. Where summer nights are warm and humid, 'Turkey Craw' and 'Mayflower' make outstanding cornfield beans provided they reach maturity in dry fall weather.

Runner beans (*Phaseolus coccineus*) produce sweeter immature pods compared with other dry beans, and the plants' showy flowers entice bumblebees. Runner beans benefit from cool nights and are easier to grow than lima beans in moderate climates. The dry seeds are big, colorful, and meaty, resembling lima beans but possessing a sweeter flavor. 'Scarlet Emperor' bears purple-and-black seeds. The seeds of peach-blossomed 'Sunset' are almost entirely black, while those of 'Streamline' are speckled black and brown. Runner beans prefer soil with a near-neutral pH between 6.0 and 7.0.

Lima beans (*Phaseolus lunatus*) thrive in warm, humid weather and are often resistant to pests that bother regular beans. Pole-type varieties, including 'Christmas' ('Large Speckled Calico') and white-seeded 'King of the Garden', can return huge yields if supplied with a secure trellis. Bushy 'Jackson Wonder' can be grown as a dry bean too. Dried limas are easier to shell than tender green ones. Lima beans favor slightly acidic soil with a pH between 5.8 and 6.5.

Cowpeas or crowder peas (*Vigna unguiculata*), collectively known as southern peas or field peas, originated in Africa and have retained their need for warm weather. Glossy cowpea leaves are of no interest to common bean pests, and the purple blossoms set fruit even in humid heat, making this crop ideal for areas

TIPS FOR GROWING DRY BEANS AND PEAS

- If you're tight on space, grow dry beans as a succession crop by planting them directly after you harvest spring crops.

- Never soak bean seeds in water to speed germination, as this can seriously damage the growing bean embryo by depriving it of needed oxygen.

- Go light with fertilizer, because overfed dry beans grow into monstrous plants that don't produce well. Lima beans are especially sensitive to overfertilization.

- In a Three Sisters garden—which includes beans, squash, and corn or sunflowers—dry beans will work better than snap beans because they can be harvested late, requiring less disturbance of the squash vines.

- If legume pods get so dry that they shatter when you pick them, lightly dampen the plants with water before gathering, or harvest in the morning when plants are wet with dew.

There are a number of different bean varieties to grow and cook.

'Streamline' runner beans   'Christmas' lima beans

with hot, humid summers. 'Early Scarlet' and other bushy varieties set their pods high, which allows for easy picking, but you will get more peas per square foot via semi-vining varieties such as 'Pinkeye Purple Hull', 'Mississippi Silver' brown crowder, and 'Peking Black' crowder. Small-seeded, almost-white 'Zipper Cream' is much loved for its creamy culinary attributes and grows in a bush form. Cowpeas grow best in slightly acidic soil with a pH between 5.5 and 6.5.

Tepary beans (*Phaseolus acutifolius*) are native to the Southwest and Mexico, where they have been part of the traditional diet for thousands of years. Tepary beans are planted during the summer rainy season. They have smaller leaves than regular beans and adapt well to the alkaline soils found in many arid climates. Tolerant of heat and drought, tepary beans can produce well in any climate that has plenty of late-summer warmth and limited humidity. White-seeded 'Tohono O'odham White' and more colorful 'Blue Speckled' make excellent low-care crops in areas with hot summers. Tepary beans grow best in a neutral to alkaline soil with a pH near 7.0.

WHEN TO PLANT DRY BEANS AND PEAS

In early spring, sow soup peas in fertile beds 4 to 6 weeks before your last frost. All other dry beans and peas are warm-weather crops best sown in late spring and summer. Sow these seeds in fertile soil starting no earlier than 2 weeks after your last frost date. In areas with long summers, later plantings made in June may have the advantage of ripening during the typically dry weather of early fall, when scant rain reduces chances that pods will rot. In any climate, traditional dry beans with a bush habit can be planted up to 90 days before your first fall frost date.

HOW TO PLANT DRY BEANS AND PEAS

Loosen well-drained soil to at least 12 inches deep. Mix in a 1-inch layer of mature compost and, if you have it, a spadeful of soil from a bed where the same species of beans or peas grew the year before (to help inoculate the soil with nitrogen-fixing bacteria). Plant seeds 1 inch deep and 3 inches apart. Do not thin soup peas, as these grow best when crowded. Thin bush beans to 4 to 6 inches apart; thin pole beans, limas, and semi-vining cowpeas to 10 inches apart. Dry beans and peas bear all at once on spreading branches, so they need wider spacing than snap beans do.

'Yin Yang' dry beans   'Dwarf Horticultural' dry beans   'Pinkeye Purple Hull' cowpeas

When growing dry beans up cornstalks or sunflowers, wait until the support crop is 18 inches tall and plant bean seeds on the sunniest side of the corn or sunflowers. As the support crop topples from the weight of the beans, you may need to install stakes to give wandering vines a place to twine. Place 4- or 5-foot-tall stakes every 2 feet in rows of semi-vining cowpeas to support and boost the productivity of the plants, which often reach heights of 4 feet. Pole-type lima beans are a full-season crop that requires a sturdy trellis at least 6 feet tall.

HARVESTING AND STORING DRIED BEANS AND PEAS

Harvest beans and peas for drying anytime after the pods have become leathery up to when they have dried to their mature colors. (For example, the pods of 'Dwarf Horticultural' beans turn ivory with red stripes when the seeds inside reach maturity, while the pods of 'Pinkeye Purple Hull' cowpeas turn dark purple.) You can harvest green beans and peas for fresh cooking sooner, but seeds you intend to store must be fully ripe.

Leave drying pods on the plants as long as you can, but harvest them before a period of prolonged rain. If damp weather sets in just when your beans should be drying, pull up the plants and hang them upside down in a dry place until the beans are dry enough to pick and sort. Collect drying pods from pole varieties and runner beans as they change to tan or brown, and let the pods dry until crisp in a shallow tray or box kept indoors.

Threshing, or shelling, is the process of removing bean seeds from the pods, and you can do it either by machine or by hand. On a home-garden scale, shell a large crop of dry beans or peas by placing the dry pods on a tarp and crushing them by walking over them. Gather the heavy seeds that drop from the pods, and remove debris by pouring the beans back and forth from one bowl into another in front of a fan for a few minutes. Another option for small harvests is to put the pods in a pillowcase, tie the pillowcase closed tightly, and tumble it in a warm (not hot) clothes dryer.

After shelling and winnowing out debris, place your beans or peas in open bowls and let them dry at room temperature for 2 weeks, stirring often. When the seeds are hard and glossy, remove any shriveled beans (dumping the beans over a screen can help), and store your sorted beans in airtight containers. If you suspect bean weevils or other insects may be present in your stored beans or peas, keep the sealed containers in the freezer.

Handpick Mexican bean beetles in all life stages, and try spraying Neem to control light infestations.

PROPAGATING DRIED BEANS AND PEAS

Select the largest, most perfect seeds from your stored beans to keep with your cache of garden seeds for replanting. Because the seeds of legumes are self-pollinating, varieties are not likely to cross-pollinate provided varieties of the same species aren't grown side by side. When stored in an airtight container in a cool, dark place, dry bean and pea seeds will remain viable for at least 4 years.

PEST AND DISEASE PREVENTION TIPS

Brick-colored, black-spotted Mexican bean beetles often lay clusters of yellow eggs on leaves of *P. vulgaris* beans, and the eggs then hatch into yellow larvae that will rasp tissues from leaves. Handpick this pest in all life stages, and try spraying Neem on the insects and the leaves they are eating to control light infestations. In large plantings of more than a quarter-acre, try releasing beneficial *Pediobius* wasps. Mexican bean beetles do not bother cowpeas and are only slightly keen on limas.

Night-feeding cutworms sometimes fell bean seedlings by severing them at the soil line. Diatomaceous earth (DE) sprinkled over the soil's surface can help reduce losses.

Wait until foliage is dry to pick or weed beans because bean rust and other leaf-spot diseases can spread between plants when the leaves are wet.

Dry beans and peas are naturally short-lived plants. Promptly pull up and compost any plants that are past their prime in order to interrupt the life cycles of pests and diseases.

IN THE KITCHEN

Dry beans and peas share an impressive nutritional profile: a 1-cup serving of cooked dry legumes provides about 15 grams of protein plus lots of manganese, fiber, B vitamins, and iron. Rinse dry beans well in cool water before cooking. If using a pressure cooker, cook the rinsed beans for 15 to 30 minutes. If you plan to cook dry beans on the stovetop, soak them in room-temperature water for 6 to 12 hours, depending on size. Drain, then cook at a low simmer for 2 to 3 hours. Season slow-cooked beans generously with garlic, bay leaf, or thyme. Cooked beans can be simmered for a warm soup or chili, marinated for salads, puréed into dips or spreads, or mashed for filling burritos or enchiladas.

grow your own container gardens

by Ed Smith

IF YOU DON'T have the space or time to have a garden in the earth, you still can grow a significant amount of healthy, tasty food . . . in containers. Any sunny spot will do, whether it's in your yard, on your patio, deck, or balcony, or even inside your home or apartment. Not only is growing a container garden possible, it's fun and fairly easy to grow virtually anything grown in a conventional garden.

In some ways, gardening in containers is easier than gardening in the ground. Container-grown vegetables have slightly smaller yields than plants grown in the ground, but there are fewer, if any, weeds. Some pests are less likely to be a problem, because your container garden is in a location that pests don't expect to find food. Diseases also are easier to avoid because your potting soil is less apt to harbor them than ground soil. You need few tools beyond a trowel, and you don't need to cultivate the soil. Container gardens, at least the smaller ones, can be moved around and brought indoors when frost threatens. And you can set your container garden at whatever height is comfortable and convenient; you can even garden sitting down if you like!

A GARDEN IN A FLOWERPOT

There are two container options. The first is what I'll call a traditional container, which consists of anything that can hold some soil and has a hole in the bottom to drain excess water. The second option is a self-watering container, which arrived on the market a few years ago. These have a reservoir for water that is connected to the soil in the rest of the container, which ensures that the water is continually available to the growing plants. As long as there's water in the reservoir, soil throughout the container is evenly moist.

For vegetable plants, most of which are larger than the flowers typically grown in containers, a suitable container can be either a large flowerpot or something originally meant for some other use: an old washtub, a pail or sap bucket, half of a whiskey or wine barrel, or a plastic bucket that once held doughnut filling or Sheetrock compound. And because they can be recycled objects, traditional containers often are inexpensive or free. Just avoid containers that previously held chemicals.

Containers, both traditional and self-watering, allow you to grow just about anything you would normally grow in the ground on a patio, deck, or balcony.

Choose a container large enough for the plant you want to grow—the bigger the plant, the bigger the pot. A large tomato plant needs about 30 to 40 quarts of soil; a pepper or eggplant can make do with 15 to 20. Fill the container with moist container soil (see "Selecting Soils" on page 124) and add water. Then add more water.

You can grow large plants such as corn or squash in containers, but make sure your container garden site has full sun. The same is true for tomatoes, peppers, and eggplant. You can get away with partial shade for spinach, lettuce, bok choy, and other leafy greens.

WATER, WATER, ALL THE TIME

Because vegetable plants tend to be bigger and grow faster than most flower and herb plants, they need much more water. And they need it all the time in order to grow well and produce tasty and nutritious vegetables. The soil in even a large traditional container simply cannot receive and hold as much water as many vegetable plants need on a daily basis.

If you use traditional containers, plan to water at least once a day, and more often for large plants or during hot, dry, or windy weather. A mature tomato plant needs a gallon of water a day. There's no wiggle room here; vegetable plants that don't get enough water when they need it become stressed and don't produce as well. This means that a traditional container gardener has to be available to water the garden once a day—or more than once—every day.

Traditional containers are best watered just before they need it. You want to avoid stressing the plants by letting the soil go dry, but you don't want to water more frequently than is necessary because you *do* have other things to do. In my experience the critical variable here is time; it takes a certain number of hours for a plant of a certain size in a container of a certain size to use up the available water. Because water use varies with the age and size of a plant, I usually water everything whenever the thirstiest plants need water, just to keep things as simple as possible.

GARDENS THAT WATER THEMSELVES

Looking for a way to cut back on how often I had to water my container garden, I tried self-watering containers and found that I needed to water much less often. Self-watering containers with big tomato or squash plants, or closely spaced lettuce or mesclun mixes, needed water every 3 or 4 days, but younger, smaller plants got by with water once a week. No plants needed daily watering.

Container gardens need a lot of water. Self-watering models such as these can eliminate some of the work and worry of container gardening.

These containers make it possible for the container gardener to have a life beyond the garden.

I also got a nice surprise: I found that virtually all the vegetable plants I grow in my regular gardens grow at least as well in self-watering containers. Some grow better. Artichokes or eggplant can't be conventionally grown in my area due to the short season, but in a self-watering container, they grow fast enough. Why?

It appears that water is the key. As long as there is water in the reservoir, the soil throughout the container is always moist and the plants growing in it always have enough water, but not too much. In a traditional container, the soil contains as much water as it can hold only for a short time after watering. From then on, the soil—and the plants growing in it—have progressively less water available. Plants become stressed and suffer some interruption of growth whenever they have insufficient water, and self-watering containers eliminate that possibility.

Most self-watering containers are rectangular plastic, in some shade of green or brown. But there also are round, square, and hanging containers in many other colors. They have various ways to get the water from the reservoir to the soil and different ways to add water to the reservoir and register the water level. And, in my experience, they all work, although some inexpensive containers advertised as self-watering have reservoirs that are too small to offer any advantage over traditional containers.

The critical differences have to do with size: how much soil can it hold (and how deep is the soil?), and how much water? Big plants need big pots (I like about 40 quarts of soil for artichokes or summer squash). Soil 8 inches deep satisfies most plants, and 5 or 6 inches is enough for salad greens, but carrots need 12 inches. Reservoirs need to be big enough to allow at least 3 or 4 days between waterings. I like at least 1 quart of water for every 8 quarts of soil, but more is better.

Self-watering containers greatly simplify things. If there is water in the reservoir, there's enough water in the soil, period. Simply refill the reservoir before it's empty—unless rain is in the forecast. If excess water flows out the overflow hole(s), it will take valuable nutrients with it.

SELECTING SOILS

Soil in either a traditional or a self-watering container provides plants with water and food. In a traditional container, the soil needs to receive and hold as much water as possible. In a self-watering container, the soil needs to be able to absorb water from the reservoir and disperse it evenly throughout the container. Both tasks are best accomplished by a soil containing peat moss and some perlite and/or vermiculite. Peat has a unique ability to absorb and hold moisture.

I like to re-create as nearly as I can the conditions that work best in my regular garden, so I use soil that contains about 50 percent compost. I've had excellent results using a 50-50 mix of good compost and sphagnum peat–based potting soil. If you have any doubts about the compost quality, add about a cup of balanced organic fertilizer per 40 quarts of soil mix. I make my own fertilizer blend:

DIY SELF-WATERING CONTAINER

You can make your own self-watering container from a couple of 5-gallon plastic buckets. (From our food co-op, I've scored free buckets that had housed peanut butter and other such things.)

Materials
- Two 5-gallon plastic buckets
- One plastic funnel (from hardware or home supply stores)

Tools
- Drill with a ¼-inch bit
- Saber saw

1. Fit one bucket inside the other bucket. The space between the respective bucket bottoms is the reservoir.

2. Mark an oblong hole in the side of the outer bucket about 1 inch high and 2 inches long, so the top of the hole is even with the bottom of the inner bucket. Cut it out with the saber saw. This hole serves triple-duty as the fill hole, the overflow hole, and the place to stick a finger to gauge how full the reservoir is.

3. Cut a hole in the bottom of the inner bucket large enough so the funnel will project into the reservoir all the way to the bottom.

4. If necessary, cut the bottom off the funnel so it is about ½ inch longer than the space between the bucket bottoms.

5. Drill a dozen or so holes at random in the bottom of the inner bucket.

6. Fit the inner bucket into the outer bucket; insert the funnel. Fill the top bucket with moist container soil, making sure that the funnel is filled but not packed with soil. Fill the reservoir with water, and you're ready to plant!

⅓ cup each of greensand, rock phosphate, or bonemeal and a nitrogen source such as alfalfa or soybean meal. I add a tablespoon of Azomite—a rock dust that provides micronutrients and trace minerals.

Note: When peat-based soil dries out, it does not reabsorb water well, and it does not properly wick water. A dry traditional container must be watered, then watered again in a few minutes until the soil is evenly moist. A dry self-watering container needs water on the soil surface until even moisture is restored. Then fill the reservoir.

Best of luck with your new versatile, low-maintenance container garden!

Keep your soil consistently moist to provide the best growing conditions for your lettuce varieties.

all about growing lettuce

by Barbara Pleasant

GROWING LETTUCE, FROM baby leaf lettuce to big crisp heads, is easy in spring and fall, when the soil is cool. Leaf color and texture vary with variety. All types of lettuce grow best when the soil is kept constantly moist and outside temperatures range between 45 and 75°F.

TYPES OF LETTUCE TO TRY

Loose-leaf varieties grow tender leaves in dense rosettes but seldom form crisp inner heads. Some loose-leaf lettuce varieties have superior heat tolerance.

Butterhead and Bibb types quickly form small heads of leaves with stout, crunchy ribs. Some varieties have superior cold tolerance.

Romaine lettuce has elongated leaves with stiff ribs. Romaines often tolerate stressful weather better than other types of lettuce.

Crisphead lettuce includes familiar iceberg types, as well as lush and leafy Batavian, or French crisp, varieties that have great flavor and color, and are easy to grow.

WHEN TO PLANT LETTUCE

In spring, sow lettuce in cold frames or tunnels 6 weeks before your last frost date. Start more seeds indoors under lights at about the same time, and set them

LETTUCE AT A GLANCE

TYPE	DESCRIPTION	CULTURAL TIPS	VARIETIES
Loose-leaf 45 to 55 days	Fast-growing plants in a range of colors and leaf types. Frilly 'Lollos' are among the first to bolt in spring; oakleaf varieties are among the last.	Direct-sow a mixture in a covered frame for your first salad greens of spring. Gradually thin to 5 inches apart. Sow again in late summer to harvest around your first fall frost date.	'Green Ice' 'Oakleaf' 'Lollo Red' 'Red Sails' 'Salad Bowl'
Butterhead 45 to 60 days	Vigorous and cold tolerant, but the delicate leaves need protection from hail, ice, and heavy rains. Easy to grow beneath row covers in spring or fall.	Direct-sow and thin to 6 inches apart, or start seedlings indoors and transplant when they are 3 weeks old. Use row covers or cloches to shield transplants from cold and wind.	'Buttercrunch' 'Four Seasons' 'Kwiek' 'Optima' 'Pirat' 'Tom Thumb'
Romaine 50 to 60 days	Retains texture and flavor well through hot spells, provided the plants never run short of water.	Direct-sow and thin to 6 inches apart, or start seedlings indoors and transplant when they are 3 weeks old.	'Freckles' 'Jericho' 'Romulus' 'Rosalita' 'Rouge d'Hiver'
Crisphead 80 to 90 days	This crunchiest type of lettuce needs a long period of cool weather, but is worth the wait. Grow a few plants in spring and more in the fall.	Start seedlings indoors and transplant when they are 3 weeks old. Add mulch to keep soil cool and moist. Provide shade during hot spells.	'Minetto' 'Nevada' 'Red Iceberg' 'Sierra' 'Summertime'

out when they are 3 weeks old. Direct-seed more lettuce 2 weeks before your average last spring frost date. Lettuce seeds typically sprout in 2 to 8 days when soil temperatures range between 55 and 75°F.

In fall, sow all types of lettuce at 2-week intervals starting 8 weeks before your first fall frost. One month before your first frost, sow only cold-tolerant butterheads and romaines.

HOW TO PLANT LETTUCE

Prepare your planting bed by loosening the soil to at least 10 inches deep. Mix in an inch or so of good compost or well-rotted manure. Sow lettuce seeds ¼ inch deep and 1 inch apart in rows or squares, or simply broadcast them over the bed.

Indoors, sow lettuce seeds in flats or small containers kept under fluorescent lights. Harden off 3-week-old seedlings for at least 2 or 3 days before transplanting. Use shade covers such as pails or flowerpots to protect transplants from sun and wind during their first few days in the garden.

HARVESTING AND STORING LETTUCE

Harvest lettuce in the morning, after the plants have had all night to plump up with water. Wilted lettuce picked on a hot day seldom revives, even when rushed to the refrigerator. Pull (and eat) young plants until you get the spacing you want.

Gather individual leaves or use scissors to harvest handfuls of baby lettuce. Rinse lettuce thoroughly with cool water, shake or spin off excess moisture, and store it in plastic bags in the refrigerator. Lettuce often needs a second cleaning as it is prepared for the table.

PROPAGATING LETTUCE

Lettuce varieties are open-pollinated, so you can save seeds from any plants you like. Be patient as your strongest plants develop yellow flowers followed by ripe seedpods. Stake plants if necessary to keep the ripening seedheads from falling over. Gather the dry seedheads in a paper bag, and crush them with your hands. Winnow or sift to separate the seeds from the chaff, and store the seeds in a cool, dry place for up to a year. In some climates, plants grown in spring will reseed themselves in fall.

Fast-growing loose-leaf lettuce comes in a range of colors and leaf types, such as oakleaf.

PEST AND DISEASE PREVENTION TIPS

Slugs chew smooth-edged holes in outer leaves. Collect them with a gloved hand during drizzly weather, or trap them in pit traps baited with beer. You also can spray cold coffee on slug-infested plants to stop feeding.

Aphids sometimes feed in groups between the folds of lettuce leaves. Try rinsing them away with a spray of cool water. Natural predators such as syrphid fly larvae often bring the problem under control.

Prevent soilborne diseases by growing lettuce in the same spot no more than once every 3 years.

IN THE KITCHEN

Bumper crops of lettuce can't be preserved, so plan ahead for daily salads when lettuce is in season. Stock up on big flavor toppings such as olives, dried fruits, nuts, and smoked salmon. Be generous with snippings of fresh herbs as you create original salads.

TIPS FOR GROWING LETTUCE

- As the seedlings grow, thin leaf lettuce to 6 inches apart; thin romaines to 10 inches and allow 12 inches between heading varieties. After thinning, mulch between plants with grass clippings, chopped leaves, or another organic mulch to deter weeds and retain soil moisture.

- Replace old lettuce seed yearly, because low germination is usually caused by dead seeds. Expect spotty germination from lettuce seeds that are more than 1 year old.

- In late winter, grow lettuce inside a cold frame or plastic tunnel. Seedlings often survive temperatures below 20°F when they are protected with sheet plastic or glass.

- For extra flavor from your salad bed, sprinkle in a few seeds of dill, cilantro, or other cool-season herbs.

- If your garden is small, try miniature lettuce varieties such as 'Tom Thumb' or 'Minetto'.

- Should hot weather hit just as crisphead lettuce is reaching its peak, cover the plants with a shade cover made from lightweight cloth (such as an old sheet) held aloft with stakes. If possible, cool down the shaded plants by watering them at midday.

- Never allow the soil to dry out while lettuce is growing. In most soils, you'll need to water lettuce every other day between rains.

- Perfect lettuce does not last long in the garden, especially when the weather gets hot. Harvest lettuce when conditions are good, then store it in the refrigerator.

all about growing onions

by Barbara Pleasant

PACKED WITH VIBRANT flavor, onions are a staple food throughout the world. Familiar bulb onions are easy to cultivate as long as you plant varieties adapted to your climate, and you can expand your onion season by growing leeks, scallions, and other non-bulbing varieties. Fertile, well-drained soil that's slightly acidic (a pH between 6.0 and 6.8) is best for growing onions of all types.

For gardeners interested in growing onions, shown here from left to right are 'Bianca di Maggio', 'Red Torpedo', scallions, and a yellow onion with its stalk buds. The robust, exceptional flavor they add to meals is worth the few teardrops that may end up on your cutting board.

TYPES OF ONIONS TO TRY

Bulb onions mature in response to changing amounts of daylight. The longer the plants grow before they begin forming bulbs, the bigger and better those bulbs will be. In North America, days become shorter after the summer solstice, about June 21. Summer days are longer in the North than in the South.

Short-day varieties grow best in the South. They begin forming bulbs in late spring, so they need to be planted in fall in the far South and in late winter in colder climates in order to produce large bulbs.

Intermediate-day varieties are the best main-crop onions for the country's midsection (Washington, DC, to northern Arizona), and they can be grown as early onions in the North.

Long-day varieties are best grown in the North. These onions have spicy, well-rounded flavors and store well.

TIPS FOR GROWING ONIONS

- Choose the least-weedy section of your garden for growing onions.

- You can start seeds early, because onion seedlings are easy to hold in containers until it's time to plant them.

- Delay planting until the last cold spell has passed. Exposure to prolonged cold can cause bulb onions to bolt, and plants grown from sets are more prone to bolting than those grown from seedlings.

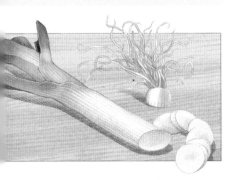

Leeks can play all sorts of scrumptious roles in the kitchen. They are great for drying and also give a tasty punch to soups, stews, and other dishes that cook for a long time.

WHEN TO PLANT ONIONS

In late winter, start seeds of all types of onions—bulb onions, leeks, scallions, and shallots—indoors under bright fluorescent lights. Make additional sowings until early spring. Set out bulb onion seedlings 3 weeks before your last frost, and set out seedlings of non-bulbing onions 6 weeks before your last frost.

In spring you can also plant sets, which are small dormant onions. Small sets produce better bulbs than large sets do.

In fall, short-day varieties can be planted in many mild-winter areas. Seedlings should be ready to set out in mid-October.

HOW TO PLANT ONIONS

Choose a sunny site with fertile, well-drained soil, and loosen the planting bed to at least 12 inches deep. Mix in a 1-inch layer of mature compost. Make a 4-inch-deep V-shaped furrow in the prepared bed. Fill the bottom of the furrow with 1 inch of rich compost or a light dusting of dry organic fertilizer, and then water the prepared furrow. Set out seedlings or sets 3 to 6 inches apart, depending on the plants' mature size.

HARVESTING AND STORING ONIONS

The tops of bulb onion plants fall over naturally once the bulbs have matured. When half of the tops in a planting have fallen over, lift all of the bulbs and place the pulled plants in a warm, dry place away from direct sunshine to cure.

Cure short-day onions for just a few days before clipping off roots and tops and storing the onions in the refrigerator. Cure intermediate- and long-day onions for 2 to 3 weeks. When the onions feel paper-dry on the outside, clip off tops and roots, and lightly brush off loose soil before storing the onions in a cool, dry place. Arrange them in a single layer or hang them in mesh bags. Properly cured onions will store for 6 to 8 months in a root cellar or cool basement. Check them weekly to sniff out signs of spoilage.

PROPAGATING ONIONS

Several of the alternative onions can be handled as perpetual crops by digging and dividing them, or by replanting bulbs or bulblets.

Big bulb onions are grown from seed. To grow your own from an open-pollinated variety, select three perfect onions and store them through winter. Replant them in early spring. After the plants bloom and black seeds begin to fall from the flower heads, gather the heads in a paper bag. Allow the seeds to air-dry for a few days before storing the largest seeds for up to 2 years.

PEST AND DISEASE PREVENTION TIPS

Onion root maggots eat onion roots and bulbs. The adult flies are attracted by rotting onion tissues, so rotate onions with other crops and compost all refuse after harvesting. Planting late can help you avoid this pest, or you can use row covers in spring, which is when the egg-laying females are most active.

ALTERNATIVE ONIONS

Not every climate is great for growing bulb onions, and in some years, unusual weather can lead to substandard crops. You can keep plenty of garden-fresh onion flavor on hand by growing these alternative onions. Many are perennials that will come back or can be replanted for many years.

TYPE	DESCRIPTION	VARIETIES
Bunching onions scallions, green onions (*Allium fistulosum*)	Instead of forming bulbs, these cold-hardy, disease-resistant plants multiply by division, forming clumps of scallions. Established plants often bloom and produce seed. Start seeds indoors in late winter. Divide in spring or fall.	'Evergreen White Nebuka' is hardy to Zone 4. 'Beltsville' and 'White Spear' are hardy to Zone 5. Some Japanese varieties are winter-hardy, but handle others as cool-season annuals.
Egyptian onions topset, walking, or multiplying onions (*A. cepa proliferum*)	These plants develop bulblets atop tall stems in early summer, and often multiply by division too. Replant bulblets in fall for spring scallions. Dig and divide parent plants, or make new plantings in spring or fall.	The 'Catawissa' strain is popular in the Northwest. These perennial onions are usually sold as Egyptian or multiplying onions and are hardy to Zone 5.
Leeks (*A. porrum*)	Leeks are easy to grow from seed. When grown from seed as cool-season annuals, they develop long, thick shanks. Summer crops can be dried. Start seeds indoors from late winter to early summer.	Fast-growing summer leeks to harvest young include 'King Richard' and 'Lincoln'. 'Bandit' and 'Blue Solaize' are more cold-hardy but slower to mature.
Potato onions nest, hill, or pregnant onions (*A. cepa aggregatum*)	Planted in fall, these hardy storage onions produce a "nest" of 2- to 3-inch onions in midsummer. Potato onions are easier to grow and store than larger bulb onions, and they are more productive than shallots. Replant saved bulbs or make new plantings in fall or early spring.	Yellow-skinned strains are popular and productive. Some varieties produce topsets (like Egyptian onions do) and nests of small bulbs.
Shallots (*A. cepa aggregatum*, *A. oschaninii*)	Highly renowned for flavor, shallots look like elongated potato onions, with some selections appearing nearly round. Plant them in fall as you would garlic, or set out bulbs in early spring. Several newer varieties can be grown from seed started in late winter. Young shallot greens can be substituted for scallions in any recipe.	Gray shallots excel in cold-hardiness, while most other varieties grow well in long-day, northern climates. In the South, look locally for 'Delta Giant' and other "Louisiana" varieties, which stay green nearly year-round.

Keep areas near onions mowed to reduce the weedy habitat that onion thrips prefer. Use a spinosad-based biological pesticide to control serious infestations.

Pink root and several other soilborne diseases can cause onions to rot. Use resistant varieties, and grow all onions in well-drained sites.

IN THE KITCHEN

Does a cook ever have enough onions? Pungent bulb onions and mild leeks are best for soups, stews, and other dishes that cook for a long time. Use tender young scallions when you need bright punches of raw onion flavor. Leeks are great for drying. Flawed bulb onions that are not likely to store well can be added to summer pickles.

all about growing radishes

by Barbara Pleasant

FAST, CRISP, EASY-TO-GROW spring and fall radishes sown directly in the garden are ready to eat in less than a month! For best quality, grow them in cool weather, keep the soil constantly moist, and harvest them as soon as the roots become plump. Radishes grow best when temperatures range between 50 and 70°F.

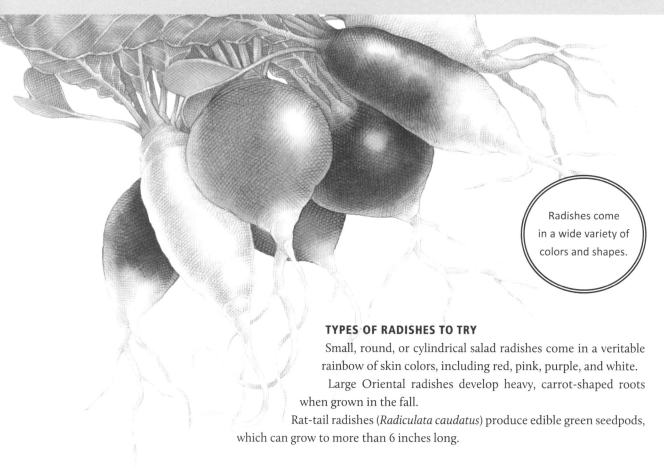

Radishes come in a wide variety of colors and shapes.

TYPES OF RADISHES TO TRY

Small, round, or cylindrical salad radishes come in a veritable rainbow of skin colors, including red, pink, purple, and white.

Large Oriental radishes develop heavy, carrot-shaped roots when grown in the fall.

Rat-tail radishes (*Radiculata caudatus*) produce edible green seedpods, which can grow to more than 6 inches long.

WHEN TO PLANT RADISHES

In spring, sow salad radishes at 10-day intervals starting 2 weeks before your average last spring frost, continuing to 3 weeks after your last frost date. Sow rat-tail radishes around your last spring frost date.

In fall, sow all types of radishes at 2-week intervals starting 8 weeks before your first fall frost, continuing up until 3 weeks before your first frost date.

HOW TO PLANT RADISHES

When preparing the planting bed, loosen the soil 6 to 10 inches deep and mix in good compost or well-rotted manure. Sow seeds ½ inch deep and 1 inch apart in rows spaced 12 inches apart. After the seedlings appear, thin salad radishes to 3 inches apart; thin Oriental radishes to 8 to 10 inches apart. Seeds typically sprout in 3 to 7 days when sown in 60°F soil.

HARVESTING AND STORING RADISHES

When pulling radishes in warm weather, cool them right away by dropping them into a pail of cold water. Use a sharp knife or kitchen shears to remove the leaves, then store in the refrigerator for up to 3 weeks. Large Oriental varieties can be left in the ground well into fall and dug just before the soil freezes.

Harvest salad radishes once they are bigger than grapes. Radishes left in the ground too long develop a pithy texture and often crack following heavy rains.

Hot weather and drought encourage the development of spicy flavor compounds, which are similar to those found in horseradish.

Slice or grate radishes into salads and slaws or layer them onto sandwiches.

RADISHES AT A GLANCE

TYPE	DESCRIPTION	CULTURAL TIPS	VARIETIES
Small Round (*Radiculata* group)	Commonly used in salads, slaws, and sandwiches, these radishes also can be cooked. Young leaves are edible, but not very tasty.	Use frames or tunnels to warm soil to favorable germination range (above 55°F) in spring. Keep soil constantly moist. Check daily after 3 weeks, and harvest promptly. Remove tops before storing in refrigerator.	'Champion' 'Easter Egg' 'Hailstone' 'Pink Beauty' 'Plum Purple' 'Scarlet Globe'
European (*Radiculata* group)	Round or cylindrical radishes often are served with bread and butter in France, or mustard and pretzels in Germany.	Same as small round type (see above).	'Bartender Red Mammoth' 'D'Avignon' 'French Breakfast' 'White Icicle'
Large Oriental (*Longipinnatus* group)	Most varieties grow to carrot size or larger; a few varieties are round. Very easy to grow. Varieties with cylindrical roots often push up out of the ground as they mature.	Loosen soil at least 14 inches deep. Thin to 10 inches apart. Dig gently to avoid broken roots. Remove tops after harvesting. Store in refrigerator or pack in damp sand and store in root cellar or unheated garage.	'Minowase' 'Minowase Summer Cross' 'Misato' 'Miyashige' 'Red Meat'
Winter Storage (*Radiculata* group)	Crisp roots have dense flesh, dark skin, and a complex, spicy flavor.	Quality is best when roots mature in cool fall soil. Remove tops after harvesting. Store in refrigerator or pack in damp sand and store in root cellar or unheated garage.	'Neckarruhn Red' 'Nero Tondo' 'Rex' 'Round Black Spanish'
Edible Pod (*Caudatus* group)	Grown for seed pods only, though the 'Münchener Bier' variety also produces good roots.	Harvest immature seed pods when crisp and tender, like spicy snow peas.	'Münchener Bier' 'Rat's Tail'

TIPS FOR GROWING RADISHES

- In spring, cover newly seeded beds with a cold frame or plastic tunnel to warm the soil.

- To save space, sow radishes between rows of slow-germinating vegetables such as carrots, parsley, or parsnips.

- To reduce weed competition, place strips of wet newspaper along the edges of the seeded furrow and cover them with grass clippings or another biodegradable mulch.

- Thin radishes early, when they have only two or three leaves. Early thinning minimizes disturbance to nearby plant roots.

- Keep the soil constantly moist while radishes are growing. Cool, moist soil is the key to growing a good crop. Root quality is best when the plants are thoroughly drenched with water every 3 days throughout their growing season.

- Radishes need full sun, but they benefit from partial shade during spells of hot weather. To help the plants get through a spring heat wave, cover them with a shade cover made of lightweight cloth held aloft with wooden stakes.

- High-nitrogen fertilizers will make radishes grow lush leaves, but the roots may never swell into plump radishes. Stick with compost when preparing space for radishes.

- If your soil is heavy clay, salad radishes may grow thin ropelike roots rather than large, crisp ones. Lightening the soil's texture by mixing in compost and sand can help, or you can stick with Oriental varieties, which adapt well to clay soil.

- Don't be discouraged if a spring crop doesn't meet your expectations. Your best shot at perfect radishes comes in fall, when the soil is getting cooler rather than warmer.

- Radishes make a good fall cover crop. Plant them after beans, peas, or another nitrogen-fixing legume and they will utilize nitrogen left behind in the soil. Later, when the plants are killed by cold winter weather, nitrogen and other nutrients will be returned to the soil.

PROPAGATING RADISHES

To save seeds from open-pollinated varieties, allow three or more plants to bloom together and wait until the seedpods dry and turn brown before harvesting the seeds. Crush the pods with your hands, winnow or sift them to separate seeds from chaff, and store the seeds in a cool, dry place for up to 5 years.

PEST AND DISEASE PREVENTION TIPS

Flea beetles make numerous small holes in radish leaves. Cabbage root maggots and cutworms sometimes rasp holes or channels into radish skins. All of these pests are easily prevented by covering the plants with lightweight floating row covers.

When sown early and exposed to cold weather, some radishes will bolt (rush to produce flowers) before they develop plump roots. Bolting is rare in radishes grown in late summer and fall.

IN THE KITCHEN

Slice or grate radishes into salads and slaws, or layer them onto sandwiches. You also can try eating radishes the European way—with bread and butter. Radishes braised in butter or sesame oil until they just begin to brown have a mellow flavor and succulent texture. Substitute sliced or diced radishes for water chestnuts in stir-fries. A handful of salad radishes provides about 20 percent of your daily quota of vitamin C, along with about 2 grams of fiber, lutein, and a range of minerals.

Green, Asian, pointed, and red cabbages all make beautiful additions to your garden as well as nutritious options at your table.

all about growing cabbage

by Barbara Pleasant

DEPENDABLE, NUTRITIOUS, AND delicious raw or cooked, both green and red cabbage are among the most productive cool-season crops. Gardeners growing cabbage in cool climates can grow huge blue-ribbon-winning heads. Where hot summers divide the cool seasons, fast-maturing varieties do well in spring and again in fall. All types of cabbage are at their best in late fall, after exposure to light frosts.

TYPES OF CABBAGE TO TRY

Green cabbage varieties vary in their earliness and mature size. Smaller varieties can be grown at close spacing.

Red cabbage provides higher levels of vitamins A and C than other types of cabbage do, and its bright color is always beautiful on the plate.

Savoy cabbage produces a crisp heart and crinkled dark green outer leaves.

Pointed cabbage develops conical instead of rounded heads. Its upright growth habit and tight outer leaves protect pointed cabbage from insects and sun.

Napa cabbage (or Chinese cabbage) matures quickly and produces crisp, mild-flavored leaves.

WHEN TO PLANT CABBAGE

In spring, start seeds indoors or in a cold frame 8 to 10 weeks before your last spring frost, and set out hardened-off seedlings when they are about 6 weeks old. Seeds germinate best at 65 to 75°F.

In summer, start seeds 12 to 14 weeks before your first fall frost, and transplant the seedlings to the garden when they are 4 to 6 weeks old. Plant early and late varieties to stretch your harvest season.

HOW TO PLANT CABBAGE

Growing cabbage plants requires regular feeding and abundant sun. Choose a sunny, well-drained site with fertile soil that has a pH between 6.0 and 6.5.

Loosen the planting bed and mix in a 2-inch layer of compost along with a standard application of a balanced organic fertilizer or well-composted manure. Water the fertilized bed thoroughly before setting out seedlings. Allow 18 to 20 inches between plants for 4-pound varieties; larger varieties may need more room. Varieties that will produce heads that weigh less than 2 pounds (check your seed packet) can be spaced 12 inches apart.

CABBAGE AT A GLANCE

Open-pollinated (OP) and hybrid (F1) cabbage (*Brassica oleracea* var. *capitata*) varieties have a range of sizes and maturation times. Varieties marked with an asterisk can be grown at close spacing and produce softball-sized heads.

TYPE	DESCRIPTION	RECOMMENDED VARIETIES
Green cabbage	You'll need plenty of space to grow big heads. Crowding reduces head size, but miniature varieties such as 'Gonzales' fit in tight spaces in the garden and the refrigerator.	'Farao'* (F1), 63 days 'Golden Acre' (OP), 62 days 'Gonzales'* (F1), 66 days 'Kaitlin' (F1), 94 days
Red cabbage	These stunning red heads with white cores are slightly more nutritious than green cabbage.	'Red Express'* (OP), 62 days 'Ruby Perfection' (F1), 85 days 'Super Red 80'* (F1), 80 days
Savoy cabbage	Dramatic ruffled leaves surround a tender heart. Fast-maturing varieties do well in spring, but savoy cabbage tastes sweetest in fall.	'Alcosa'* (F1), 70 days 'Deadon' (F1), 105 days 'Des Vertus' (OP), 95 days 'Famosa' (F1), 68 days
Pointed cabbage	Small, elongated heads are surrounded by buttery leaves with a crisp heart. Easy to grow and loads of fun for the cook.	'Caraflex'* (F1), 68 days 'Early Jersey Wakefield' (OP), 63 days 'Filderkraut' (OP), 95 days

To locate sources for these varieties, use our online Seed and Plant Finder at *www.MotherEarthNews.com/Custom-Seed-Search*.

HARVESTING AND STORING CABBAGE

Begin harvesting cabbage when the heads feel firm, using a sharp knife to cut the heads from the stem. Remove and compost rough outer leaves, and promptly refrigerate harvested heads. If cut high, many varieties will produce several smaller secondary heads from the roots and crown left behind.

Cabbage will store in the refrigerator for 2 weeks or more, and you can keep your fall crop in cool storage for several months. Clean cabbage carefully because heads may harbor hidden insects.

Cabbage yield is generally about 1 pound per foot of row. For the spring crop, three cabbage plants per person is probably sufficient for fresh eating. Grow another four plants per person in fall if you plan to store your cabbage or make sauerkraut.

PROPAGATING CABBAGE

Cabbage is a biennial crop that produces seed in its second year, after it has been exposed to cold weather. Most commercial cabbage seed is grown in Washington State, where winters are mild enough to allow the survival of seedlings set out in late summer. These plants form only small, loose heads before blooming and producing seeds the following summer. In colder climates, growers dig cabbage plants and move them to a cool root cellar for winter, burying the plants' roots in buckets of moist sawdust. The stored heads are trimmed and replanted in early spring. Isolation is often required to keep cabbage from crossing with its close cousins, so you should grow only one type of cabbage for seed in a given year. Cabbage seeds will keep for 5 years if stored under excellent conditions.

PEST AND DISEASE PREVENTION TIPS

- Tender cabbage seedlings may be felled in the night by soil-dwelling cutworms. To protect young seedlings, enclose their stems with stiff collars made from plastic cups, shallow cans, or aluminum foil pushed 1 inch into the soil.
- Leaf-eating caterpillars—including armyworms, cabbage loopers, and velvety green cabbageworms—frequently damage cabbage leaves. In summer, brightly marked harlequin bugs and grasshoppers can devastate young plants. The best way to prevent all of these problems is to install floating row covers the day you transplant the seedlings.
- Unless you have a heavy infestation, you can often keep plants healthy by watching them closely and handpicking pests. (Look closely—tiny green cabbageworms are very hard to see.) Biweekly sprays with a biological pesticide—Bt (*Bacillus thuringiensis*) or spinosad—will control cabbageworms and other caterpillar-type cabbage pests. Handpick slugs and snails, which can often be found hiding on the undersides of the cabbage leaves closest to the ground.
- Cabbage plants that suddenly collapse may have been hit by root maggots (rice-sized fly larvae that feed on cabbage roots). You can deter fly larvae by pressing the soil down firmly when setting out the seedlings. Rotate cabbage-family crops to deter this pest. In areas where canola is grown, use row covers to escape these ever-present maggots.

TIPS FOR GROWING CABBAGE

- Use cloches, row cover tunnels, or other season-stretching devices to get your spring cabbage crop growing a few weeks early. In summer, use temporary shade covers after transplanting fall seedlings into hot summer soil.

- Experiment with varieties, which can make a huge difference in the success of your crop. Fast-growing cabbage that forms small heads is great for space-squeezed gardens.

- Give plants extra nitrogen just as small heads begin to form by drenching them with a liquid organic fertilizer.

- Heavy rain can cause almost-ready cabbage heads to split. Prevent this by using a sharp spade to sever roots on opposite sides of the plant before an expected rain.

High in vitamins A and C, cabbage adds a nutritional boost to any meal.

IN THE KITCHEN

Various types of slaw made from raw chopped cabbage are popular accompaniments for seafood and barbecue. Cooked cabbage recipes number in the thousands, from crunchy stir-fries to slow-cooked braises. Tame strong-flavored cabbage by chopping and then blanching it for 1 minute before proceeding with your recipe. Include a few fennel seeds in the cooking liquid to reduce cabbage's cooking aroma. Large outer leaves may be blanched and frozen for later use when making cabbage rolls. Chopped cabbage can be blanched and frozen, or fermented into sauerkraut.

Cabbage is a good source of vitamins A and C. Red cabbage and green cabbage that has tight, white cores typically contain high levels of vitamin C, while dark outer leaves offer an abundance of vitamin A. Homemade fermented sauerkraut (or refrigerated kraut that hasn't been heat-processed) contains health-enhancing nutrients and bacteria.

all about growing asian greens

by Barbara Pleasant

FROM CRUNCHY CHINESE cabbage to buttery bok choy, Asian greens offer an array of flavors and textures for your fall table. Just a small plot of garden space can yield a bountiful assortment of leafy greens, crisp stems, and even edible flowers. Most Asian greens prefer shorter, cooler days, so growing them is an easy way to keep producing your own food well into autumn.

Depending on which part of the plants you use, fast-growing Asian greens can slip into several culinary roles, and all plants are excellent sources of calcium and vitamins A, C, and K. Shown here, from right to left, are Chinese cabbage, red mustard, mizuna, bok choy, and edible chrysanthemum.

TYPES OF ASIAN GREENS TO TRY

Leafy greens of Asian ancestry include mustard cousins such as mizuna, mustard spinach, and tatsoi. Red-leafed mustards and garland chrysanthemum offer more variations in flavor and texture.

Leaf ribs or crisp stems of Chinese cabbage and bok choy bring plenty of crunch to stir-fries and salads. Miniature forms of both are great for small gardens.

Tender flower buds come from special varieties of flowering brassicas, which may have a broccoli or a mustard pedigree.

WHEN TO PLANT ASIAN GREENS

In late summer (6 to 12 weeks before your first fall frost), sow seeds indoors or direct-sow them in the garden if the weather is hot and dry. Transplant seedlings when they are 4 weeks old. Some Asian greens can also be grown in spring, but because spring crops are prone to bolting, be sure to choose bolt-resistant varieties, which will hold in the spring garden about 10 days longer than other varieties.

HOW TO PLANT ASIAN GREENS

All Asian greens grow best in moist, fertile, well-drained soil with a pH between 6.0 and 6.5. Choose a sunny site, loosen the soil to at least 12 inches deep, and

ASIAN GREENS AT A GLANCE

Many leafy green types can be harvested young. The days to maturity shown below range from edible baby greens to mature plants.

TYPE	DESCRIPTION	VARIETIES
LEAFY GREENS		
Asian mustards (*Brassica juncea, B. rapa*) Variations include mizuna, mustard spinach, tatsoi, red mustards and more.	Vigorous, fast-growing plants rarely have pest problems. New leaves regrow from plant crowns after harvest. Cool weather triggers the production of sugars in leaves, which serve as natural antifreeze. The sugars balance out bitterness, improving flavor.	'Kyoto Mizuna' (30 to 50 days) 'Osaka Purple' (30 to 50 days) 'Tatsoi' (40 to 55 days) 'Vitamin Green' (21 to 45 days)
Garland chrysanthemum (*Chrysanthemum coronarium*) Also called shungiku and choy suy.	Fragrant greens can bring a floral note to soups, stir-fries and sushi. Flowers also are edible. Try them scattered over soup.	'Round Leaf' (21 to 59 days) 'Shungiku' (21 to 45 days) 'Tiger Ear' (21 to 45 days)
STEMS AND RIBS		
Chinese cabbage (*B. rapa*) Also called Napa cabbage and celery cabbage.	Plants mature quickly and are easier to grow than heading cabbage. Their crisp, mild-flavored leaf ribs make great slaw.	'Fun Gen' (45 days) 'Minuet' (F1) (48 days) 'Soloist' (F1) (50 days)
Bok choy (*B. rapa*) Also spelled "pac choi" and "pak choi."	Among the best of all miniature vegetables and quite easy to grow, bok choy is exceptional if stir-fried whole, halved, or chopped.	'Ching Chang' (40 days) 'Green Fortune' (F1) (48 days) 'Violetta' (F1) (30 to 50 days)
FLOWER BUDS		
Chinese broccoli (*B. oleracea*) Also called sprouting broccoli and flowering broccoli.	Cool weather and cooking tame plants' slightly sharp flavor. Plants produce sprouts for several weeks and can be grown through winter in Zone 7 and warmer.	'Green Lance' (F1) (45 days) 'Green Sprouting' (60 days) 'Purple Peacock' (70 days)
Flowering mustard (*B. rapa*) Also called choy sum and choi sum.	Slender stems with delicate flowers taste best if they mature in cool weather. A small family will need only a few of these highly productive plants to keep the kitchen sufficiently stocked.	'Choy Sum' (50 days) 'Hon Tsai Tai' (37 days) 'Kosaitai' (50 days)

thoroughly mix in a layer of mature compost. Sow seeds about 2 inches apart and ¼ inch deep, then water well to settle the seeds into the soil. After seeds germinate (often in less than 5 days), gradually thin them to proper spacing. Large Chinese cabbage, Chinese broccoli, and flowering mustard should be thinned to 14 inches apart, but small bok choy plants do well with just 6 inches between plants.

HARVESTING AND STORING ASIAN GREENS

You can eat the young seedlings you pull while thinning your crops. As leafy types mature, harvest individual leaves or cut away fistfuls of greens, leaving the plants' central crowns intact. New leaves will quickly replace the harvested ones. Pull whole Chinese cabbage or bok choy plants as you need them, and gather or protect them all before your first hard freeze. Most Asian greens can survive for several weeks in early winter if they're inside a row cover or plastic tunnel. Whole heads that are trimmed, rinsed, and refrigerated will keep for up to a month. Cut 4- to 6-inch stems from sprouting brassicas when the green flower buds just begin to show yellow, and promptly chill them in the fridge. Bumper crops of any Asian vegetables can be blanched and frozen.

PROPAGATING ASIAN GREENS

Plants that survive winter in Zone 7 and warmer begin blooming first thing in spring. In cooler zones, make small sowings in early spring for seed-saving purposes. Grow two or three plants of the same type together in a clump, and allow them to flower freely. When the elongated seedpods mature to tan, collect the largest pods in a paper bag. Dry them indoors in a warm room until the seeds fall from the pods if you crush them with your hand. Select your most robust-looking seeds for storage. If stored in a cool, dry place, the seeds of most Asian greens will remain viable for up to 5 years.

PEST AND DISEASE PREVENTION TIPS

Small holes in leaves are most often the work of flea beetles, but this damage is usually minor and disappears when the greens are cooked. Aphids occasionally feed in clusters in crinkled Chinese cabbage leaves, but you can easily control them with two applications of insecticidal soap, applied 1 week apart. Slugs chew holes in leaves and stems and leave a slimy trail behind them. Handpick the big ones, and pull back mulches that may provide daytime hangouts for slugs and snails. Use iron phosphate baits as a last resort.

IN THE KITCHEN

Young plants that grow in cool weather are mild enough to be eaten raw in salads and sandwiches, but with the exception of Chinese cabbage and bok choy, most Asian greens (at any stage of growth) should be cooked until they are well wilted (at least 2 to 3 minutes). Cooking tames the flavor of greens that may taste bitter if sampled raw. Sesame oil or toasted sesame seeds are great flavor accents, and you can use your chopped cooked greens as a spinach substitute in most recipes. All Asian greens are good sources of calcium and vitamins A, C, and K.

TIPS FOR GROWING ASIAN GREENS

- **Colorful Ornamentals:** Red-blushed varieties of Asian greens (such as 'Osaka Purple' mustard) make beautiful, edible ornamentals. Try pairing them with yellow marigolds or chrysanthemums.

- **Easy Chicken Feed:** Mizuna and mustard spinach grow back so quickly after harvesting that they make great additions to poultry forage mixtures.

- **Container Cultivation:** Baby bok choy is petite enough to be grown in containers, or you can use the small upright plants to fill small spaces in beds.

Among the best of all and quite easy to grow, bok choy is exceptional if stir-fried whole, halved, or chopped.

all about growing fruit trees

by Barbara Pleasant

NO PLANTS GIVE sweeter returns than fruit trees. From cold-hardy apples and cherries to semitropical citrus fruits, fruit trees grow in nearly every climate. Growing fruit trees requires a commitment to pruning and close monitoring of pests, and you must begin with a type of fruit tree known to grow well in your area.

There are many types of fruit trees, and with a little research you can easily find the best variety for your region and tastes. Try growing apples for homemade cider or peaches for a heavenly summer treat.

Choose varieties recommended by your local extension service, as some varieties need a certain level of chill hours (number of hours below 45°F).

TYPES OF FRUIT TREES TO TRY

Even fruit trees described as self-fertile will set fruit better if grown near another variety known to be a compatible pollinator. Extension publications and nursery catalogs often include tables listing compatible varieties.

Apples (*Malus domestica*) are the most popular tree fruits because they are widely adapted, relatively easy to grow, and routine palate-pleasers. The ideal soil pH for apples is 6.5, but apple trees can adjust to more acidic soil if it's fertile and well drained. Most apple varieties, including disease-resistant 'Freedom' and 'Liberty', are adapted to cold-hardiness Zones 4 to 7, but you will need low-chill varieties such as 'Anna' and 'Pink Lady' in mild-winter climates. No matter your climate, begin by choosing two trees that are compatible pollinators to get good fruit set. Mid- and late-season apples usually have better flavor and store longer compared with early-season varieties.

Cherries (*Prunus avium* [sweet] and *P. cerasus* [sour]) range in color from sunny yellow to nearly black and are classified in two subtypes: compact sweet varieties such as 'Stella' and sour or pie cherries such as 'Montmorency' and 'North Star'. Best adapted to Zones 4 to 7, cherry trees need fertile, near-neutral soil and excellent air circulation. Growing 12-foot-tall dwarf cherry trees of either subtype will simplify protecting your crop from diseases and birds because the small trees can be covered with protective netting or easily sprayed with sulfur or kaolin clay.

Citrus fruits (*Citrus* hybrids), including kumquat, mandarin orange, satsuma, and 'Meyer' lemon, are among the easiest fruit trees to grow organically in Zones 8b to 10. Fragrant oils in citrus leaves and rinds provide protection from pests, but cold tolerance is limited. 'Nagami' kumquat, 'Owari' satsuma, and 'Meyer' lemon trees may occasionally need to be covered with blankets when temperatures drop below freezing, but winter harvests of homegrown citrus fruits will be worth the trouble.

Peaches and nectarines (*Prunus persica*) are on everyone's want list, but growing these fruit trees organically requires an excellent site, preventive pest management, and some luck. More than other fruit trees, peach and nectarine trees need deep soil with no compacted subsoil or hardpan. Peaches and nectarines are best adapted to Zones 5 to 8, but specialized varieties can be grown in colder or warmer climates. Peach and nectarine trees are often short lived because of wood-boring insects, so plan to plant new trees every 10 years.

Plums (*Prunus* species and hybrids) tend to produce fruit erratically because the trees often lose their crop to late freezes or disease. In good years, plum trees will yield heavy crops of juicy fruits that vary in color from light green to dark purple. Best adapted to Zones 4 to 8, plum trees need at least one compatible variety nearby to ensure good pollination. In some areas, selected native species, such as beach plums in the Northeast or sand plums in the Midwest, may make the best homestead plums.

When learning how to grow fruit trees, be sure to research trunk guards and pruning techniques.

Pears (*Pyrus* species and hybrids) are slightly less cold hardy than apples but are easier to grow organically in a wide range of climates. In Zones 4 to 7, choose pear varieties that have good resistance to fire blight, such as 'Honeysweet' or 'Moonglow'. In Zones 5 to 8, Asian pear trees often produce beautiful crisp-fleshed fruits if given routine care. Most table-quality pears should be harvested before they are fully ripe.

HOW TO PLANT FRUIT TREES

The best time to plant fruit trees in Zones 3 through 7 is early spring, after the soil has thawed. Fruit trees that are set out just as they emerge from winter dormancy will rapidly grow new roots. In Zones 8 to 10, plant new trees in February. Choose a sunny site with fertile, well-drained soil that's not in a low frost pocket. Dig a planting hole that's twice the size of the rootball of the tree. Carefully spread the roots in the hole and backfill with soil. Set trees at the same depth at which they grew at the nursery, taking care not to bury any graft union (swollen area) that's on the main trunk. Water well, and install a trunk guard made of hardware cloth or spiral plastic over the lowest section of the trunk to protect it from insects, rodents, sunscald, and physical injuries. Stake the tree loosely to hold it steady. Mulch over the root zone of the planted trees with wood chips, sawdust, or another slow-rotting mulch. Water particularly well during any dry spells for the first 2 years.

One year after planting, fertilize fruit trees in spring by raking back the mulch and scratching a balanced organic fertilizer into the soil surface (follow application rates on the product's label). Then add a wood-based mulch to bring the mulch depth up to 4 inches in a 4-foot circle around the tree. After 2 years, stop using trunk guards and instead switch to coating the trunks with white latex paint to defend against winter injuries. Add sand to the paint to deter rabbits and voles.

PRUNING FRUIT TREES

Pruning is a key aspect of growing fruit trees. The goal of pruning fruit trees is to provide the leaves and fruit access to light and fresh air. The ideal branching pattern varies with species, and some apple and pear trees can be pruned and trained into fence- or wall-hugging espaliers to save space. Begin pruning fruit trees to shape them in their first year, and then prune annually in late winter, before the buds swell. Pruning a little too much questionable growth is better than removing too little.

Many fruit trees set too much fruit, and the excess should be thinned. Asian pear trees should have 70 percent of their green fruits snipped off when the pears are the size of a dime, and apples should be thinned to 6 inches apart before the fruits are the size of a quarter. When any type of fruit tree is holding a heavy crop, thinning some of the green fruits will increase fruit size, reduce limb breakage, and help prevent alternative bearing (a tree setting a crop only every other year).

HARVESTING AND STORING TREE FRUITS

With the exception of pears, tree fruits should be harvested just as they approach full ripeness and then kept chilled to slow spoilage. The flavor of most apples improves after a few weeks in cold storage, so a second refrigerator or a root cellar may be useful. Apples and pears can be kept for several months in a refrigerator, but softer stone fruits (cherries, nectarines, peaches, and plums) must be canned, dried, frozen, or juiced within a few days of harvest for long-term storage.

PEST AND DISEASE PREVENTION TIPS

Some types of fruit crops attract a large number of insect pests and can succumb to several widespread diseases for which no resistant varieties are available. For example, all of the stone fruits are frequently affected by brown rot, a fungal disease that overwinters in mummified fruit. Apply early-season sulfur sprays to suppress brown rot and other common diseases. Some apples have good genetic resistance to scab and rust, but you will still need to manage insect pests such as codling moths.

Allowing chickens to forage beneath fruit trees can help suppress insects. Many organic growers also keep their fruit trees coated with kaolin clay during the growing season to repel pests.

IN THE KITCHEN

Managing the hefty harvests from mature fruit trees will require a range of food-preservation skills. Manual fruit-processing equipment, such as a cherry pitter or an apple peeler/corer, can be excellent investments. At each picking, a number of bruised fruits will need attention right away, while you can refrigerate and forget about sound fruits until your next preservation project. In addition to making jams, jellies, and chutneys, try freezing or canning homemade fruit juices. Packets of frozen fruit are handy for baking or in smoothies, and dried fruit can be quickly rehydrated in warm water or munched as a snack.

Special fruit-processing equipment, such as a cherry pitter, is useful when growing cherries on your homestead.

how to make cheap garden beds

by Cheryl Long

SOMETIMES GARDEN WRITERS make things involve more work and expense than necessary. Raised garden beds are one example. Your crops will grow fine whether your beds are level, raised, or even sunken (a good choice in dry, windy regions).

Maintaining dedicated beds where you plant crops and dedicated pathways where you walk is the important piece.

Compacted soil is the enemy of strong plant growth. The more easily a plant can send roots into the soil, the faster the plant can absorb the nutrients it needs and the more drought-resistant it becomes. If the plant has to spend energy pushing roots into hardened soil, the plant has less energy to grow and produce well.

In nature, meadow mice, moles, earthworms, and other critters tunnel throughout the soil—and thus counteract compaction—and humans and other large critters do not walk over the soil often. But in a garden, we walk back and forth a great deal, and our footsteps definitely compact the soil. "One winter, we took a shortcut across a fallow field, using the path almost daily," reports market gardener Anthony Boutard in his splendid book *Beautiful Corn*. "When I looked at an aerial photograph taken 3 years later, I could still see that pathway reflected in the reduced growth of the crop planted there."

The best way to minimize soil compaction is to lay out defined areas for growing and defined areas for walking. First, measure the entire area and make a drawing on paper. Choose a bed width that lets you easily reach to its center from the path. Think about where you want composting areas, where you will want gates if you fence the garden, and where to leave room for a worktable or two and a bench with a nice view.

You can make paths as narrow as 1 foot if your space is limited, but always make a few main paths wide enough to accommodate a garden cart or wheelbarrow comfortably. If your garden area slopes, arrange the permanent garden beds across the slope rather than down it to minimize erosion. Build most of your beds the same size so you can use row covers, critter protectors, and chicken tunnels interchangeably. Use wooden stakes, pipes, or rebar to mark the corners of the beds. The stakes can do double duty as hose guides—simply slip a length of plastic pipe loosely over each, and hoses will slide around them easily.

Growing vegetables in garden beds is far more efficient than maintaining single rows of crops. From the paths on either side of a bed, you can easily weed and harvest crops in a bed 3 to 4 feet wide. When you plant several rows next to each other in a wide permanent bed without a pathway between them, crops grow together to shade the soil and thus reduce weeds. But if you placed pathways on either side of single rows, you would compact more of your garden soil as well as leave more area open to sunlight, which permits weed growth. Permanent beds and paths also let you apply fertilizer and water more efficiently.

We hear a lot of talk about raised bed gardening, but unless your site has drainage problems, there's really no reason for garden beds to be raised. In fact, choosing raised beds may have as many cons as pros. Feel free to skip raised beds and just go for the cheap garden beds. You'll be glad you did.

Here's how—and why—to create permanent garden beds and paths, and why framed or raised beds may be optional.

SIX WAYS TO GET A CHEAP GARDEN BED GROWING

Here are half a dozen methods for creating garden beds from scratch while easily incorporating what we see as the most important tenet of building new beds: keeping your planting areas separate from your walking areas.

1. **Instant Gardens:** For areas that are currently in grass or weeds, one of the simplest ways to create new beds without any tilling is to use bags of topsoil laid out to cover your bed areas, with sheets of cardboard or newspapers covering the pathways. Cut out the tops of the bags, use a long knife to punch

Straw on paths will be "sheet compost" by season's end.

drainage holes in the bottoms, and you're ready to plant smaller crops such as lettuce, bush beans, and basil. Use grass clippings or straw to conceal the edges of the bags and the cardboarded paths—then go get the garden hose! Over the summer, the bags and mulches will kill all of the grass and weeds. You won't need to do any digging until the end of the season, when you can gradually remove the plastic bags and work the topsoil into your native soil. Instant beds probably won't give you a harvest as good as other methods we cover here, but the advantage is the ability to create new beds quickly, with no initial tilling.

2. **Lasagna Gardens:** If you have access to a good supply of grass clippings, fall leaves, straw, or hay, you can start "lasagna" garden beds. Stake out your beds and pathways, lay cardboard down in the pathways, and then mulch the beds heavily with layers of whatever organic materials you have to smother the grass. If you use the lasagna technique in fall, the beds will be ready to plant in spring. Set transplants into the soil under the still-decomposing layers of mulch. To sow seeds, you'll need to spread soil over the mulch, or dig to mix the thick mulch (which is slowly turning to compost) with the native soil.

3. **Till and Rake:** Bagged topsoil isn't cheap, and sometimes it isn't even as good as your native soil. Another less-expensive way to convert lawn into garden—without buying soil—is to use a tiller to kill the grass. If you don't own a tiller, you can rent one or—perhaps even better—hire someone to till the area thoroughly for you. (Tilling sod is best done with a large tiller—check local classified ads or Craigslist to find someone who offers this service.) After the area has been tilled, use a garden rake (not a leaf rake) to go over the area thoroughly and remove clumps of grass and roots to the compost pile. Next, use stakes to mark out where you want each bed and pathway. Rake loosened soil from the

pathways into the bed areas, and you'll have tidy, slightly raised beds without having to spend money to bring in soil.

4. **Buy Some Soil:** If your native soil is poor, you may decide to hire a landscaping company to bring in a load of soil to spread out where you want permanent garden beds. If you go this route, choose a reputable company, ask for a product that includes compost blended with the soil, and verify that the company guarantees the mix is free of noxious weeds (especially nutsedge and morning glory) and herbicide residues. If possible, till the growing beds before you spread the soil.

5. **Turn with a Spade:** This method is probably the best because it loosens the soil deeply, but it requires more physical work than other methods. Mark out the garden beds and pathways, and then use a good spade to cut and turn the sod in the bed areas. Take your time, digging maybe one bed per day. Pave the pathways with cardboard or newspaper covered with grass clippings or other mulch. If you can, apply several inches of compost or mix a good layer of grass clippings into the beds. Rake them smooth, and you're ready to sow seeds or set out transplants.

6. **Chickens in the Garden:** If you have chickens and a portable coop, the birds can do a nice job of killing sod and scratching up the top few inches of soil in new or existing beds. They also add manure to the soil.

Depending on how much time and money you have, you can combine these six techniques. For instance, turn a few beds with a spade the first year and build the rest of the permanent garden beds using topsoil bags or lasagna layers. Then, after the season has ended, you can dig the remaining beds deeply as you have time, or move chickens onto them to add fertility and eat weed seeds.

THE ESSENTIAL BROADFORK

I recommend that you eventually buy a broadfork so you can loosen the soil before planting each crop. A spade or garden fork will work, but a broadfork will do the job faster and more deeply. I've found that broadforks made entirely of metal are more rigid and work better than those with wooden handles. With a broadfork, you work the long tines into the soil and then pull the handles back so that the tines lift the soil to loosen it without actually turning it over. That way, the soil is aerated for better root growth and faster warming in spring. By not turning over or mixing the soil (as happens when gardens are plowed or tilled), you've minimized disruption to the layers of soil-dwelling critters that create fertility.

SHOULD BEDS BE FRAMED?

Framing is strictly optional. Frames can make your garden look tidier and provide locations to attach hoops for mini-greenhouses and row covers, but depending on the framing materials you choose, this can add significantly to your startup

RAISED GARDEN BEDS PROS AND CONS

Numerous articles and websites claim that raised bed gardening is easier and more productive than non–raised bed gardening, but I believe most of those claims are misleading. For example, some writers assert that soil in raised beds is better. Your soil's fertility is a function of the amounts of compost and other amendments you use; raised bed soil is not automatically more fertile. As long as you continually improve the soil in dedicated beds, whether the beds are raised, sunken, or level doesn't matter.

If you have poor or contaminated native soil, you may want raised beds with better soil brought in from elsewhere, but the soil (and probably frames) will be quite expensive. If you raise beds extra high to make them easier to reach, they will cost even more. Raised beds are a good choice if your soil drains poorly, but they'll require more watering in most climates.

costs. New lumber is pricey, and most boards will begin to rot after a few years. (If you do choose to make board frames, 2-by-4s will work just as well as more expensive 2-by-6s and will require less soil to fill.)

Rather than buying lumber, look for low- or no-cost frames. For instance, my neighbor gave me a load of cedar fence rails he was replacing, and they have made perfect frames for my beds. I simply raked tilled soil from pathways into low raised beds and laid the cedar rails down on the long sides of each. Even with no end pieces, the fence rails stay right where I put them, and I can easily adjust a bed's width if need be. Fencing companies replace rail fences constantly and would probably be happy to have you take used rails off their hands.

Four- to five-inch-diameter logs also work well as frames—not on the ends, but just laid on the long sides of the beds. Shorter logs work well to form curves if any of your beds are not rectangular. If you don't have a place where you can cut logs, call a firewood company to ask whether it will deliver what you need—logs should cost less (and last longer) than boards. Rocks, reclaimed bricks, or concrete blocks are other framing options.

BEST MULCHES FOR VEGETABLE GARDENS

Long-lasting bark mulches can be okay in pathways if you have the right kind of hoe to cut out weeds.

In the growing beds, however, you'll be happier using mulches that are finer and decompose over the season. Top choices are grass clippings, fall leaves, hay, straw, or aged fine wood chips or sawdust. Clippings and leaves are free.

If you have weed problems, simply put down cardboard or newspaper before you apply mulch.

easy plant propagation

by Barbara Pleasant

THE MOST COMMON way to grow new plants is to sow seeds, but many plants also can be propagated vegetatively by rooting cuttings or stems, or dividing clumps. If you already have a healthy plant, plant propagation is often faster, easier, and cheaper than growing more plants from seeds. It takes 6 weeks to grow a tomato seedling to transplanting size, but you can root a stem tip cutting in half that time. With plant propagation, you can multiply one petunia or coleus into several happy plants, and it will cost you nothing to start a new planting of grapes by sticking pruned branches into a bed of moist soil.

No special equipment is needed to become an accomplished plant propagator, though it helps to carry a spirit of adventure into each new project, because each species responds differently to various techniques and plant propagation often involves a serious injury or near-death event followed by recovery. Plants that are easy to propagate know how to handle this unnatural disaster.

GREEN INTELLIGENCE

If you were being chased by someone with a knife or about to be trampled by a herd of buffalo, you would run away or hide. Plants cannot, so they have devised

fundamental ways to survive common catastrophes. On a cellular level, most plants stock their stems with "undifferentiated" cells that begin multiplying into specialized cells if the plant "decides" that its best shot at survival requires new stems, leaves, or roots. These undifferentiated cells are most numerous in nodes—the places where branches and buds emerge from stems—and in buds that form on shallow roots and low-growing stems. Your job as a plant propagator is to identify where the plant is holding its caches of undifferentiated cells, and then provide perfect conditions to help those cells morph into beautiful new roots.

To get an up-close look at this process, start with a sprig of supermarket mint. Clip or pinch the lowest leaves from a 4-inch-long stem, stick them in a small water-filled glass or bottle for 10 days, and you should see the beginnings of tiny white roots emerging from the nodes and the sections of the stem between them. You can transplant the cutting to a pot as soon as the roots are ½ inch long.

Many plants root readily in water, including tomatoes, hydrangeas, coleus, and many culinary herbs such as rosemary, marjoram, and oregano. Keep in mind that warm temperatures are crucial to fast rooting in water. Basil and other plants that aren't supposed to root from stem cuttings often do when kept in a sun-warmed window. And, though glass containers make it easy to keep an eye on rooting (or rotting) cuttings, dark-colored heavy pottery vases work even better because they absorb and retain solar heat while shielding the roots from light.

Rooting in water is quick and easy for plants that can be propagated this way. Other plants will root best in soil or a soil-like medium such as perlite or vermiculite. Roots that form in water are structural wimps compared to those that grow in soil. Either of these mediums, or a mixture of half peat moss and half sand, will reduce problems with disease when you're working with slow-rooting woody cuttings. To speed things up, many people use rooting powders or gels, which provide synthetic forms of several common plant hormones. However, research studies show that plants that root readily do not benefit from hormonal stimulation, plus there are natural alternatives you can make yourself at home. If you are working with a challenging plant (such as blueberries or another slow-growing woody plant), the Rooting Database hosted by the University of California–Davis is a magnificent source of information on success rates using various rooting mediums, rooting hormones, and much more. Hundreds of challenging trees, shrubs, and perennials are listed by common or botanical name. With the right technique, you can propagate almost any plant from a cutting.

IMPROVING YOUR LUCK

Herbaceous, or green-stemmed, cuttings (the most common type gardeners handle) root as readily in compost-amended potting soil as they do in sterile soil-less mediums as long as six key factors receive close attention.

1. Choose a donor plant that has not yet begun flowering but is approaching mature size. If the cuttings do have buds or flowers, snip them off. Rooted cuttings retain the general maturity level of their parents, but until they have enough roots to support reproduction, you should remove flowers that try to form.

2. Make sure the donor plant is in good condition. Water it the day before collecting cuttings, which are at their best during the morning hours.

3. Keep cuttings small—no more than 6 inches long—and remove all but the top-most three to four leaves. A few leaves help the cutting survive on light-derived energy, but too many will suck the cutting dry.

4. Temperatures must be kept warm, around 75°F, so bottom heat from a warming mat (or heating pad) is especially beneficial. Outdoors, wait until after your last frost passes to try rooting anything (other than root-bearing divisions) directly in the garden.

MORE PLANT PROPAGATION TECHNIQUES

- When pruning grapes in early spring, set aside 12- to 14-inch-long sections of stem that have three or more nodes. Being careful to keep them right side up, push the ends that grew closest to the parent plant 6 inches deep in fertile, well-drained soil and keep them moist. Those that take will be well rooted and ready to train or move by midsummer.

- In spring, just as roses leaf out, take 6-inch-long cuttings from the tips of your favorites, remove the leaves from the bottom halves, and stick them 3 inches deep in a moist, fertile spot. Cover with quart canning jars for 3 to 4 weeks. You will know which cuttings are successful when they show new growth.

- You can root cuttings while they are still on the plant using the method called simple layering. Bend down a branch, and nick or scratch the stem where it touches the ground. Bury the "distressed" stem section beneath 2 inches of moist soil. If necessary, use a stone or U-shaped wire pin to hold the stem in place. Wait until new roots emerge to sever the cutting from the parent plant. This method works great with thyme, rosemary, and other stiff-stemmed herbs, as well as raspberries, forsythia, and most perennial vines.

5. Light levels should be low at first (around 50 percent) to suppress growth of new stems and leaves. The combination of warm soil temperatures and low light levels pushes the cuttings to send energy to developing roots.

6. Moisture around the buried stems must stay constant at all times. To reduce evaporation and increase humidity, use containers you can enclose in glass or plastic to keep humidity high. Until the cuttings can take up water through their yet-to-grow roots, high humidity is the best way to prevent moisture loss from the leaves and rooting medium.

For years I fashioned tents from plastic produce bags to make little greenhouses for rooting cuttings, but these days I use shoebox-sized plastic storage boxes with clear or translucent lids. Filled with 3 inches or so of moist soil (or plastic cellpacks reused from bedding plant purchases), the boxes become mini-greenhouses that can be propped open during the day and closed at night. When I'm propagating only one or two tidbits, I use a 3-inch-wide, 6-inch-tall clear glass candleholder. To keep humidity high and light low during the first week or so, I cover the container with a small plate. After the plate is removed, the container's tall sides help create humid conditions, like an open terrarium. A glass or translucent plastic cake cover makes a great impromptu propagation greenhouse too.

It is not unusual to have 100 percent success with willing rooters such as mint, tomato, or chrysanthemum, but with other plants you should expect significant failures. I often hope for a 50 percent success rate when propagating a plant for the first time, so I start twice as many cuttings as I think I need. Successful cuttings keep their color while failed ones slowly fade or flat-out collapse. Promptly remove corpses to prevent the buildup of root-devouring fungi. When you see signs of new growth, check for resistance from new roots by gently pulling on the cuttings. When it's clear that cuttings have anchored themselves with new roots, get ready to move them to your garden.

MULTIPLYING THE MASSES

Many perennial plants grow into colonies that expand with each passing season, so they are prime candidates for digging and dividing—the most straightforward way to make more plants. Simply dig up a clump of asters, echinacea, chives, or strawberries, break or cut the mass into pieces with a few intact roots and at least one growing bud, and replant the divisions in hospitable spots. Thousands of plants can be propagated this way, including asparagus, bunching onions, horseradish, rhubarb, and all types of groundcovers. The appearance of new stems and leaves aboveground is usually accompanied by the growth of new roots down below, so plants divided in spring are usually nicely rooted by late summer.

Digging and dividing does destroy roots, so it's good to relieve divided plants of at least half of their leaves and stems as you replant them—and to keep them well-watered for about a month after transplanting. As soon as new roots form, the plants should produce a nice flush of healthy new foliage.

6

SPRING/
EARLY
SUMMER

maintain a weedless organic garden

by Lee Reich

WEEDLESS GARDENING! THAT'S an oxymoron, an impossibility, right? Well, my gardens may not be 100-percent weed-free, but they are 100-percent free of weed problems.

I've achieved this happy state in four ways: (1) never tilling or otherwise disturbing the soil, so dormant weed seeds stay asleep, away from light and air; (2) designating permanent areas for walking and for planting to avoid compaction and the need for tillage; (3) maintaining a thin mulch of weed-free organic material to snuff out any weed seeds that blow in or are dropped into the garden by birds; (4) using drip irrigation whenever watering is called for to avoid promoting weed growth in paths and between widely spaced plants.

Those are the basics of keeping my gardens free of weed problems. Over the years I've honed some details of this weedless gardening system, and I'd like to share them with you.

ORGANIC FERTILIZERS AND MULCHES

A particularly nice aspect of this weedless gardening system is how much it simplifies fertilization. I rarely use commercial fertilizer. It's not that my plants don't need food, it's just that the slow and steady decomposition of the organic mulches fulfills most of my plants' nutrient needs.

Where extra nitrogen might be needed, I use soybean meal, which supplements the diet of young trees, bushes, and intensively grown vegetables. The soybean meal is inexpensive, readily available at farm and feed stores, and only needs to be applied once a year. The nitrogen in soybean meal applied anytime from late autumn to late winter will not leach out of the soil during the cold months, but it begins to release as spring's moisture and warmth awakens hungry plants. For plants that regularly need that extra nitrogen, I spread 1 to 2 pounds per 100 square feet. Other meals, such as cottonseed or alfalfa meal, can be used similarly but generally cost a little more.

If your soil is naturally poor, you may want to apply other nutrients as fertilizers, such as phosphorus and potassium, until organic mulches decompose and build up a reserve of those nutrients in the soil. Bonemeal, seaweed, and wood ashes are all good sources of phosphorus and potassium.

Because most of my gardens' fertility comes from organic mulches, I tailor which mulch I use to the particular plant's needs. Generally, this involves nothing more than using nutrient-rich mulches for plants that are heavy feeders and other mulches for light feeders. Two nutrient-rich mulches for my vegetables are compost and grass clippings; I make both at home.

If you're not up to making your own weed-free compost, you usually can buy good bulk compost locally. I often spread a thin layer of grass clipping on top of the compost in my vegetable beds. The thin layer of grass clippings helps smother any weed seedlings that survived composting and keeps the compost moist to make the nutrients in it more readily available. Be careful about using neighbors' grass clippings, however. I found this out the hard way 30 years ago as I watched my potato vines wilt overnight after using what I later learned were clippings from a lawn that was treated with weedkiller.

Wood chips or leaves (whole or shredded) are good mulches for plants that aren't particularly heavy feeders, such as established trees and shrubs, most flowers (delphiniums and roses are notable exceptions), and just about everything

Grass clippings are a nutrient-rich choice for organic mulch.

Grow cover crops in early autumn to replenish your soil after the main growing season. By using frost-tolerant cool-season varieties, the plants will grow until the soil freezes—this photo was taken in the author's New York garden in November.

else. I get wood chips from local arborists and "harvest" bags of leaves from my neighbors, who call me when it's time to pick them up. I occasionally supplement this supply with a truckload of leaves from a local landscaper.

COVER CROPS

Over the years, I've become increasingly interested in living mulches, also known as cover crops—plants specifically grown to protect and improve the soil. Like traditional mulches, cover crops smother weeds; enrich the soil with humus, which increases nutrient availability; and, in the case of leguminous cover crops, add nitrogen to the soil.

Two big advantages of using cover crops as mulch are that the cover crop roots improve the soil as they grow and die, plus you only have to carry a small bag of seeds out to the garden rather than hauling garden carts full of bulky materials.

You can set aside part of the garden to plant a season's worth of cover crops, or try my approach: squeeze in cool-season cover crops at the end of summer and again in early autumn. Because I never till my soil, I grow cover crops such as oats, peas, and barley, which naturally succumb to winter cold here in New York. By winter's end, I just rake up the stems and leaves on top of the soil, leaving the dead roots intact along with the myriad channels they've created.

Crops that don't naturally winterkill can also be used. Just mow them over when they're about to flower or dispose of them with repeated mowing.

DRIP IRRIGATION

Drip irrigation helps keep my garden weed-free because it doesn't water weeds along the paths or between rows the way regular sprinklers do. Slowly dripping water onto the crop's root zone also conserves water. In fact, drip systems can reach 95 percent application efficiency and save up to 75 percent of the water used by sprinkler systems.

You can buy drip irrigation system installation kits at garden centers, hardware stores, and home improvement stores. For larger systems, consider hiring a landscape professional. A basic drip irrigation system consists of five elements:

Blueberry bushes are a perfect candidate for drip irrigation since they have shallow root systems.

1. **Feeder Tubes:** Often called emitters or drip tape because they're sold flattened on a roll, these tubes are made from black polyethylene plastic with holes spaced at regular intervals to dispense water at a relatively constant rate, even with changes in elevation and water pressure. For widely spaced plants, individual emitters can be plugged into mainline piping as needed.

2. **Mainline Piping:** Also called a lateral line, this piping connects the water supply to feeder tubes.

3. **Fittings:** You'll need a variety of fittings such as valves, connectors, and end caps to connect irrigation lines, close them off, control the flow of water, and keep it from flowing back into the main water source.

4. **Filters:** Sand or screen filters pull impurities from the main water supply to keep feeder tubes from clogging.

5. **Pressure Regulators:** Spring or valve regulators help reduce water pressure to the feeder tubes.

I use a drip irrigation system in parts of my garden that need regular watering, such as vegetable beds and around young blueberry bushes.

In my vegetable garden, I run ½-inch mainline piping perpendicular to the 3-foot-wide beds. Then I plug in a ¼-inch barbed transfer fitting and attach ¼-inch feeder tubing and run it down the length of the bed. The tubing comes with emitters at 6-inch intervals, each dripping ½ gallon of water per hour. For wider beds in drier climates or locations with lighter soils, you might want to run two dripper lines down each bed.

Young blueberry bushes require at least 1 inch of water a week since they have shallow root systems. To water them, I run ½-inch mainline piping along the row of plants, then I plug a ¼-inch barbed transfer fitting into the mainline piping at each bush. I attach a short length of ¼-inch solid tubing to the mainline, which is terminated by an emitter that drips ½ gallon per hour at the roots of each bush.

Use vinegar as a homemade organic herbicide to kill back grass and weeds, and keep them from encroaching on your garden.

EFFECTIVE WEEDING

Weeds constantly threaten to invade the edges of any garden. The most direct way to thwart interloping weeds is to just grab them by hand and pull them out. I also maintain a 6-inch-wide bare soil "Maginot Line" of defense around parts of my garden with a Winged Weeder hoe, which has a sharp blade that lies parallel to the ground as you work with it. In a more formal part of the garden, I created a low-maintenance weed barrier with half cinder blocks laid flat right next to each other in a fitted, shallow depression so I can run the wheel of my lawnmower along it.

If you have ever chopped the tops off dandelions with a hoe, you know that it's only a short time before they sprout yet again from their robust roots. To eliminate the possibility of an encore, I pull out these weeds individually to be sure I get their roots along with their tops.

Removing one weed at a time would be too tedious where a colony of young weed seedlings has sprouted. When this happens, I recommend using a hoe to kill the small seedlings. I think the traditional garden hoe that most gardeners have hanging in their garage is far better at mixing concrete than killing weeds. A better choice is a collinear hoe, stirrup hoe, or the Winged Weeder. With a Winged Weeder, a few simple strokes back and forth (like mopping a floor), just a hair beneath the soil's surface, will do the job quickly while you barely break a sweat.

A SAFE, NATURAL HERBICIDE

For larger areas, such as my brick terrace and beneath fruit trees, I resort to herbicide—not the toxic stuff that lines shelves of nurseries and hardware stores, but household strength (5 percent to 6 percent) vinegar. For maximum effectiveness, I spray vinegar on small plants, which have weaker root systems and fewer leaves to "shade" them from the spray. Established weeds will resprout new leaves following a vinegar spray, but if you kill back the leaves several times, eventually the plant will starve to death.

You can increase the vinegar's ability to spread and stick to leaves by adding 1 tablespoon of dish detergent and 2 tablespoons of canola oil per gallon of vinegar. The vinegar is most effective at temperatures above 70°F, and while it will burn just about any greenery, it's most effective against grasses. Early in the season, once the weather warms, spray weekly then progress to a biweekly or monthly schedule, depending on the weather and weed growth.

My final attack on weeds entails (dare I say it?) regular weeding. I'll hoe or pull weeds here and there as I walk through the garden and as I harvest and plant. Just think of your hoe as your walking stick. For all the negative connotations of weeding, I consider it part of any pleasant visit to the garden, probably because the few weeds I have are neither ominous nor demanding these days.

all about growing broccoli

by Barbara Pleasant

As THE MOST popular member of the cabbage family, broccoli is always in high demand at the table. Because it's a cool-weather crop, you'll see your best results from growing broccoli in the spring or fall. Florets that mature in autumn when nights turn chilly taste the sweetest. Broccoli seeds sprout best when soil temperatures range between 60 and 70°F.

Tasty in each of its many varieties, broccoli is easier to grow than cauliflower or brussels sprouts and can produce bountiful crops for even novice gardeners.

TYPES OF BROCCOLI TO TRY

Large-headed varieties produce the familiar domed heads that are composed of numerous clustered florets. Many large-headed varieties produce smaller side shoots after the primary head is harvested.

Sprouting varieties grow into bushier plants that produce numerous small heads. These varieties are at their best when grown from fall to spring in mild-winter climates.

Romanesco varieties produce elegantly swirled heads composed of symmetrically pointed spirals. These large plants need plenty of space, excellent soil, and good growing conditions to do well.

Broccoli raab is grown for its immature flower buds, which have a stronger flavor than regular broccoli. Broccoli raab (closely related to turnips) is popular in Asian and Italian cooking.

WHEN TO PLANT BROCCOLI

For a summer harvest, start seeds indoors 6 weeks before your last spring frost and set out hardened-off seedlings when they're about 4 weeks old. You can also seed broccoli directly into a nursery bed and transplant the seedlings to your garden. Direct-sow broccoli raab starting 3 weeks before your last frost.

For a fall harvest, start seeds indoors 12 to 14 weeks before your first fall frost and set the seedlings out when they're 4 to 6 weeks old. Direct-sow broccoli raab starting 8 weeks before your first fall frost.

HOW TO PLANT BROCCOLI

Broccoli is a heavy feeder, and plants take up nutrients best when the soil pH is between 6.0 and 7.0. Choose a sunny site with fertile, well-drained soil. Loosen the planting bed and mix in up to 1 inch of mature compost. Unless your soil is very fertile, also mix in a high-nitrogen organic fertilizer such as alfalfa meal or composted poultry manure. Water the bed thoroughly before setting out seedlings. Allow 18 to 20 inches between plants. Dwarf varieties can be planted 12 inches apart.

BROCCOLI AT A GLANCE

TYPE	DESCRIPTION	VARIETIES
Large-headed broccoli (*Brassica oleracea*, *Botrytis* group) 50 to 70 days, spring 65 to 90 days, fall	Big heads need plenty of space to grow. Crowding reduces head size, but miniature varieties such as 'Munchkin' work well in tight spaces. Many varieties produce side shoots after the primary head has been harvested.	'Arcadia' 'Belstar' 'Munchkin' 'Nutri-Bud' 'Packman'
Sprouting broccoli (*B. oleracea*, *Italica* group) 50 to 70 days, spring 65 to 90 days, fall	Small heads are very tender. Cut often to encourage steady production. Best grown from midsummer to fall in most climates, or from fall to spring where winters are mild.	'Calabrese' 'De Cicco' 'Purple Peacock' 'Purple Sprouting'
Romanesco broccoli (*B. oleracea*, *Botrytis* group) 75 to 90 days, spring 85 to 100 days, fall	Large upright plants need plenty of elbow room, rich soil, regular water and temperatures in the 80°F range. Satisfied plants produce spiraled heads with the crunch of cauliflower.	'Natalino' 'Romanesco Italia' 'Veronica'
Broccoli raab (*B. rapa*, *Ruvo* group) 40 to 55 days, spring 50 to 75 days, fall	A fast-growing crop for cool weather. Vigorous plants produce continuously for several weeks. The leaves and stems are as tender and edible as the buds.	'Early Fall Rapini' 'Sessantina Grossa' 'Sorrento' 'Zamboni'

Broccoli is a nutritional superfood that will strengthen your immune system, help maintain strong bones, and help protect you from cancer and heart disease.

HARVESTING AND STORING BROCCOLI

Harvest broccoli heads when the florets around the edges of the head begin to show slight loosening but the beads in most of the crown are still tight.

Cut the stems at an angle—this will keep water from pooling inside the cut stem and causing rot. Refrigerate the cut heads immediately. To get top home-preserved quality, steam-blanch broccoli before freezing it. Continue to water the plants after harvest, as most varieties will produce secondary heads.

Watch broccoli raab closely, and harvest just as the first flowers show their yellow petals. Sprouting broccoli and broccoli raab are also "cut-and-come-again" crops that produce a second flush of buds after the first ones have been harvested.

When plants are spaced 18 inches apart, average yields are about 1 pound of broccoli per foot of row. Three to four plants per person are sufficient for fresh summer eating, but you should triple that number if you want a freezer crop for winter.

PROPAGATING BROCCOLI

Most broccoli varieties must be exposed to winter chilling before they will flower heavily, but plants die if exposed to single-digit temperatures. Because of this, most seed is produced in mild-winter areas.

Isolate plants to keep broccoli from crossing with cabbage, kale, and other close cabbage cousins. Broccoli raab will cross with turnips.

Harvest seeds when the slender pods dry to tan and the seeds inside are dark brown or black. Select the largest, most perfect seeds for planting.

Broccoli seeds will keep for 5 years when stored in cool, dry, dark conditions. Test seeds that are more than 3 years old before relying on them for a main crop—just put a few in a wet paper towel for 5 days to confirm they will sprout.

PEST AND DISEASE PREVENTION TIPS

Leaf-eating caterpillars, including armyworms, cabbageworms, and cabbage loopers, like to feast on broccoli leaves. In summer, harlequin bugs and grasshoppers

TIPS FOR GROWING BROCCOLI

- Experiment with planting dates, which vary widely by climate. Striving for very early crops can backfire, as seedlings exposed to cold often "button," meaning they produce tiny heads. Start by trying spring and fall planting dates recommended by your neighbors or your local extension service.

- Grow several varieties to extend your harvest and to help buffer your crop from stressful weather. Varieties react differently to wet, dry, hot, or cold periods.

- If you have less-than-ideal soil, give plants extra nitrogen just as small heads begin to form. You can drench them with an organic mix-with-water fertilizer, mulch with well-rotted manure, or scratch a dusting of any high-nitrogen organic fertilizer into the soil around the plants.

- Weed often and mulch deeply to get the highest yields from your broccoli. Two inches of grass clippings or any other biodegradable mulch will keep the soil cool, the way broccoli likes it.

can devastate young plants. Prevent these problems by growing plants beneath row covers. Read "Row Covers: The No-Spray Way to Protect Plants" on page 195 for details on using row covers.

When insect pressure is light, keep plants healthy by watching them closely and picking pests by hand. Weekly sprays with Bt (*Bacillus thuringiensis*) or spinosad will control cabbageworms, the most serious broccoli pest.

Plants that suddenly collapse may have been hit by cabbage root maggots, which are rice-sized fly larvae that feed on broccoli roots. In areas where this pest has been seen before, plant seedlings deeply, pressing the soil firmly around the stems. Prevent adults from laying eggs by covering the ground around each plant with a square of window screen or lightweight cloth.

IN THE KITCHEN

Broccoli is a nutritional superfood that will strengthen your immune system, help maintain strong bones, and help protect you from cancer and heart disease. Broccoli is delicious raw, or you can steam florets for a minute and then plunge them into ice water before serving as finger food. Eat the stems by peeling away the chewy outer skin, slicing them, and then cooking them along with the florets. Garden-fresh broccoli is tender, so be careful not to overcook it.

Learn how to grow carrots in your garden. Carrot varieties vary greatly in color and shape. The different colors range from dark red to light yellow.

all about growing carrots

by Barbara Pleasant

CHOOSING TO GROW crisp, delicious carrots of unique varieties in spring and fall can lead to great nutritious eating right from your backyard. Find out how to grow several varieties such as Nantes, Chantenay, Imperator, miniature, and Danvers in your garden at home. By knowing the basics of when and how to plant, you can produce a successful harvest and have enough carrots to store throughout the year.

TIPS FOR GROWING CARROTS

- Keep the soil moist for at least 10 consecutive days after sowing, because carrots take longer to germinate than other vegetables. To reduce surface evaporation during the germination period, cover newly seeded soil with boards or old blankets for 5 to 6 days. Check daily, and remove the covers as soon as the first seeds germinate. Seeds germinate best when soil temperatures range between 60 and 70°F.

- Reduce weed competition by sowing carrot seeds in shallow furrows filled with weed-free potting soil. Cover the ground between rows with newspapers topped by a mulch or grass clippings.

- Sow carrots with a "nurse crop" of radishes. The fast-growing radishes will shelter tiny carrot seedlings while helping to suppress weeds.

- Be stingy with nitrogen: among fertilizers, carrots favor compost or vermicompost worked into the soil prior to planting; they respond to abundant phosphorous and potassium more than to high nitrogen levels. Carrots take up nutrients best in soil with a pH between 5.8 and 7.0. Use lime to raise the pH of acidic soil.

- Harvest carefully: before pulling carrots, use a digging fork to loosen the soil just outside the row.

- Harvest small blossom clusters from overwintered plants to use as cut flowers. Thinning the blossoms helps the plants channel energy to the biggest seed-bearing umbels (flower clusters springing from the same point).

- Max out the season: to eat carrots year-round, grow fast-maturing varieties in spring and make summer sowings for a season-stretching fall crop.

- Use soaker hoses or drip irrigation lines to keep the soil constantly moist.

- Cover the shoulders of all maturing carrots with mulch to keep them from turning green.

TYPES OF CARROTS TO TRY

Nantes are fast and easy to grow, and adapt to a range of climates and soils.

Chantenay carrots develop stocky roots that become sweeter as the soil cools in the fall.

Miniature carrots have small, shallow roots that are often quite sweet. They're good for heavy clay soil. Imperator carrots are *long* and need deep, sandy soil to thrive. Danvers carrots make great juice, and the sturdy roots store well too.

WHEN TO PLANT CARROTS

In the spring, sow carrot seeds in fertile, well-worked soil about 2 weeks before your last frost date. In cool climates, continue planting every 3 weeks until midsummer.

In summer, begin sowing seeds for fall and winter carrots 10 to 12 weeks before your average first fall frost. Many gardeners plant carrots after their spring peas are finished.

HOW TO PLANT CARROTS

Prepare the planting bed by loosening the soil to at least 12 inches deep. Thoroughly mix in a 1-inch layer of mature compost or ½-inch layer of vermi-compost (carrots love what earthworms leave behind).

Sow your seeds about ¼ inch deep and 2 inches apart, in rows spaced at least 10 inches apart; carrots do well in double or triple rows. Thin seedlings to 4 to 6 inches apart, depending on the variety's mature size.

HARVESTING AND STORING CARROTS

Pull or dig spring-sown carrots when roots reach mature size and show rich color. Taste improves as carrots mature, but do not leave mature carrots in warm soil any longer than necessary (many critters like carrots). Summer-sown carrots that mature in cool fall soil can be left in the ground longer but should be dug before the ground freezes to preserve their quality. Remove tops to prevent moisture loss, rinse clean, and store in a refrigerator or cold root cellar. Most varieties keep for several months in the fridge. Carrots also may be canned, pickled, dried, or frozen.

PROPAGATING CARROTS

Carrots are biennial and therefore won't flower and make seed until their second year. In cold climates, open-pollinated carrots kept in cold storage through winter can be replanted in early spring for seed production purposes. When the seed clusters have ripened to brown, collect them in a paper bag. Then allow them to dry for another week indoors before crushing the clusters and gathering the seeds. Discard the smallest seeds. Store the largest seeds in a cool, dry place for up to 3 years.

CARROTS FOR YOUR GARDEN

TYPE	DESCRIPTION	CULTURAL TIPS	VARIETIES*
Nantes 55 to 70 days (spring) 60 to 75 days (fall)	Easy and widely adapted; straight, cylindrical roots 5 to 7 inches long; sweet flavor and crisp texture; limited storage potential.	Grow in loose, sandy soil or in raised beds enriched with plenty of organic matter, but no fresh manure.	'Early Nantes' 'Nelson' 'Mokum'
Chantenay 55 to 70 days (spring) 70 to 110 days (fall)	Conical roots with broad shoulders and rounded tips; rich, sweet flavor and good storage potential.	Excellent type to grow from summer to fall, and not as picky about soil as other types. Usually sizes up well in clay soils with high organic matter content.	'Red Core' 'Kuttiger' 'Kurota'
Miniature/Baby 50 to 60 days (spring) 60 to 70 days (fall)	Round, cylindrical or tapered roots less than 5 inches long; crisp texture and frequently quite sweet when mature; limited storage potential.	Grows in any fertile soil that drains well. Makes a good "marker" plant to separate sowings of salad greens.	'Thumbelina' 'Little Finger' 'Parmex'
Imperator 55 to 100 days (spring) 80 to 110 days (fall)	Long, tapered roots with stocky shoulders and strong tops; slightly fibrous texture. Stores well.	Roots size up best in deep, sandy loam. When pleased with their site, roots can become quite large.	'Yellowstone' 'Purple Haze' 'Sugarsnax'
Danvers 70 to 80 days (spring) 80 to 110 days (fall)	Thick-rooted cylindrical shape, often with yellowish core; widely used in processing, good for juicing. Stores well.	Grow in raised beds or in deep, sandy loam. Good main crop type for cool climates.	'Danvers' 'Healthmaster' 'Danvers Half Long'

* To find sources for these varieties, use our Seed and Plant Finder at www.MotherEarthNews.com/Custom-Seed-Search.

When cooking carrots, simply grill until tender or chop up and add to soups and stir-fries.

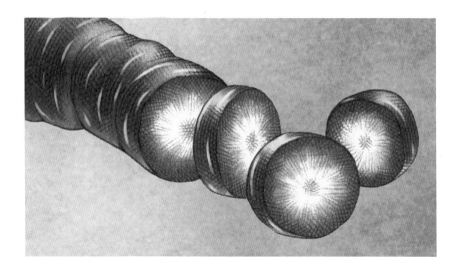

PEST AND DISEASE PREVENTION TIPS

Aster leaf-hoppers look like ⅛-inch green slivers that hop about when the foliage is disturbed. Leaf-hopper feeding causes light damage, but leaf-hoppers can spread aster yellows, a disease caused by a tumor-forming bacterium sometimes present in otherwise healthy soils. Trying to eliminate it would be unwise because of its close family ties with nitrogen-fixing rhizobia that benefit legumes. Instead, grow carrots in compost-enriched soil far from grapes and nut or fruit trees, which often host the parasitic bacteria. Use row covers to exclude the leaf-hoppers.

Row covers also protect a crop from carrot rust flies and carrot weevils, which make grooves and tunnels in carrots as they feed.

Hairy or misshapen roots can be caused by excessive nitrogen or aster yellows disease.

IN THE KITCHEN

Carrots will caramelize in their own sugars when braised in a little oil or grilled until tender. Grate raw carrots into muffins, cakes, or pancakes to provide moisture and extra vitamin A. Use carrots generously to bring nutritious color to salads, stir-fries, and soups. Try steamed carrots with fresh mint and a dab of honey or brown sugar. Orange and yellow carrots are great as nutritious raw snacks, but red carrots taste best cooked.

all about growing tomatoes

by Barbara Pleasant

THE EXQUISITE FLAVOR and irresistible juiciness of homegrown tomatoes put them at or near the top of most gardeners' planting lists. Fruit size, color, and flavor differ with each variety, but all tomatoes grow best under warm conditions. For the best flavor, provide fertile, organically enriched soil with a pH between 6.0 and 6.5, and plant your tomatoes in a site that gets plenty of sun.

Try growing some of these beautiful tomato varieties in your vegetable garden (from left to right): 'Green Zebra', 'San Marzano', 'Brandywine', 'Cherokee Purple', 'Mr. Stripey', 'Juliet', 'Yellow Pear', and 'Black Cherry'.

TYPES OF TOMATOES TO TRY

Many organic gardeners include varieties of the following three types of tomatoes in their gardens each year.

Cherry tomatoes and salad tomatoes produce small fruits in a rainbow of colors and an array of shapes, including round, pear-shaped, and teardrop-shaped.

Slicing tomatoes are round and juicy, making them ideal for eating fresh. Fruit size and color vary, and some varieties produce surprisingly large fruits.

Paste tomatoes, also called canning tomatoes, have dense flesh and little juice, so they are the best type for cooking, canning, and drying.

WHEN TO PLANT TOMATOES

Start seeds indoors under bright fluorescent lights in early spring, about 6 to 8 weeks before your last spring frost. If kept moist and warm (above 70°F), tomato seeds should sprout within a week. Transplant the seedlings to larger containers when they are about 6 weeks old. Harden off seedlings by gradually exposing them to outdoor weather for a few hours each day for at least a week before transplanting them. Transplant seedlings to the garden (or to large containers) after your last frost has passed, during a period of warm weather.

HOW TO PLANT TOMATOES

Choose a sunny site with fertile, well-drained soil, and loosen the planting bed to 12 inches deep. Mix in a layer of mature compost. Dig planting holes at least 18 inches apart, and enrich each with a spadeful of additional compost mixed with a balanced organic fertilizer (follow application rates on the fertilizer label). Plant tomatoes deeper than they grew in their containers, so that only the top five or six leaves show at the surface. Additional roots will grow from the buried section of stem.

HARVESTING AND STORING TOMATOES

Tomato flavor declines at temperatures below 55°F, so never keep them in the refrigerator. If kept in a warm place, fruits picked when they're showing stripes or blushes of ripe color will continue to ripen. Bumper crops can be preserved by canning, drying, or freezing. Tomatoes don't need to be blanched before they are dried or frozen.

Tomato sauce, salsa, chutney, and ketchup can be processed in a water bath canner or a pressure canner, depending on acidity levels (always follow recipes when canning). You will need a pressure canner to can tomato soup that includes other vegetables.

TOMATOES FOR YOUR GARDEN

The varieties listed below ranked highest in our recent nationwide tomato survey (go to *www.MotherEarthNews.com/Best-Tomatoes* to read the full results for your region). To ensure that you have some early ripening, disease-resistant tomatoes, and some with exceptional flavor, include hybrid (F1) and open-pollinated (OP) tomato varieties in your garden.

TYPE	DESCRIPTION	RECOMMENDED VARIETIES
Cherry tomatoes and salad tomatoes	Small fruit size gives these varieties an edge over diseases and weather-related problems. Most varieties mature early and have a long harvest period. Flavor differs by variety, but sweet, fruity taste is common in cherry tomatoes. Preserve by cutting in halves or quarters and drying.	'Black Cherry' (OP, 65 days) 'Juliet' (F1, 60 days) 'Stupice' (OP, 55 to 60 days) 'Sungold' (F1, 57 days) 'Super Sweet 100' (F1, 65 days) 'Yellow Pear' (OP, 70 days)
Slicing tomatoes	Try early-maturing hybrids and open-pollinated varieties famous for flavor. Large-fruited slicing varieties have a higher risk of diseases and nutritional disorders (such as blossom-end rot) compared with smaller-fruited types. Slicing tomatoes may be canned, dried, or frozen.	'Beefsteak' (F1 and OP, 80 to 90 days) 'Better Boy' (F1, 75 days) 'Brandywine' (OP, 80 to 90 days) 'Cherokee Purple' (OP, 80 to 90 days) 'Early Girl' (F1, 75 days)
Paste (canning) tomatoes	Many of these versatile tomatoes are vigorous determinates, which means they produce ripe fruits in two or three concentrated flushes. The low moisture content of these varieties makes them ideal for canning, drying or freezing.	'Amish Paste' (OP, 74 to 80 days) 'Opalka' (OP, 85 days) 'Roma' (F1 and OP, 75 days) 'San Marzano' (F1 and OP, 78 days) 'Viva Italia' (F1, 75 days)

TIPS FOR GROWING TOMATOES

- Stake or cage tomatoes to raise them above damp conditions close to the ground. Cages support plants from all sides, so they are preferred for large, vigorous varieties. All tomato cages become top heavy after the plants set fruit, so plan to anchor them to sturdy stakes to prevent toppling.

- Include early and midseason varieties in your garden to ensure a long harvest season. In long-season regions, root the stem tips from healthy plants in early summer and they'll quickly grow new plants for a fall crop.

- Prevent cracked fruits and blossom-end rot by mulching tomatoes heavily in early summer, after the soil has warmed. Place a soaker hose beneath the mulch if summer droughts are common in your area.

PROPAGATING TOMATOES

To save seeds from open-pollinated varieties, allow perfect fruits to ripen until they become soft. Cut them in half and squeeze the gel and seeds into a small jar. Cover with 3 inches of water and shake well. Allow the mixture to sit at room temperature for 24 hours before pouring out the liquid. Rinse the big seeds at the bottom of the jar in a strainer, and then dry them on a paper plate for about 2 weeks (write the variety name on the plate). If handled this way and given cool, dry storage conditions, tomato seeds usually stay viable for 4 to 6 years.

If you're growing tomatoes for seed-saving, keep in mind that wind and insects can transfer pollen, creating crosses between varieties. For pure seed, save seeds from plants that were grown apart from other tomato varieties.

PEST AND DISEASE PREVENTION TIPS

Most tomatoes are susceptible to a fungal disease called early blight (*Alternaria solani*), which develops in early summer and causes leaves near the ground to develop dry brown patches surrounded by concentric black rings. Good genetic resistance is not available, although 'Plum Dandy', a Roma type, offers noticeable tolerance. The best intervention is to prune off affected leaves as soon as you see them. Removing all leaves within 18 inches of the ground can reduce or delay outbreaks. Most tomato plants produce well despite losing leaves to early blight.

Hard black or brown patches on the blossom ends of ripening tomatoes indicate a physiological disorder called blossom-end rot, which is most common in large-fruited varieties. Prevent this problem by growing tomatoes in fertile soil generously enriched with compost, and mulch heavily to keep soil moisture levels as constant as possible.

Tomato hornworms (large green caterpillars with white stripes) are the larvae of a large moth. Handpick them starting in early summer (follow the trail of pebbly caterpillar droppings to find them). In extremely bad years, control hornworms using Bt (*Bacillus thuringiensis*) or spinosad, two widely available biological pesticides.

The devastating fungal disease called late blight (*Phytophthora infestans*) may strike following a prolonged period of cool rain. Affected leaves develop light brown water-soaked patches, and entire plants can wilt within a few days. Provide excellent light penetration and air circulation to keep plants dry, reducing the

Use your juicy, homegrown tomatoes to make the perfect tomato sandwich. Bread, mayo, and fresh tomato slices are all you need!

risk of late blight. Reliable genetic resistance is not available, though a few varieties, such as 'Juliet', have shown some tolerance. In climates where late blight is a problem every year, try growing tomatoes in high tunnels—the best way to keep the plants dry.

IN THE KITCHEN

Tomato sandwiches dripping with juice capture tomato cuisine at its purest, but summer wouldn't be complete without salsa, tomato basil soup, or hot pasta tossed with chopped tomatoes, basil, garlic, and a good hard cheese.

Tomatoes that ripen to black, green, orange, or yellow add visual appeal to dishes and often have unusual textures and flavors ranging from the firm and citrusy 'Green Zebra' to the soft and smoky 'Black Krim'. Use green tomatoes gathered at season's end to make tomato chutney or other condiments to enjoy year-round.

All tomatoes are good sources of vitamins A and C, and red tomatoes provide lycopene, a powerful antioxidant that may help prevent some types of cancer. Green tomatoes also have high nutritional value.

the best homemade tomato cages

by Jennifer Kongs

YOU'LL ENJOY A bigger tomato harvest if you use stakes or tomato cages to help your plants grow vertically, saving space in the garden while keeping fruits off the ground and preventing rot. Store-bought tomato cages tend to be flimsy and too small. For a sturdier option, consider building your own. We think these four plans are especially good choices for creating durable, low-cost tomato cages. Find the best fit for your garden and start building! (The cost estimates for each design are based on current prices from Lowe's and Tractor Supply Co.)

LIVESTOCK PANEL TRELLIS

Rigid metal livestock panels (sold at farm stores) make a strong, durable trellis. Simply stand up the panels and attach them to steel T-posts, and you're on your way to your own wall of tomatoes. Livestock panels typically come in 16-foot lengths, but with a pair of bolt cutters or a hacksaw, you can cut them to whatever length you want.

As the tomatoes grow, weave the plants between the openings of the panel for better support. You can use the panels for other crops, including beans, cucumbers, and peas. You can even bend the panels to make a trellised archway, which you can cover with plastic for use as a cheap greenhouse or livestock shelter.

Supplies
1. One 16-foot livestock panel
2. Steel T-posts (use one for about every 4 to 6 feet of panel)

Estimated cost: about $2 per tomato plant (assumes four T-posts, plus $20 for a 16-foot panel, with eighteen tomato plants spaced 2 feet apart on both sides)

FOLDING WOODEN TOMATO CAGES

These tall wooden tomato cages add a beautiful vertical accent to your garden. They also work well with other vining crops. To construct a cage, build two tomato "ladders" with three rungs and a brace to stabilize the sides against strong winds. Connect the two ladders at the top with a piece of scrap wood, which you can easily remove to fold the ladders for storage at the end of the season.

Supplies

- Six 1-by-3-inch wooden pieces, each measuring about 8 feet long
- One 8-inch 2-by-4
- Two 3-inch deck screws
- About 30 1½-inch galvanized deck screws

Estimated cost: about $20 per cage (less if you use recycled materials, or maybe saplings)

WIRE MESH TOMATO CAGES

Constructing cages from 4- or 5-foot-wide concrete-reinforcing wire is quick and simple—and the materials are cheap, which makes these cages an especially good choice if you're growing on a large scale. They're also a good bet for people with little DIY experience, because the only tool you'll need to put them together is a pair of wire cutters.

Concrete wire mesh is stiffer than most other fence wire, and its openings are large enough that you can easily reach through to pick the tomatoes. Cut sections about 5 to 6 feet long to form circular cages 19 to 23 inches in diameter. To make storage easier, vary the diameters so that two or three cages will nest together, one inside the other.

These lightweight cages will blow over easily unless you stake them, so anchor them firmly to the ground with steel T-posts. You can extend your growing season by wrapping each cage with plastic or row cover. This type of tomato cage also works well as a trellis for cucumbers, beans, and other vining crops.

One of the simplest tomato cages is a rigid metal livestock panel used as a trellis. Another option: build these simple wooden "tomato ladders." They're easy to construct from scrap wood and can be folded up for easy storage.

Left: Wire mesh tomato cages are cheap and easy to make. Be sure to stake them to the ground with steel T-posts to prevent them from blowing over.

Right: Building with plastic pipe creates a super-durable tomato cage. This isn't the cheapest tomato cage option, but it may well be the sturdiest.

Supplies
- Rolls of 6-by-6-inch concrete-reinforcing wire mesh
- Steel T-posts

Estimated cost: about $8 per cage (based on making thirty cages from a 150-foot roll of concrete mesh, with one steel post per cage)

THE INDESTRUCTIBLE TOMATO CAGE

This cage earns the name "indestructible" because it's made of sturdy plastic pipes, which are easy to work with and won't rot or rust. To construct these cages, drill three sets of corresponding holes in each of three equal lengths of plastic pipe. Form the cages by placing horizontal metal rods (electrical conduit) through the holes in the plastic uprights. Make sure the plastic pipes have a large enough diameter to hold the metal conduit you use. The metal crossbars can be removed at the end of the season, making breakdown a breeze and requiring minimal storage space. A bonus: by pouring water into the tops of the vertical pipes, you can deliver moisture directly to your plants' roots—where they need it most—without providing surface water to competing weeds.

To make drilling the holes in the plastic pipes easier, *MOTHER EARTH NEWS* contributing editor Steve Maxwell recommends using a step bit. "As the name suggests, a step bit is shaped into a series of steps and designed for use in drilling thin metal," he says. "They also happen to work really well on plastic. Because each level is incrementally larger, they go into the surfaces gently, with little chance of grabbing and splitting."

Supplies:
- Three 4-foot (or longer) pieces of 3-inch-diameter plastic pipe
- 15 feet of electrical conduit
- Estimated cost: about $25 per cage

organic pest control strategies for the garden

by Barbara Pleasant

ACCORDING TO AN ancient Chinese proverb, "If you would be happy all your life, plant a garden." Modern gardeners know this to be true, but unfortunately our gardens also seem to inspire delight in grasshoppers, squash bugs, and countless other hungry insects. There's at least one serious insect enemy for every crop, so knowing how to prevent and treat pest problems is fundamental to maximizing the rewards you can reap from your gardening efforts.

When faced with a pest problem, gardeners—new ones in particular—often reach for a solution that comes in a spray bottle. It's true that many poisons sold in garden centers will kill any, and often all, insects in your garden. But spraying chemicals is rarely the best option for getting rid of pests. Many pesticides are hazardous to humans and wildlife, and most will kill beneficial insects right along with the pests you're targeting.

ORGANIC PEST CONTROL STRATEGIES

Before you march into your garden armed for an insect Armageddon, answer these three important questions:

1. **Are there natural predators capable of controlling this pest?** In many cases the answer is yes, but you will never see your garden's homeland defenses in action unless you actively encourage beneficial insects and adopt a wait-and-see attitude when new pest problems arise. Always watch what happens for at least 5 days after you see a pest become active. This can be a wonderfully fascinating show.

2. **Can you control this pest by using preventive methods?** You can prevent attacks from many nonflying insects—as well as diseases—by rotating your crops (not planting them in the same place more than once every 3 years), cleaning up and composting dead plants, eliminating habitats such as weedy host plants, or growing resistant varieties. Learning to use methods that prevent pest problems does not happen overnight, and even the most experienced organic gardeners pick up new strategies with each passing season. When it comes to learning what works and what doesn't, your garden is often your best teacher.

3. **Are there easy ways to capture the pest or to install barriers that will protect the plants?** Some insects are easy to pick off and drown in a pail of soapy water, or perhaps you can nab them with pieces of duct tape or a rechargeable vacuum. If you see a certain pest returning to your garden year after year, you often can keep the hordes at bay by covering plants with lightweight floating row covers.

All of the possible answers to these three questions are called cultural controls, which can be remarkably effective. When Cornell University brought together five horticulture experts to summarize the effectiveness of organic pest-control options for thirty-six vegetable insect pests and diseases, they found that twenty often could be handled using cultural controls. In your garden, the ratio between problem pests and cultural solutions can get tighter as you learn to make use of practical preventive measures.

KNOW THY ENEMIES: IDENTIFY COMMON GARDEN PESTS

It's important to understand that most garden pests are only capable of damaging a very narrow range of closely related plants. For example, little black flea beetles may make holes in potato leaves in spring then hop to tomatoes or eggplant in summer, but they won't veer far from plants that are members of the nightshade family. In similar fashion, the squash bugs that invade your pumpkin patch cannot digest juices sucked from lettuce or broccoli. A few pests do have broad feeding ranges (Japanese beetles eat the leaves and flowers of more than two hundred plants, and some grasshopper species have equally varied tastes), but for the most part, garden pests require the presence of specific host plants—that's where you can target your efforts.

It's wise to learn as much as you can about the life cycles and physiques of the pests that are damaging plants in your garden. Invest in a handheld magnifying

Above: Wasps are an excellent ally against garden pests.
Left: An American toad eyes a potato beetle.

glass and a good insect identification book such as *Garden Insects of North America: The Ultimate Guide to Backyard Bugs* by Whitney Cranshaw. Also bookmark useful online resources. Two excellent places to start are Cornell University's Resource Guide for Organic Insect and Disease Management and the University of California's Integrated Pest Management Program.

To find local information, begin with the U.S. Department of Agriculture's guide to regional integrated pest management centers. The Ontario Ministry of Agriculture, Food, and Rural Affairs is bursting with good information on insect identification and control.

The more you know about your problem pests, the better job you can do in choosing an intervention that will prevent or stop the damage without sabotaging the important work done by beneficial life forms. Before you get excited about any pest control product, read that last phrase again and consider this story: Last summer, out of the blue, thousands of aphids appeared on my eggplants. Three days later, ladybugs arrived and began eating the aphids and laying clusters of orange eggs on the undersides of leaves. As I anxiously waited for the eggs to hatch, I examined a few leaf samples with my 20× microscope. Two other beneficials—predatory mite larvae and syrphid fly larvae—had beaten the ladybugs to the punch. Within a week, the aphids were gone. If I had sprayed those aphids with insecticidal soap, I would have wiped out the food supply for three major predators. It was a lesson I will not soon forget.

all about growing cucumbers

by Barbara Pleasant

THE CRUNCH OF fresh cucumbers (*Cucumis sativus*) has helped cool down summers for more than 3,000 years, and cucumbers were likely one of the first vegetables to be preserved by pickling. Growing cucumbers is easy in fertile, organically enriched soil. Productive and fast to mature, cucumbers are a rewarding crop for new and veteran gardeners.

Cucumber varieties come in different sizes, shapes, colors, and even flavors. You'll need to pick often because cucumbers can double in size in just one day!

TYPES OF CUCUMBERS TO TRY

The size, shape, color, and flavor of cucumber fruits differ by variety, but all grow best under warm conditions. Growing more than one type each year is the best way to extend your cucumber season and ensure more diverse uses in the kitchen.

American slicing cucumbers are the oblong dark green cukes you see in supermarkets. Varieties of this type have been bred for uniformity, productivity, and strong disease resistance.

Pickling cucumbers bear smaller fruits with bumpy, slightly wrinkled rinds that make them naturally crisp and firm. Some varieties resist bacterial wilt, a widespread cucumber disease (see "Pest and Disease Prevention Tips" on page 181).

Asian cucumbers are long and slender, with small seed cavities. Non-bitter Asian cucumbers are easy to digest and are also not preferred by cucumber beetles.

Greenhouse cucumbers produce self-fertile female flowers, so you can grow many varieties of this slightly shade-tolerant type under row covers or in high tunnels.

Other *Cucumis* species include 'Armenian' and 'Indian Poona Kheera' cucumbers (both *C. melo*), 'West Indian' gherkin (*C. anguria*), and jelly melon (*C. metuliferus*, also called African horned melon).

WHEN TO PLANT CUCUMBERS

Sow seeds directly into prepared rows or hills 1 to 2 weeks after your last spring frost, and make a second planting a month later. Where summers are short and

CUCUMBERS FOR YOUR GARDEN

TYPE	DESCRIPTION	RECOMMENDED VARIETIES
American slicers 50 to 65 days to maturity	Uniform, oblong shape with dark green skin. Plants tend to produce all at once. Good fresh or pickled.	'Marketmore 76' (OP) 'Straight Eight' (OP) 'Sweet Success' (F1)
Pickling 52 to 65 days to maturity	Small, oblong fruits with thin skins that are often bumpy. Plants produce all at once and must be picked daily. Good fresh and great pickled.	'Boothby's Blonde' (OP) 'County Fair' (OP) 'Cross Country' (F1) 'Little Leaf' (OP)
Asian 52 to 65 days to maturity	Long, slender fruits with small seed cavities and sweet flesh. Skins usually lack the bitter compounds that attract cucumber beetles. Need trellising.	'Shintokiwa' (OP) 'Suyo Long' (OP) 'Tasty Jade' (F1)
Greenhouse 52 to 65 days to maturity	Produce self-fertile flowers, which do not require pollination by insects. Fruits have thin skins and small seed cavities. Produce best if trellised.	'Beit Alpha MR' (OP) 'Cool Breeze' (F1) 'Diva' (F1) 'Green Finger' (OP)
Other species ('Armenian', jelly melon, others) 55 to 120 days to maturity	Rampant, heat-resistant plants bear distinctive fruits that hold their flavor and pickling quality in hot weather. Best in warm climates.	'Jelly Melon' (OP) 'Poona Kheera' (OP) 'Yard Long Armenian' (OP)

cool, start seeds indoors under bright fluorescent lights 2 weeks before your last spring frost. If kept moist and warm (above 70°F), cucumber seeds should sprout within 5 days. Set out 3- to 4-week-old seedlings after your last frost has passed.

HOW TO PLANT CUCUMBERS

Choose a sunny site with fertile, well-drained soil with a pH between 6.0 and 6.5. Grow cucumbers in rows or hills spaced 6 feet apart, or try increasing yields by training vines up a vertical trellis.

Mix a 2-inch layer of rich compost into the planting site along with a light application of an organic fertilizer. Thoroughly water the soil before planting seeds ½ inch deep and 6 inches apart. When the seedlings have three leaves, thin them to 12 inches apart, which is the spacing you should use if transplanting seedlings.

HARVESTING AND STORING CUCUMBERS

Cucumbers self-regulate how many fruits they carry at a time. To maximize production, harvest fruits as soon as they reach picking size. Pick daily, because under ideal conditions, cucumber fruits can double in size in just 1 day. Use scissors or small shears to snip fruits with a short stub of stem attached. Lightly scrub, pat dry, and refrigerate harvested cucumbers right away.

Depending on variety and size of the fruit, one cucumber plant will typically bear ten to twenty fruits, which would total about 2 to 3 pounds. A pound of cucumbers yields about a pint of pickles, and six healthy plants of a pickling variety will produce enough cucumbers in one season to make more than a dozen pints of pickles.

PROPAGATING CUCUMBERS

To save seeds from open-pollinated varieties, allow perfect fruits to ripen on the vine until they develop leathery yellow or brown rinds. Slice away the rinds without cutting into the seeds, place the cores in a pail of water, and mash with your hands. After 2 days, remove the seeds that have accumulated at the bottom of the pail and spread them out to dry on newspaper or paper plates (discard any floating seeds). Allow seeds to dry at room temperature for 2 weeks before storing your largest, plumpest ones in a cool, dry place. Cucumber seeds should stay viable for at least 5 years.

PEST AND DISEASE PREVENTION TIPS

Grow cucumbers under row cover tunnels for pest protection. After plants begin blooming heavily, remove the covers so insects can pollinate the flowers.

You can control cucumber beetles using yellow sticky traps, but the traps may also snare small beneficial insects and pollinators. In large plantings, perimeter trap crops of 'Blue Hubbard' winter squash can be an effective cucumber beetle control strategy. Because the beetles prefer the squash plants, you'll intercept the pests before they can wreak havoc on your future pickle supply. Nearby

TIPS FOR GROWING CUCUMBERS

- Use a trellis or a wire tomato cage to increase the leaf-to-fruit ratio of your cucumbers, which will increase yields of flawless, flavorful fruits that are easier to pick. To further increase your yields, mulch beneath cucumbers with organic material.

- Make two plantings a month apart to stretch your season, and try to plant different varieties. If your area has super-hot summers, grow a second crop in early fall using row covers.

- If you're planning crop rotations, note that cucumbers often do well following cabbage-family crops.

- A popular intercropping technique is to seed crimson clover between cucumber rows just as the plants begin to "run" (send out vines). The clover will germinate and grow beneath the cucumber vines, and will become well rooted before winter.

A bumper crop of cucumbers calls for mixing up a batch of crunchy dill pickles.

plantings of borage may also help suppress cucumber beetle populations: I suspect they are intimidated by the large bumblebees and other insects that hang out in the borage.

Bacterial wilt is a common disease spread by cucumber beetles. Initially, a single stem wilts, followed by another, and within a week infected plants are barely alive. The best defense is to grow resistant varieties such as 'County Fair' or 'Little Leaf' or to protect plants with row covers.

Powdery mildew often infects old cucumber plants, turning leaves dull gray and halting plant growth. Many varieties offer some genetic resistance, such as 'Little Leaf' and 'Marketmore 76'. Pull up and compost badly infected plants.

IN THE KITCHEN

Cucumbers are 96 percent water, so they are low in calories but do provide abundant vitamin C and fiber if eaten with their skins. For a refreshing summer drink, grate cucumber and a bit of onion into a cold glass of buttermilk. Cucumbers quickly pick up the flavors of marinades to become refrigerator pickles, and they partner well with any type of salad dressing. Gazpacho, a cold vegetable soup from Spain, is always in order if ripe cucumbers abound. You can make cucumbers into pickles by canning them in various brines using a water bath canner or by fermenting them in a salt brine.

all about growing peppers

by Barbara Pleasant

PEPPERS PRESENT SOME of the summer garden's biggest flavors and brightest hues, and these striking fruits are simple to store and have a wealth of delicious uses in the kitchen. Plus, sweet and specialty peppers are among the most expensive produce at the grocery store, so growing peppers of your own can be a money-saving move.

Growing peppers will color your garden with dazzling, eye-catching fruit. Shown here from right are 'Sante Fe' (yellow), pimento (dark red), 'Marconi' (bright green with a blush of red), 'Apple' (mid-range red), poblano (deep green), 'Jimmy Nardello' (bright red), and cayenne (orange red).

TYPES OF PEPPERS TO TRY

Sweet bell peppers come in various sizes and colors, and the fruits' colors change as they mature. They grow best where summers are long and warm.

Specialty sweet peppers include pimentos, frying peppers, and other sizes, shapes, and flavors. Small-fruited varieties are among the easiest peppers to grow.

Southwestern chile peppers have complex flavors with varying degrees of heat. Many varieties bear late and all at once, so they can be a challenge to grow in climates with short summers.

Specialty hot peppers range from moderately spicy jalapeños to hotter cayennes to hottest-of-all habaneros. Most are easy to grow.

Ornamental peppers may feature spicy, brightly colored fruits, purple or variegated foliage, or both.

WHEN TO PLANT PEPPERS

Start seeds indoors under bright fluorescent lights in early spring, 8 to 10 weeks before your last spring frost date. If possible, provide bottom heat to keep the plants' containers near 80°F. Make sure the seeds stay slightly moist. Seeds should sprout within 3 weeks. Transfer seedlings to larger containers when they are about 6 weeks old. Don't set peppers outside until at least 2 weeks after your

PEPPERS FOR EVERY PALATE

Experiment with different types of peppers to find a good fit for your garden and your kitchen. Days to maturity given below are for fully ripe peppers that have begun to show mature color.

TYPE	DESCRIPTION	VARIETIES
Sweet bell peppers (*Capsicum annuum*)	Fruits may start out green, lavender, or yellow, and ripen to red, orange, or yellow. Miniature or other small-fruited varieties work best in cool climates. Choosing disease-resistant varieties is crucial in warm climates.	'Ace' (70 days) 'California Wonder' (75 days) 'Yum Yum Gold' (75 days) 'King Arthur' (79 days)
Specialty sweet peppers cubanelle, frying pepper, pimento (*C. annuum*)	These peppers are great for beginners. They tend to mature faster than bells, and they produce good crops over an extended period of time. Varieties that produce fruits less than 6 inches long are usually extremely productive.	'Gypsy' (70 days) 'Sweet Banana' (72 days) 'Lipstick' (73 days) 'Carmen' (80 days)
Southwestern chile peppers Anaheim, ancho, poblano (*C. annuum*)	Most varieties carry a little heat over a rich, smoky-sweet pepper flavor. These are great for grilling, pan-frying, stuffing, or drying. They usually ripen all at once quite late in the season.	'Anaheim' (76 days) 'Ancho San Luis' (85 days) 'Holy Mole' (85 days) 'Numex Joe E. Parker' (95 days)
Specialty hot peppers cayenne, habanero, jalapeño, serrano (*C. annuum, C. chinense*)	Most small-fruited hot peppers are so prolific that only a few plants are needed. Varieties with less heat—such as 'Garden Salsa', 'Mariachi', and 'Señorita'—are more versatile in the kitchen.	'Serrano del Sol' (75 days) 'Early Jalapeño' (80 days) 'Hungarian Hot Wax' (83 days) 'Mariachi' (85 days)
Ornamental peppers (*C. annuum*)	These make great edible ornamentals in beds or containers. Fruits may be round marbles or pointed fingers, and color may be yellow, orange, purple, or black. These peppers are usually very hot.	'Riot' (50 days) 'Demon Red' (80 days) 'Black Pearl' (85 days) 'Purple Flash' (85 days)

TIPS FOR GROWING PEPPERS

- Be careful with nitrogen when preparing your planting holes, as overfed peppers produce lush foliage but few fruits. Use a high-nitrogen fertilizer only if you're growing peppers in poor soil.

- In cool climates, use black plastic mulch in addition to row covers to create warm conditions for peppers. In warm climates, use shade covers during summer to reduce sunscald damage to ripening peppers.

- Provide stakes or other supports to keep plants upright as they become heavy with fruits. Cover surrounding soil with a mulch of clean straw or grass clippings so ripening peppers don't come in contact with soil, which can cause them to rot.

- Always wear gloves if handling hot peppers, and avoid touching your eyes or nose. If you do handle hot peppers bare-handed, immediately scrub hands with soap and warm water, rub them vigorously with vegetable oil, then wash them again.

average last frost date, during a period of warm weather. Always harden off seedlings by gradually exposing them to outdoor weather a few hours each day for at least a week before transplanting them outdoors.

HOW TO PLANT PEPPERS

All peppers grow best under warm conditions, but gardeners in cool climates can keep peppers happy by using row covers. Choose a sunny site that has fertile, well-drained soil with a pH between 6.0 and 6.5. Loosen the planting bed to 12 inches deep, and thoroughly mix in a 1-inch layer of mature compost. Dig planting holes 12 inches deep and at least 18 inches apart, and enrich each with a spadeful of additional compost. Partially refill the holes and situate plants so they are planted slightly deeper than they were in their containers. Water well.

HARVESTING AND STORING PEPPERS

You can eat peppers when they are mature yet still green (green peppers), although the flavor and the vitamin content of peppers improve as they ripen to red, yellow, or orange. Use pruning shears to snip ripe peppers from the plant, leaving a small stub of stem attached. Bumper crops can be briefly steam-blanched or roasted and then frozen, either whole (for stuffing) or chopped. Peppers are also easy to dry. Dried peppers quickly plump if soaked in hot water, or you can grind them into powders for your spice shelf.

PROPAGATING PEPPERS

Harvesting seeds from open-pollinated pepper varieties couldn't be easier. Allow a perfect fruit to ripen until it begins to soften. Cut around the top of the pepper, and use the stem as a handle to twist out the core. Use the tip of a knife to flick out the largest, most mature seeds. Allow them to air-dry until a test seed breaks if folded in half. Store seeds in a cool, dry place for up to 3 years.

When growing peppers for seed-saving, keep in mind that insects can transfer pollen, creating crosses between varieties. Genes that create a pungent flavor are dominant in peppers, so it is best to ban insects from plants being grown for seed. The easiest way to do this is to use "cages" made of row covers or lightweight

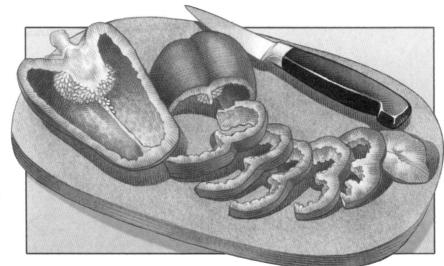

Cooking your way through harvests of 'Gypsy' or other specialty sweet peppers should (happily) be a lengthy task, as these peppers produce good crops over an extended period of time.

cloth such as tulle. The cages can be removed after the plants have set several perfect fruits.

PEST AND DISEASE PREVENTION TIPS

Tobacco etch virus (TEV), cucumber mosaic virus (CMV), and potato virus Y (PVY) can infect peppers grown in warm climates. Transmitted by thrips and aphids, these viruses cause leaves to become thick and crinkled or narrow and stringy. The best defense is to grow resistant varieties such as 'Tam Jalapeño'.

Margined blister beetles may suddenly appear in large numbers in midsummer, especially in warm climates. These large beetles are black with gray stripes, and they devour pepper foliage. Handpick beetles, making sure to wear gloves to prevent skin irritation. Use a spinosad-based insecticide to control severe outbreaks.

Pepper weevils can also be a serious problem in warm climates. Clean up fallen fruit daily to interrupt the life cycle of this pest, and trap adult pepper weevils with sticky traps.

IN THE KITCHEN

Pasta, pizza, salads, sandwiches, chili, salsa—shall we continue? Bring refrigerated ripe peppers to room temperature to enhance their flavors before eating them. Peppers' flavors become richer and more succulent when they are grilled, roasted, or smoked. If you bite into a pepper that sets your mouth ablaze, reach for milk or sour cream to quell the heat.

all about growing sweet potatoes

by Barbara Pleasant

SWEET POTATOES (*Ipomoea batatas*) are productive, delicious, and super nutritious. Few staple crops keep as well as these flavorful tubers, which can be stored for months in a cool, dry place. This crop is a staple in climates with hot, muggy summers, but growing sweet potatoes is also possible in cooler climates if you adjust to meet the plants' requirement for warm temperatures.

Sweet potatoes belong in the *Convolvulaceae*, or morning glory, family, as is evident by their morning glory–type blossoms.

SWEET POTATOES AT A GLANCE

TYPE	DESCRIPTION	RECOMMENDED VARIETIES
Orange-fleshed	Popular and nutritious, orange sweet potatoes have moist flesh, and the available varieties suit a range of climates.	'Beauregard' (90 to 100 days) 'Georgia Jet' (90 to 95 days) 'Nancy Hall' (120 days)
White-fleshed	The creamiest sweet potatoes have white flesh with less moisture than orange sweet potatoes. They're an excellent substitute for regular potatoes.	'Bonita' (90 to 100 days) 'O'Henry' (90 to 100 days) 'Sumor' (100 to 110 days)
Purple-fleshed	Originating in Asia, purple sweet potatoes need a long growing season, but can produce huge yields of straight, starchy tubers that can be stored until spring.	'All Purple' (120 days) 'Stokes Purple' (120 days) 'Violetta' (120 days)

Locate sources for these sweet potato varieties with our Seed and Plant Finder at *www.MotherEarthNews.com/ Custom-Seed-Search*.

TYPES OF SWEET POTATOES TO TRY

Sweet potato varieties differ in skin and flesh color and texture, as well as in leaf shape and vine length. The flavor and nutritional qualities of sweet potatoes vary with flesh color: orange-fleshed sweet potatoes are rich sources of fiber and vitamins A and C. White-fleshed varieties contain less vitamin A but are a good source of minerals and B vitamins. Purple sweet potatoes contain a little vitamin A but are loaded with antioxidants.

Orange-fleshed sweet potatoes are the most popular. Tried-and-true 'Beauregard' is productive and disease resistant. Some short-vined varieties such as 'Georgia Jet' make good crops in areas where summers are brief. In warmer areas, grow slower-maturing heirlooms famous for flavor, such as 'Nancy Hall'.

White-fleshed sweet potatoes are easier to grow and store in warm climates compared with regular "Irish" potatoes. Fun to use in the kitchen, white sweet potatoes are distinctly creamy, making them a favorite for soups and baby food. Varieties of this type also make excellent potato salad.

Purple-fleshed sweet potatoes need a long, warm season to produce a good crop, but the starchy deep-purple roots of varieties such as 'Violetta' and 'All Purple' are worth the wait. The dry flesh of purple sweet potatoes makes them perfect for roasting and frying. The anthocyanin pigments that give purple sweet potatoes their color also enhance their nutritional value.

WHEN TO PLANT SWEET POTATOES

To grow sweet potatoes, begin with rooted stem cuttings, called slips, which sprout from the ends of stored tubers. When the stems are more than 4 inches long and the weather is consistently warm, break off the slips from the parent sweet potatoes and plant them.

HOW TO PLANT SWEET POTATOES

Sweet potatoes grow best in warm, well-drained soil with a slightly acidic pH between 5.6 and 6.5. Choose a site with fertile soil in full sun. Where summers are mild, place plastic—either black (which heats soil and prevents weeds) or clear (which heats more than black but does not control weeds)—over the site in spring to warm the soil. Plant slips into small holes cut in the plastic, and leave the plastic on the site until harvest time. Sweet potatoes benefit from a generous helping of fully rotted compost dug into the soil before planting, along with a light application of balanced organic fertilizer. Space bush-type varieties 12 inches apart, but allow 18 inches between varieties that grow long, vigorous vines. Space rows at least 3 feet apart; long-vined varieties may need even more space. Situate sweet potato slips diagonally in the prepared soil so that only the top two leaves show at the surface.

Water well and frequently for the first several days and be patient. After about 2 weeks, the plants should be well-rooted and showing hardy growth.

HARVESTING AND STORING SWEET POTATOES

Begin checking the root size of fast-maturing varieties 90 days after planting. Sweet potatoes can be left in the ground as long as the vines are still growing and nighttime temperatures are above 50°F. One sign sweet potato plants are done growing is when the leaves and vines turn yellow. Starting from the outside of the row, loosen the soil with a digging fork before pulling up the plants by their crowns. Some sweet potato varieties develop a cluster of tubers right under the plants, but others may set roots several feet from the main clump.

Before storing sweet potatoes, you will need to cure them, a process that creates a second skin that is an incredibly effective seal. To cure sweet potatoes, gently arrange them in a single layer in a warm, humid place where temperatures can be held at 80°F for 7 to 10 days. In warm climates, a well-ventilated outbuilding is ideal. In cooler climates, a bathroom or closet with a space heater makes a good curing place (put a bucket of water in the room to increase humidity). Another option is to place jugs of hot water in a large cooler with your tubers; add new hot water to the jugs daily to keep the space warm and humid.

After curing, choose damage-free sweet potatoes for long-term storage in a dry place where temperatures will stay between 55 and 65°F. The flavor and nutritional content of sweet potatoes improve after a couple of months of storage. If conditions are ideal, well-cured sweet potatoes will store for up to 10 months.

PROPAGATING SWEET POTATOES

If you want to grow your own slips, move parent potatoes to a warm room in early spring. A month before your last frost date, soak the tubers in warm water overnight, and then plant them sideways or diagonally in shallow containers, covering the tuber only halfway with sandy potting soil. After danger of frost has passed, move the sprouting sweet potatoes to a warm spot outdoors and keep

TIPS FOR GROWING SWEET POTATOES

- Some sweet potato varieties produce morning glory–type flowers in late summer, followed by tiny seeds. Plant breeders work with the seeds, but for gardeners, propagating sweet potatoes by growing them from slips is more practical.

- With adequate moisture, shabby-looking slips usually recover quickly.

- You can also increase your supply of plants by taking 4-inch-long stem-tip cuttings, clipping off all but the top two leaves, and rooting the cuttings in moist potting soil.

Baked sweet potatoes slathered with butter and brown sugar are so sweetly warming that many people would consider them a dessert rather than a side dish.

them moist. When handled this way, stems (the slips) will emerge from both ends of the sweet potato, with each potato producing six or more. They're ready to plant when the stems are at least 4 inches long.

PEST AND DISEASE PREVENTION TIPS

Slightly acidic soil conditions help suppress sweet potato diseases, and the plants' lush vine growth naturally smothers many weeds. Rotating sweet potatoes with grains, cowpeas, or marigolds helps prevent disease problems, especially from root knot nematodes, which infect tomatoes, peppers, and many root crops. Avoid growing sweet potatoes in areas recently covered with grass, because ground-dwelling grubs and wireworms—often numerous in grass-covered soils—chew holes and grooves into the tubers. Deer love to eat sweet potato leaves, so you may need row covers or other deterrents. Stored sweet potatoes are a favorite of hungry mice, so stash your harvest in a secure location.

IN THE KITCHEN

Sweet potatoes can be baked, boiled, mashed, or used in stir-fries. Cooked, mashed sweet potato can be substituted for pumpkin in any recipe, and few desserts are as nutritious as sweet potato pie. In breads and puddings, use cinnamon, nutmeg, cloves, or orange to add complexity to sweet potato flavor. In savory dishes, sweet potatoes' flavor is enhanced by a range of spices, including garlic, ginger, and curry, and sweet potato salads can carry big handfuls of chopped parsley or cilantro. Thin slices of sweet potato are great for grilling, or you can make sweet potato chips in a hot oven. Don't overlook the new leaves on stem tips, which make excellent cooked greens.

From watermelons and muskmelons to honeydew and Asian melons, you'll be stunned by the variety of colors and shapes melons can bring to your garden.

all about growing melons

by Barbara Pleasant

DELICIOUS AND PACKED with nutrition, melons have delighted gardeners for about 2,500 years. Their rambling vines grow best in warm weather, and fruit flavor and texture improve if rain becomes less frequent as the fruits mature. Melons come in a wide range of sizes, shapes, and colors, providing a multitude of options for summertime fare. All melons grow best in fertile, well-drained soil with a pH between 6.0 and 7.0.

TYPES OF MELONS TO TRY

Finding the right melons for your garden will take some experimenting, because varieties that thrive in dry climates may fail under moist conditions, and vice versa.

Watermelons mature after 80 to 100 days in hot, humid climates—they won't grow well or taste good without plenty of warmth and sun. Because of their pest and disease resistance, watermelons tend to be the easiest melons to grow in organic gardens.

American cantaloupes, properly called muskmelons because of their fruity fragrance, produce 75 to 85 days after planting. Some varieties have smooth rinds, but the most popular and nutritious varieties have orange flesh beneath heavily netted rinds.

Honeydew melons have smooth rinds over white or green flesh. Most varieties need about 100 days of warm weather to make a good crop.

Casaba and crenshaw melons are oblong with wrinkled rinds and juicy salmon-pink flesh. Most varieties need more than 100 days of warm weather to produce high-quality fruits.

Specialty melons vary in size and maturation time, and some are much sweeter than others. Asian melons are fast growing and productive, but they aren't as sweet as European or Middle Eastern varieties.

WHEN TO PLANT MELONS

Sow muskmelons, honeydew, and other *Cucumis melo* varieties in prepared beds or hills after your last frost has passed, or sow seeds indoors under fluorescent

MELONS AT A GLANCE

TYPE	DESCRIPTION	RECOMMENDED VARIETIES	
Watermelons (*Citrullus lunatus*)	Need summer heat, but otherwise easy to grow. Small-fruited varieties that mature quickly make great homestead crops.	'Crimson Sweet' (OP) 'Orangeglo' (OP)	'Moon and Stars' (OP) 'Sugar Baby' (OP)
American cantaloupes (Muskmelons) (*Cucumis melo*)	Sweet orange flesh with netted rinds. Most varieties slip from the vine when ripe. Choose varieties resistant to powdery mildew for top flavor and productivity.	'Ambrosia' (F1) 'PMR Delicious 51' (OP)	'Hannah's Choice' (F1) 'Sweet Granite' (OP)
Honeydew and other green-fleshed melons (*C. melo*)	Less fragrant and nutritious than orange-fleshed muskmelons, but their flesh tends to be sweeter. Dry weather enhances flavor.	'Haogen' (OP) 'Sakata's Sweet' (OP)	'Passport' (F1) 'Venus' (F1)
Casabas and Crenshaws (*C. melo*)	Long, hot summers bring out the best in these melons, which have smooth flesh with hard rinds. Not for short-season climates.	'Crenshaw' (OP) 'Lily' (F1)	'Early Crenshaw' (F1) 'Twice as Nice' (F1)
Specialty melons, including Asian and novel hybrids (*C. melo*)	Interesting variations in shape and flavor, including some varieties that grow well on a trellis and others you can grow for both fragrance and flavor.	'Brilliant' (F1) 'Honey Yellow' (F1)	'Early Silver Line' (OP) 'Savor' (F1)

light and set the seedlings out after about 3 weeks. Direct-sow watermelon seeds in late spring or early summer, when your soil feels warm to the touch. In short-season climates, plant watermelon seedlings started indoors to get a jump-start on the growing season.

HOW TO PLANT MELONS

Fertile, well-drained soil is essential to growing great melons. Prepare raised planting hills within wide rows or along your garden's edge. Space 3-foot-wide hills 5 to 6 feet apart. Loosen the soil in the planting sites to at least 12 inches deep. Mix in a 2-inch layer of compost and a light application of organic fertilizer. Melons love composted manure (from cows, horses, or poultry), which eliminates the need for supplemental fertilizer. Use a rake to shape the hills into 6- to 8-inch-high flat-topped mounds, and water well. Plant six seeds per hill, poking them into the soil 1 inch deep. Ten days after sowing, thin plants to three per hill. If planting seedlings, set out three seedlings for each hill.

Consider installing protective row covers after you finish planting melons. Row covers benefit melons by raising soil surface temperatures, taming wind, and excluding insects. Remove covers a week after plants begin to bloom so insects can pollinate the flowers.

HARVESTING AND STORING MELONS

Most muskmelons naturally separate ("slip") from the vine when ripe, which means you can pick these melons with just a gentle tug. The rinds of some varieties of honeydew and watermelon change color when ripe, making it easier to learn the melon-picker's art. Watermelons are ripe when the curled tendril nearest to the melon dries to brown and the melon sounds deep and solid if thumped. Pecking from birds often indicates imminent ripeness.

Keep muskmelons at room temperature for 2 to 3 days after harvesting to help bring out flavors, and then move them to a refrigerator. Always keep honeydew and Asian melons in the refrigerator. Watermelons stored in a cool place (about 55°F) will keep for several weeks.

PROPAGATING MELONS

To keep seed quality high, select a perfect fruit from the densest part of a planting of open-pollinated melons and mark the fruit for seed saving. You can set aside seed from all melons as you eat the fruits, then rinse the seeds and allow them to dry at room temperature for about 3 weeks. Select the largest, plumpest seeds for replanting and store them in a cool, dry place. If given good storage conditions, melon seeds can stay viable for at least 5 years.

PEST AND DISEASE PREVENTION TIPS

Melons often face challenges from insects, namely aphids and squash bugs. Cucumber beetles also pose a threat, spreading bacterial wilt when their waste comes in contact with feeding wounds in the plants' leaves. Watermelons are

TIPS FOR GROWING MELONS

- Learn how to grow melons using vigorous, disease-resistant hybrids. As your skills develop, switch to open-pollinated varieties so you can save your own seed.

- All melons love rich compost, so try planting them in an old compost pile.

- Grow honeydew and small-fruited Asian melons on trellises to save space: they're great for vertical culture.

Fresh, lightly chilled chunks of melon need no further accompaniment on a hot summer day. Making smoothies and other liquid concoctions is a refreshing way to use a bumper crop of melons.

resistant to bacterial wilt, but other types of melons are susceptible. Your best defense is to use protective row covers.

Melon plants that stay full and leafy until the fruits ripen produce better crops, but powdery mildew can rob plants of their energy, which in turn reduces sugars, flavor, and nutrition. In addition to using resistant varieties, some gardeners ward off powdery mildew by using a spray made of 1 part milk to 6 parts water, applied every 2 weeks during the second half of summer.

IN THE KITCHEN

Fresh, lightly chilled chunks of melon need no further accompaniment on a hot summer day, but they do mix well with a variety of flavors. Melon salads often include mint, although oregano and basil also marry well with melon. Salty proteins such as sardines, cheese, cured meats, and smoked fish work wonderfully with melons' sweet juiciness. Making smoothies and other liquid concoctions is a refreshing way to use a bumper crop of melons. Muskmelons with firm flesh can be candied and dried, or try pickled watermelon rind for an old-fashioned delight. The deeper the orange of a melon's flesh, the richer it is in vitamin A. All types of melon are good sources of vitamin C and fiber.

row covers: the no-spray way to protect plants

by Barbara Pleasant

IN MANY ORGANIC gardeners' storage sheds lurk what look like stashes of dirty bed linens. These are actually sheets of reusable fabric row covers, which serve as barriers between plants and those creatures that would destroy them. Without ever picking up a sprayer, you can use row covers to eliminate problem insects and prevent browsing by rabbits and deer too. When combined with a weed-suppressing mulch (such as straw or grass clippings spread over wet newspapers), row covers often increase yields of peppers, strawberries, and cucumber-family crops by more than one-third.

Unlike plastic, which blocks rain and quickly heats up in the sun, the zillions of tiny holes in fabric row covers let rain in and heat out. Perforated plastic row covers do vent out hot air through thousands of holes or slits, but they are much less durable than breathable fabric row covers, which can be reused for several years and serve multiple purposes. With fabric row covers in place over your spring salad patch, you can stop worrying about biting winds and hungry rabbits.

In summer, you can sleep easy knowing your melons are safe from four- and six-legged saboteurs that sneak in at night.

LESSONS IN LIGHT

Garden row covers come in different weights, with thick versions such as Agribon 50 or various "frost blankets" providing up to 8°F of frost protection. The density needed to retain heat comes at a cost, however, because heavyweight covers admit only 50 percent of available light. This level of light deprivation nearly offsets these covers' insulating benefit, though thick covers are great to use in late winter to promote heavy, early production of strawberries and fall-bearing raspberries such as the 'Heritage' variety.

Midweight row covers such as Agribon 19, Reemay, and Covertan 17 admit 75 percent to 85 percent of available light. They also provide 2 to 4°F of frost protection and excellent buffering of strong winds. The fibers in midweight row covers are dense enough to provide multiseason durability but still porous enough to admit rain and ventilate themselves on sunny days. Should a serious cold snap hit, you can simply add a sheet of plastic or throw an old blanket on top of the row cover.

As the weather cools in the fall, midweight row covers are great for wrapping around caged tomatoes or peppers that are heavy with ripening fruits, or you can use them to keep aphids, leafminers, and flea beetles from finding your leafy greens.

Very lightweight row covers give little or no frost protection, but they also retain very little heat while admitting 95 percent of available light. These covers are standard equipment for excluding squash bugs, cucumber beetles, and squash vine borers from young squash, cucumbers, and pumpkins, or for keeping cabbageworms and root maggots from finding your broccoli. Row covers do need to be left off some plants to allow for pollination. Most vegetables that produce flowers before they make a crop, such as squash, cucumbers, tomatoes, and peppers, require repeated visits from insects to spread pollen from flower to flower. Root crops and leafy greens need no pollination, so they can be grown under covers until they are ready to pick. Last August, a featherweight row cover held in place with clothespins spooked the family of deer that had taken to eating my ripening grapes for their breakfast.

One of the disadvantages of row covers is that they become soiled and dingy. Enter wedding net, often called tulle, which is sold in 60- to 90-inch widths at craft and fabric stores. In early summer, when I switch from midweight white row covers to the ones I've made from wedding net, it's as if my garden changes from peasant underwear to polished formal attire. I use the finest mesh to keep flea beetles off my eggplants, but the regular 1/16-inch mesh effectively excludes the moths whose larvae become armyworms and cabbageworms, flies whose offspring become root maggots—and marble-sized hailstones too.

Little, if any, heat builds up beneath tulle covers, which admit more sunlight than the featherweight row covers sold as insect barriers. Grasshoppers chew through the netting a little faster than they make it through regular row covers, but grasshoppers are less likely to make holes in either fabric if it is held above the plants' leaves. I also use wedding net to keep birds from taking too many blueberries. Compared to bird netting, tulle is much less likely to snag on branches or accidentally snag hummingbirds. When bushes are covered with tulle that is gathered up beneath the bushes and secured with clothespins, even the most experienced robins can't get to the fruit.

GETTING A CUSTOM FIT

Standard row cover widths range from 5½ to 8 feet, and wider is always better. When shopping for row cover, be sure to get widths that will match the dimensions of your beds. Row cover that's 83 inches wide gives you 12 inches of overhang on each side when installed over a 3-foot-wide bed held aloft with 6-foot-long hoops stuck deep in the ground. Twelve inches of overhang is perfect if you're

Robins and many other birds love black raspberries, but bird netting is hard to use with brambles because it gets stuck in the thorns. Tulle sticks some too, but not nearly as badly as bird netting.

attaching the edges to bamboo poles or weighting them with boards, bricks, or sandbags. A 2-foot-wide bed could be secured beneath a narrower 61-inch-wide piece, but such a width over a 3-foot-wide bed could be raised no more than 12 inches above the soil line.

Row covers can be allowed to rest atop many plants, though peppers, tomatoes, and others with fragile growing tips do better when the cover is held aloft. Many people support row covers with 9-gauge wire cut into 6-foot-long pieces. You also can make hoops from inexpensive plastic pipe, which costs about a dime per foot at hardware stores. The ends can be pushed into the soil, or you can slip them over sturdier rebar stakes. On one of my framed raised beds, the planks on the long sides are equipped with vertical pipe sections into which I insert hoops made from slender saplings cut from the woods.

You can support row covers with stakes as long as the tops are smooth rather than jagged. Rebar or plastic-pipe stakes topped with rounded end caps work well, or you can use "living stakes." In spring, dot the bed with a few corn or sunflower seedlings and let them lift the row cover as they grow.

TAILORING TIPS

When you run into situations where your row covers' lengths or widths come up short, you can overlap pieces (making it easy to peek inside through the slit), or you can attach pieces using an ordinary paper stapler or a needle and thread. In the interest of research, I tested the strength of seams made with basting stitches on a sewing machine, hand stitches, and staples placed 2 inches apart. After abusing the samples in a bucket of muddy water and then setting them in the sun for a few days, the stapled seams showed fewer gaps and less tearing than the sewn ones. For quick jobs, simply attaching pieces of row cover together with spring-type clothespins will do.

After the row cover is on the bed, you may still need to weight the bamboo poles with bricks, heavy stones, or sandbags—a great reuse for gallon-sized freezer or food storage bags. When loaded with 10 cups of sand and 3 cups of water, these sandbags weigh about 8 pounds and instantly mold themselves to the spot where you put them, or use wire staples to hold down the poles on each end of the cover.

Under very windy conditions, it's a good idea to further secure row covers by clamping them onto their support hoops. If you use 9-gauge wire hoops, buy a few feet of ⅜-inch vinyl tubing and use kitchen shears or wire snips to cut it into 2-inch pieces. Then slit each piece open lengthwise and pop them onto the hoops after the row cover is installed. If you use flexible pipe as support hoops, make clamps from pipe of a slightly larger diameter than the pipe used for the hoops using a utility knife to make sure, clean cuts.

MAKING THEM LAST

Clean row covers last longer because soil particles that become wedged in the fibers have an abrasive effect. Promptly gathering and storing row covers between uses will go a long way toward keeping them reasonably clean, as will using poles

or weights to hold the edges rather than burying them beneath soil or mulch. Should a piece get very dirty, hang it on a clothesline and hose it down. Allow it to dry completely before storing it (I store mine in plastic dry cleaning bags). If you have several pieces, use a laundry marker to label a corner of each one with its size and type, or label the bags in which you store them. Once row covers are crumpled on a shelf, they all look alike.

After 3 years or so of frequent use, you can cut ragged row cover into pieces to use for smaller jobs like wrapping individual tomato cages or keeping flea beetles from finding a short row of radishes. Cut into strips, worn row covers make good plant ties, or you can wrap the strips around tree trunks in need of protection from winter sun or borers. Ripening melons swaddled in row covers scrap are rarely sampled by birds or mice, and young ears of corn covered with row cover bonnets held in place with rubber bands become off limits to the moths whose larvae become corn earworms. Last fall, I went out on a chilly morning and stuffed a scrap of row cover into the entrance of a badly located yellow jacket nest so I could safely harvest my butternuts. It really worked like a charm.

Row covers work great to protect your crops from a wide variety of pests, including:

- Cabbageworms
- Flea beetles
- Squash bugs
- Colorado potato beetles
- Root maggots
- Leafminers
- Deer
- Rabbits
- Birds
- Cucumber beetles
- Armyworms
- Grasshoppers
- Squash vine borers

These lucky carrots never knew the presence of a single leaf-hopper.

From left:
Mason bees can help assure a good harvest of many fruit trees; sweat bees prefer strawberries and blueberries; bumblebees pollinate legumes; squash bees collect only cucurbit pollen grains.

how to attract native bees to your organic garden

by Barbara Pleasant

THE PLANET'S BEST pollinators are in big trouble. Wildflower meadows where native bees once gathered nectar and pollen have turned into shopping malls, and dead trees where these ancient insects nest are getting harder to find. The native bees that do manage to survive are imperiled by Big Ag's pesticides—unless they can find safe haven in diversified organic gardens.

THE FRUITS OF THEIR LABOR

Gardeners can reap huge benefits from hosting helpful pollinators, which tend to stay put when given food and a place to live. Native bees—including bumblebees, sweat bees, mining bees, and others—pollinate many crops more efficiently and completely than honeybees do, with strawberries, blueberries, and the entire squash family reliant on local pollinators to produce their best crops. Tomatoes visited by bumblebees bear bigger fruits because the big bees' buzzing action shakes loose more pollen than wind alone. Strawberries pollinated by multiple types of bees yield fewer misshapen berries, and pumpkins pollinated by native squash bees produce larger pumpkins. Pollinators play a significant role in producing 150 food crops in the United States and, according to the Xerces Society (a nonprofit wildlife conservation group), one in three mouthfuls of our food and drink requires their work.

BEE ACTIVITY

For about 70 percent of the four thousand bee species native to North America, home is a secure spot tunneled into the ground (ground nesters). The other 30 percent nest in dead trees and stems (wood nesters). Almost all native bees live alone, not in colonies. Passive by nature, bees won't usually sting unless squashed or pinched.

Young adult bees emerge from their nests at various times during the year, usually in sync with the blooming period of their favorite crops. Females quickly mate and select good nesting sites, which are often within 1,000 feet of desirable flowering plants. After making a few short flights to learn their new addresses, ground-nesting bees immediately start working to excavate a nest and stock it with eggs. Gathering the necessary pollen, nectar, and sometimes mud requires thousands of trips between flowers and the nest. The closer the flowers are to the bees' nest, the less energy the bees must expend in flight.

TYPES OF NATIVE BEES

Native bees are closely tied to their environments. The following five types provide pollination for gardens and orchards.

Bumblebees are the largest native bees, and they also tend to fly the farthest in search of food. Active from spring to fall, they pollinate a wide range of plants and are especially important to legumes. Bumblebees usually nest in the ground or in cavities in trees. Bumblebees are the only native bees that are truly social.

Mason bees are also called orchard bees because they often appear in fruit orchards in spring. These stout, bristly little bees may be black or metallic blue or green. Mason bees use mud to pack their well-provisioned eggs into the hollows of twigs and branches. They frequently accept manmade nesting blocks.

Mining bees look like slender, miniature honeybees but have long wasplike wings. Active early in the year, they are important pollinators of fruit trees. Although mining bees are solitary ground nesters, numerous closely spaced nests may appear in hospitable spots.

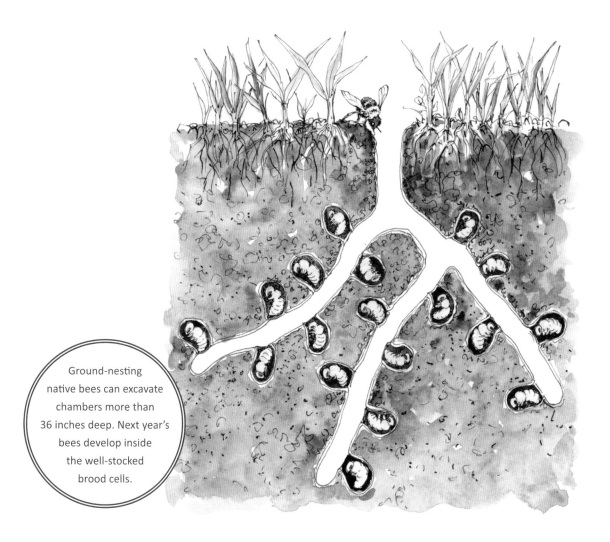

Ground-nesting native bees can excavate chambers more than 36 inches deep. Next year's bees develop inside the well-stocked brood cells.

Squash bees are the small black-and-yellow bees found in cucurbit blossoms, including those of cucumbers, summer squash, and pumpkins. Male squash bees sometimes sleep inside the blossoms in hopes of encountering a female. These solitary ground nesters do not emerge until early summer.

Sweat bees are small and often have metallic backs. You'll spy them pollinating strawberries, blueberries, and a wide range of flowers. Different species are active early and late in the year. They prefer to stay within ¼ mile of their nests, and they live alone, though several nests may be present in a hospitable location.

THE BEE SANCTUARY

Most ground-nesting bees are quite small and rely on secrecy to ensure their survival. Their entry holes in bare ground are difficult to spot and closely resemble those made by ants and solitary wasps.

Close observation is the only way to determine whether areas on your property have been inhabited by ground-nesting bees. "When they emerge from their nests as adults, they tend to start new nests near where they were reared, so preserving the area bees use for 1 year is likely to lead to continuous use of the nesting area," says T'ai Roulston, curator of the State Arboretum of Virginia, where researchers have identified 143 native bee species. "My best suggestion for maintaining ground-nesting bees is to provide areas with substantial bare soil or gaps in vegetation that will not get tilled." Sunny south-facing slopes are preferable, though some ground nesters look for vertical banks.

Bumblebees' shelters are usually well hidden and equipped with long entry tunnels. If habitat is in short supply, though, some bumblebees may take up residence too close for comfort (right next to the front door, for instance). Two to three days of intermittent soaking of the ground with a hose will usually persuade the bees to move elsewhere.

You can invite bees to your backyard by setting a low wooden frame around a pile of dirt mixed with sand, then topping it off with a couple of rotting logs or old pieces of firewood. Only allow clumping grasses to grow on the mound, and provide a diversity of bee-beckoning plants nearby to complete your bee sanctuary.

MAKE YOUR OWN BEE NESTING SITES

Some of the best bees for pollinating early-blooming fruits are wood-nesting mason bees. They nest in the soft centers of semi-hollow twigs (such as those of elderberries and bramble fruits) or in holes made in dead trees by beetles or other small insects. Other wood-nesting bees prefer rotting stumps or logs.

If your garden is near open woods that include standing dead trees and rotting logs, you may already have a good population of mason bees and other wood-nesting species. If there are no dead trees around, you can use fence posts or logs as substitutes. Use a drill to make a number of deep holes in the south side of a fence post or stump. Because different species prefer different sizes of

To build an insect hotel, stack wooden pallets and fill them with stems and logs with holes drilled in them. Add bee-friendly plants nearby.

PLANTS THAT ATTRACT BEES

These flowers, vegetables, herbs, and fruits make wonderful additions to a backyard bee sanctuary.

- **Annual flowers:** bachelor's button, cosmos, cuphea, larkspur, poppy, sunflower, zinnia

- **Perennial flowers:** achillea (yarrow), agastache (hyssop), black-eyed Susan, caryopteris (blue mist shrub), coreopsis, echinacea (coneflower), foxglove, hollyhock (single-flowered), lamb's ear, monarda (bee balm), ornamental alliums, penstemon, Russian sage, scabiosa

- **Vegetables:** artichoke and cardoon, beans, cucumber, peas, summer and winter squash

- **Herbs:** basil, borage, catnip, comfrey, coriander, dandelion, dill, fennel, lavender, low-growing clover, mint, oregano, rosemary

- **Fruits:** apple, blackberry, blueberry, cranberry, currant, melon, raspberry, strawberry

holes, drill them ranging from $\frac{3}{32}$ of an inch to $\frac{5}{16}$ of an inch (8 millimeters) wide. Drilling at a slight upward angle will keep water from entering the holes.

In Europe, many urban parks include insect hotels, which are freestanding structures stocked with habitat for wood-nesting bees and other insects. Envision a deep box artfully filled with hollow stems and logs with holes drilled in them. A simple way to make an insect hotel is to stack several wooden pallets together and then slip stems and logs with holes drilled in them into the openings.

WHICH NATIVE PLANTS ATTRACT POLLINATORS?

Many types of bees emerge at just the right time to gather pollen and nectar from specific crops (from blueberries in spring or from squash in summer, for example). They may only forage for a few weeks, so having different flowers coming into bloom all summer long is important. Recent studies have found that many native bees are more attracted to a diversity of plants than they are to large plantings of a single flower crop.

Native bees coevolved with native plants, so growing native plant species will naturally attract local pollinators. Many vegetables and herbs attract native bees, as do easy-to-grow annual and perennial flowers, flowering shrubs, and trees (see "Plants That Attract Bees" at left). Look closely and you'll likely discover that many plants in your garden are natural magnets for these winged wonders. When you find good bee plants—lo and *bee*-hold—grow more of them! That's the best way to give native bees the help they so desperately need.

7

SUMMER

the best vegetables to grow in the shade

by
Colleen
Vanderlinden

FOR MANY GARDENERS, the optimum conditions most vegetables prefer—8 to 10 hours of full sun—just aren't possible. Whether it's from trees or shadows from nearby buildings, shade is commonly a fact of gardening life. Luckily, shade doesn't have to prohibit gardeners from growing their own food. If you start with the most shade-tolerant crops, take extra care to provide fertile soil and ample water, and consider using a reflective plastic mulch, you can establish a productive shade garden and harvest a respectable variety of veggies.

HOW MUCH SHADE IS TOO MUCH?

All shade is not equal. Some shady conditions will yield much more produce than others will, while some areas are better left for hostas and moss. Gardeners should be familiar with the different types of shade but should also keep in mind that measuring how much shade your garden gets isn't always easy.

For instance, nearby trees may cast dappled shade on your garden for some or all of the day. If the tree canopy is high enough and the branches aren't too dense, the conditions nearby can be shady but still fairly bright. Trimming any low-hanging branches can help let in more sunlight.

More challenging than dappled shade is partial shade, which can be quite variable, ranging from only a couple of hours to many hours of shade. Shade from buildings is more difficult to deal with than shade from trees, as it often plunges the garden into total shade for large parts of the day. As a general rule, if you have a few hours of full sun but dark shade for the rest of the day, you can grow some crops, but the yields won't be as high as if you had bright or dappled shade during the rest of the day. Maybe your garden has a little of everything: some areas that get a couple of hours of sun, some that get dappled shade, and some areas that are in complete shade. In addition, the amounts of shade will change seasonally! It can be difficult to add up the exact amount of sun your crops get in such a scenario. Keep an open mind about what you may be able to grow in your conditions, and use our chart of the best shade-tolerant vegetables as a guide for where to start.

REFLECTIVE MULCHES AND SURFACES

Reflective mulches, including metallic mulches, are a great tool for gardeners growing in shady conditions, and for some crops in some regions, the benefits can be huge. University studies have shown increased yields in crops such as peppers, tomatoes, and strawberries.

Reflective mulches—such as the red plastic mulch some tomato growers have become fond of reflect light up onto the leaves of plants. Mathieu Ngouajio, associate professor of vegetable crops in Michigan State University's Department of Horticulture, says that under partial shading, reflective mulches have been shown to provide the following advantages: increased amount of light in the plant canopy, increased air temperature in the plant canopy, increased photosynthesis, reduced incidence of certain insects (particularly aphids and thrips), and increased produce yield and quality. Ngouajio recommends metallized reflective mulches (which look like aluminum foil) because they reflect the entire light spectrum and will have the greatest impact on increasing photosynthesis and, therefore, growth.

Creating other bright, reflective surfaces near your garden will also benefit plants. If you're growing near a wall, R. J. Ruppenthal, who shares his experiences with his small Bay Area garden in his book *Fresh Food from Small Spaces*, recommends painting the wall white or another light color.

"A bright-painted wall that faces the sun for any period of the day, particularly south-facing, will reflect an enormous amount of light and heat," Ruppenthal

BEST SHADE-TOLERANT VEGETABLES

When considering which crops to grow in shady areas, think of them in terms of leaves and roots. Crops we grow for their leaves (kale, lettuce, spinach) and those we grow for their roots (beets, carrots, turnips) will do fairly well in partially shady conditions. (The crops we grow for their fruits—such as eggplants, peppers and tomatoes—really do need at least six hours of full sun per day.)

CROP	SHADE NOTES	GROWING TIPS
Arugula	At least 3 to 4 hours of sun per day.	Arugula welcomes shade, as this crop is prone to bolting as soon as the weather turns warm if in full sun.
Asian greens	At least 2 hours of sun per day.	Asian greens such as bok choi (also spelled "pac choi" and "pak choi"), komatsuna, and tatsoi will grow wonderfully with a couple of hours of sun plus some bright shade or ambient light.
Chard	If you grow chard mainly for its crisp stalks, you will need at least 5 hours of sun per day; if you grow it mainly for the tender baby leaves, 3 to 4 hours of sun per day will be enough.	Expect chard grown in partial shade to be quite a bit smaller than that grown in full sun. Baby chard leaves are excellent cooked or served raw in salads.
Culinary herbs	At least 3 hours of sun per day.	While many culinary herbs need full sun, chives, cilantro, garlic chives, golden marjoram, lemon balm, mint, oregano and parsley will usually perform well in shadier gardens.
Kale	At least 3 to 4 hours of sun per day.	You'll notice only a small reduction in growth if comparing kale grown in partial shade with kale grown in full sun.
Lettuce	At least 3 to 4 hours of sun per day.	Lettuce is perfect for shadier gardens because the shade protects it from the sun's heat, preventing it from bolting as quickly. Often, the shade can buy a few more weeks of harvesting time than you'd get from lettuce grown in full sun.
Mesclun	One of the best crops for shady gardens. Grows in as little as 2 hours of sun per day and handles dappled shade well.	The delicate leaves of this salad mix can be harvested in about 4 weeks, and as long as you leave the roots intact, you should be able to get at least three good harvests before you have to replant.
Mustard greens	At least 3 hours of sun per day for baby mustard greens.	Mustard grown for baby greens is best-suited for shady gardens.
Peas and beans	At least 4 to 5 hours of sun.	If growing these crops in partial shade, getting a good harvest will take longer. Try bush and dwarf varieties rather than pole varieties.
Root vegetables	At least 4 to 5 hours of sun per day for decent production.	Beets, carrots, potatoes, radishes, and turnips will do okay in partial shade, but you'll have to wait longer for a full crop. The more light you have, the faster they'll mature. Alternatively, you can harvest baby carrots or small new potatoes for a gourmet treat that would cost an arm and a leg at the grocery store.
Scallions	At least 3 hours of sun per day.	This crop does well in partial shade throughout the growing season.
Spinach	At least 3 to 4 hours of sun per day.	Spinach welcomes shade, as it bolts easily if in full sun. If you grow it specifically to harvest as baby spinach, you'll be able to harvest for quite a while as long as you continue to harvest the outermost leaves of each plant.

These estimates are based on the experiences of the author and the experts mentioned in this article.

says. "This speeds up growth rates quite a bit, and can compensate for some other shade during the day."

We encourage you to try reflective mulches (aluminum foil should also work nicely) and reflective surfaces in your own shady garden.

SOIL CONSIDERATIONS

If you're going to push the envelope sun-wise, make sure your soil is well prepared. Amend your garden soil with plenty of mature compost, and loosen the soil to at least a foot before planting your crops.

The roots of nearby shade trees present a challenge all their own. The roots will wick moisture and nutrients away from your crops, causing them to need more frequent watering and fertilizing, and the roots will eventually invade your well-prepared soil. To overcome this, build raised beds or grow in containers filled with good-quality potting soil. If you're building a raised bed, try lining the bottom of the bed with discarded carpet to help keep tree roots at bay.

PESTS AND DISEASES IN SHADY GARDENS

In any garden, the key to successful pest and disease management is to pay close attention to your plants and deal with problems right away. This is doubly important in shady gardens, where some disease problems can be exacerbated by the low light levels, and pests such as slugs and snails—which thrive in damp, shady conditions—can decimate your lettuce crop in a flash.

Check your garden daily for the first signs of pests. Chewed leaves are most likely from slugs or snails. Handpick these pests whenever you see them. Also, a reflective mulch brightening your garden will do double duty as a pest deterrent: the reflective surface will confuse many pests, and they'll tend to avoid the area.

TRIAL AND ERROR

Shade gardening experts tend to champion a trial-and-error approach to growing without full sun, all offering the same advice: just try it and see! The quality of shade, your soil type and level of fertility, ambient temperature, and how much moisture the plants get all play a role in determining the success of the crops.

Regional conditions also play a part in how well your garden will handle shade. In the South and at high altitudes, some shade can be a good thing during summer to protect plants from the intense sunlight. In cooler, less-sunny areas such as the Pacific Northwest, growing in shade is a bigger challenge. Orientation can have an effect on the garden too: north-facing slopes are already cool and shady, but south-facing slopes tend to be hot and dry during the summer. South-facing gardens benefit from a bit of shade to conserve moisture and regulate temperatures slightly.

Have a blast experimenting in your garden. Rather than feeling limited by less-than-perfect conditions, try to see shade as a fun challenge to overcome, and we're betting you'll eventually enjoy plenty of delicious homegrown food!

Learn about keeping crops cool during hot weather. Some plants stop flowering and setting fruit when temperatures soar. To keep them cool, use old screens, lattice, and sheets to shade vulnerable mature plants from the effects of midsummer sun. Cover new seedlings with opaque covers to protect them from the sun until their roots are established.

keeping crops cool during hot weather

by Barbara Pleasant

IF YOU WANT to keep your garden productive well into fall, then late summer is a busy season that must be embraced. Hot temperatures are as rough on plants as on the gardeners who grow them, but here's a roundup of techniques you can use to help you and your crops cope. The sweat you invest when you seed beets or transplant broccoli will be richly rewarded in a few short weeks. The late-summer planting list is a long one with plenty of choices—chard, spinach, lettuce, kale, broccoli, kohlrabi, carrots, beets, radishes, and turnips. Now is the time to give cool-season vegetables a second run in your garden.

SIZZLIN' SUMMER: PREVENTING HEAT STRESS IN PLANTS

At this point you may be thinking it's all you can do to nurse tomatoes and other pet crops through a mean summer. We know your pain! But even if you keep the soil evenly moist by using lots of soakers or drip irrigation hoses covered with a thick mulch, many vegetables will abort their blossoms rather than set fruit in extreme heat. Temperatures in the 90s cause many beans to hold back flowers, and tomatoes, peppers, and eggplants start having trouble completing the pollination process when temperatures rise above only 86°F.

Commercial growers often use sprinkling to cool plants down. A late afternoon sprinkling may be an excellent idea, but strategically placed shading devices are often more practical, more water efficient, and much less time-consuming. For example, you can easily cool down the sunny sides of tomatoes by installing a short run of snow fencing or preassembled sections of picket fence along the south or west side of the row.

Shade covers made from lightweight cloth (such as old sheets) also will help keep struggling plants cool, though they must be held several inches above the plants to keep them from retaining heat. When using a cloth-type shade cover over plants, tie or staple the corners to wood stakes. You can probably buy shade cloth at your garden center. Scavenge before you buy. Old window screens make good shade covers too, as do narrow panels of wood lattice. If plants are so tall that installing a shade cover over them is impractical, simply situate a sun screen alongside them to shield their bases from afternoon sun.

Controlled shade also may help you grow lettuce and other leafy greens despite 90°F heat. In a 2001 study conducted on two Kansas City–area organic farms and at the Kansas State Research and Extension Center in Olathe, high tunnels covered with 40 percent shade cloth doubled the survival of transplanted lettuce seedlings and kept the plants from developing bitter flavors.

Whether you use shade screens or not, be sure to remove weeds to reduce competition for limited moisture. Ripening fruits demand huge loads of water and nutrients, so pick thoroughly and often to make it easier for the plants to keep up with the business of staying alive.

IMPROVING SEED GERMINATION

You may be able to direct-seed fast-growing kohlrabi and kale only 6 weeks before your first frost arrives. Leafy greens such as arugula, spinach, lettuce, and Asian mustards are easy and fast to grow from seeds sown right in the garden. Root crops such as carrots, beets, radishes, and turnips grow best from seeds tucked into moist garden soil. As the ground cools in September, lettuce can be put back onto the planting list too.

When choosing sites for small late-summer plantings, make use of partial shade from neighboring plants that will be sent to the compost pile soon. After the new crop is up and growing, you can remove the "screen" plants to open the site to stronger sun.

To help seeds germinate fast, soak them in water overnight, which will coax them out of dormancy. If you can't plant your plumped-up seeds right after a drenching rain, thoroughly water the bed or row the day before putting them in the ground.

To further insulate seeds from the drying effects of strong sun, it helps to plant the seeds slightly deeper than you would if planting them in spring. One trick that works every time is to plant seeds in a slightly recessed furrow, water well, and then cover the seeded furrow with a board for 3 to 4 days. When sowing in wide beds, shade the seeds with an old blanket or a piece of wood lattice held aloft over the bed with bricks for several days.

The repeated watering needed to get seeds up and growing sometimes causes a crust to form over germinating seeds, slowing or blocking their timely emergence. A light sprinkling of grass clippings will help prevent crusting, or you can cover seeds with potting soil or screened compost to keep the surface crust-free.

HOW TO KEEP COOL DURING HEAT WAVES

When summer sizzles, it's best to limit your outdoor work to the cool of the morning or late in the evening, but sometimes working in the sun is the only way to get things done. Wear a wide-brimmed hat to shade your face, and cool down your neck and wrists with loosely tied wet bandanas. A tie-on neck cooler will stay wet longer if you sew it up as a tube, fill it with a tablespoon of the same water-absorbing polymer crystals used to improve the moisture retention of potting soils (also used in diapers), and then sew up the ends. Or, thoroughly dampen clean dish or hand towels, shape them into rounded collars on cookie sheets, and pop them in the freezer. A frozen collar draped around your neck will cool you down for more than an hour.

Even with these tricks, remember that it's unwise to do hard outdoor work when both the temperature and the humidity are high. When the two numbers (temperature in Fahrenheit and humidity percentage) added together equal more than 160, stay indoors during the middle of the day.

Keep yourself cool when working outdoors by wearing a wet bandanna around your neck and a water-soaked hat.

all about growing sweet corn

by Barbara Pleasant

Isn't it time to make mouthwatering sweet corn one of your hit crops this summer? Growing sweet corn requires warm soil (above 65°F), so early summer is prime planting time. To stretch your harvest season, grow both early and midseason sweet corn varieties.

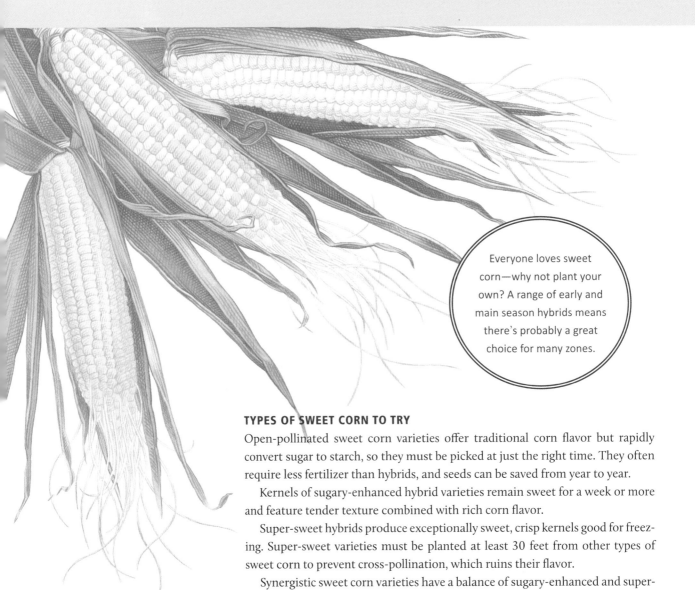

Everyone loves sweet corn—why not plant your own? A range of early and main season hybrids means there's probably a great choice for many zones.

TYPES OF SWEET CORN TO TRY

Open-pollinated sweet corn varieties offer traditional corn flavor but rapidly convert sugar to starch, so they must be picked at just the right time. They often require less fertilizer than hybrids, and seeds can be saved from year to year.

Kernels of sugary-enhanced hybrid varieties remain sweet for a week or more and feature tender texture combined with rich corn flavor.

Super-sweet hybrids produce exceptionally sweet, crisp kernels good for freezing. Super-sweet varieties must be planted at least 30 feet from other types of sweet corn to prevent cross-pollination, which ruins their flavor.

Synergistic sweet corn varieties have a balance of sugary-enhanced and super-sweet kernels.

WHEN TO PLANT SWEET CORN

In late spring or early summer, sow seeds in warm, fertile, and well-worked soil that contains plenty of nitrogen. Sow early sweet corn varieties 1 to 2 weeks before main season varieties for a longer harvest season. Many gardeners sow their early sweet corn when apple trees are in full bloom.

HOW TO PLANT SWEET CORN

Thoroughly mix in a 1-inch layer of fresh grass clippings, compost, or well-rotted manure along with alfalfa meal, soybean meal, or another high-nitrogen organic fertilizer (follow label directions). Sow seeds 1 inch deep and 4 inches apart, in blocks of at least three rows spaced about 24 inches apart. Thin early varieties to 8 inches apart; thin taller midseason and late varieties to 12 inches apart.

HARVESTING AND STORING SWEET CORN

Once an ear feels plump and full when you squeeze it, pull back the shuck near the tip and pierce a kernel with your fingernail; it's ready to harvest if the juice is milky.

Try to harvest sweet corn in the morning, when the ears are cool. Refrigerate them immediately or put the corn in a cooler and layer it with ice. Sweet corn can be canned in a pressure canner, but most people prefer the speed and convenience of freezing. Blanched corn off the cob takes up much less freezer space compared to whole ears.

PROPAGATING SWEET CORN

Most sweet corn varieties are complex hybrids, so don't expect good results from saving and replanting the seeds. To save seeds from open-pollinated varieties,

SWEET CORN AT A GLANCE

TYPE	DESCRIPTION	CULTURAL TIPS	VARIETIES
Early Hybrids 65 to 75 days	Small plants grow to less than 6 feet tall and bear one or two small to medium-sized ears per plant.	Best bets for cold climates or for growing in small gardens. With ample water and fertilizer, early hybrids can produce high-quality sweet corn.	'Early Sunglow' 'Fleet Bicolor' 'Spring Treat' 'Sugar Buns'
Main Season Hybrids 75 to 90 days	Vigorous, stocky plants typically load up with two big ears each. The best-flavored, most productive varieties are in this group.	When growing in average soil, fertilize with a high-nitrogen plant meal or other organic fertilizer when plants are 1 foot tall, and a second time when the tassels emerge.	'Argent' 'Bodacious' 'Illini Xtra-Sweet' 'Marai Bicolor' 'Miracle' 'Montauk'
Open Pollinated/ Heirloom 75 to 90 days	Plants vary in size, with some up to 8 feet tall. Expect one or two ears per plant. Sugars rapidly convert to starches as the kernels mature. Check ears daily as they approach ripeness.	Wide spacing helps older strains prosper with less fertilizer than hybrids. The tall stalks can double as trellises for snap beans and provide filtered shade for pumpkins or winter squash.	'Black Aztec' 'Double Standard' 'Golden Bantam' 'Luther Hill' 'Texas Honey June'

TIPS FOR GROWING SWEET CORN

- Precede sweet corn with a cover crop of hairy vetch or another legume to boost the soil's nitrogen supply. In warm weather, sweet corn can be sown 1 to 2 weeks after a cover crop is cut down or turned under.

- Sweet corn seed must germinate rapidly or it will rot. For best germination, soak seeds in clean water overnight before sowing in *warm* soil (65°F).

- Hybrid sweet corn is bred to grow at close spacing with heavy fertilization. To keep plants supplied with nitrogen, fertilize before planting, then side-dress them with a high-nitrogen fertilizer, such as cottonseed or blood meal, when the plants are 1 foot tall, and again when tassels appear.

- If plants are blown over by gusty summer thunderstorms, give them a few sunny days to right themselves. It won't hurt nearly mature plants to grow crooked, but you may need to prop up young plants that don't get back up by themselves. To prevent this problem, called lodging, hill up soil over the base of the plants as you hoe out weeds.

- The best way to fit sweet corn into a small garden is to grow early varieties in hills comprising six to eight plants. Corn is pollinated when wind carries pollen onto emerging strands of silk. To assure big, well-filled ears in a small planting, gather pinches of dusty pollen from corn tassels and sprinkle it onto the silks once or twice a day.

allow perfect ears to dry on the plants until the husks turn tan. Continue to dry them indoors until a few kernels fall away when you twist the ear between your hands. Store seeds in a cool, dry place for up to 2 years.

PEST AND DISEASE PREVENTION TIPS

Grublike gray to brown corn earworms feed on corn silks and kernels. They are larvae of moths that lay eggs in the tips of immature ears. To limit damage, use a squirt bottle to place five to six drops of vegetable oil in the tip of each new ear. For nearly worm-free harvests, add *Bacillus thuringiensis* (also known as Bt) organic insecticide to the oil. If earworms are minimal, simply break off the blemished tips as you shuck. Varieties with tight husk tips (such as 'Argent') often show only modest earworm damage.

A fungal disease called corn smut causes kernels to become black, swollen, and distorted. You can limit its spread by removing infected ears. Revered in Mexico as a delicacy, blobs of corn smut actually are edible and resemble mushrooms when cooked.

Inch-long striped armyworms are common pests of late corn varieties, but early maturing varieties rarely are damaged. Tachinid flies and other beneficials kill large numbers of fall armyworms, or you can use a spinosad-based pesticide.

Raccoons closely monitor sweet corn's progress and stage nighttime raids just as it reaches perfection. To protect nearly ripe ears, tape the ears to the stalk with packing tape.

IN THE KITCHEN

Immediately refrigerate sweet corn to preserve its flavor. You can boil, steam, or grill full ears; cut off whole kernels; or make creamed corn. To get kernels like those found in canned and frozen corn, blanch ears in boiling water for a few minutes, then cut off the kernels. For creamy corn kernels, cut the kernels from raw ears and use a spoon to scrape the remaining milky juice off the cobs.

all about growing summer squash

by Barbara Pleasant

FAST AND EASY to grow in a wide range of climates and soils, the many types of summer squash are among the most productive vegetables in the summer garden.

Try all the different types of summer squash, from tromboncino and zucchini to round and pattypan varieties.

TYPES OF SUMMER SQUASH TO TRY

Most summer squash are classified as *Cucurbita pepo* and vary more in appearance than taste. They come in a range of sizes, shapes, and colors, so make plantings of several types to add variety to your table.

Yellow squash are buttery yellow and elongated, and some have crooked necks. Overripe fruits turn into warted gourds.

Zucchini squash produce large crops of club-shaped fruits with skins in varying shades of green. Some zucchini squash varieties are striped or even bright yellow.

Pattypan squash are an old type of summer squash that produce fruits shaped like plump flying saucers with scalloped edges. Varieties range from dark green to bright yellow to white.

Round and oval squash produce single-serving-sized fruits on compact, bushy plants suitable for large containers or intensive raised beds.

Tromboncino and zucchetta squash (*C. moschata*) produce large curvaceous fruits with light green skins. Naturally resistant to insect pests, these rowdy vining plants grow best on a trellis.

WHEN TO PLANT SUMMER SQUASH

Sow summer squash seeds in prepared beds or hills in spring after all danger of frost has passed. You can also sow seeds indoors under fluorescent lights and then set out the seedlings when they're 3 weeks old. In Zone 5 and warmer, you can sidestep early-season squash bugs by delaying the planting of seedlings until early summer. Stop planting summer squash 12 weeks before your average first fall frost date.

SUMMER SQUASH AT A GLANCE

The chart below includes a mix of open-pollinated (OP) and hybrid (F1) varieties. In summer squash, hybridization is necessary to provide some types of disease resistance and maintain uniformity of size and color. All types of summer squash produce fruit about 50 days after being planted, although open-pollinated varieties tend to set their main crop later and produce for a longer time.

SPECIES	DESCRIPTION	RECOMMENDED VARIETIES
Yellow squash (*Cucurbita pepo*)	The classic squash for skillets and casseroles. Plants quickly produce heavy crops that require frequent picking.	'Success PM Straightneck' (OP) 'Yellow Crookneck' (OP) 'Zephyr' (F1)
Zucchini squash (*C. pepo*)	Dark rinds indicate superior nutrition, but try yellow zucchinis for color variety. Incredibly productive in good years.	'Black Zucchini' (OP) 'Dunja' (F1) 'Goldy' (F1) 'Raven' (F1)
Pattypan squash (*C. pepo*)	Also known as scallop squash, these fruits have a more solid texture. Beautiful stuffed and baked; whole, trimmed fruits can also be blanched and frozen.	'Benning's Green Tint' (OP) 'Dark Green Scallopini' (F1) 'Sunburst' (F1) 'Yellow Scallopini' (F1)
Round and oval summer squash (*C. pepo*)	Most varieties have a compact, bushy growth habit good for containers or small gardens. Small fruits are the perfect size for stuffing and baking.	'Eight Ball' (F1) 'Lemon' (OP) 'Magda' (F1)
Tromboncino and zucchetta squash (*C. moschata*)	Highly resistant to squash vine borers and not preferred by squash bugs. Slower to grow than other types. Vigorous vines benefit from trellising. Same species as butternut squash.	'Trombetta di Albenga' (OP) 'Tromboncino' (OP) 'Zucchetta Rampicante' (OP)

HOW TO PLANT SUMMER SQUASH

Choose a sunny site with fertile, well-drained soil with a pH between 6.0 and 6.5 for growing summer squash. Spots that were previously occupied by compost piles are especially desirable, or you can dig two heaping spadefuls of compost into each planting site. As you dig, loosen the soil to at least 12 inches deep and mix in a light application of a balanced organic fertilizer.

Plant summer squash seeds 8 inches apart, poking them into the soil 1 inch deep; water well. Thin seedlings to 3 feet apart. (If using transplants, set them out 3 feet apart.)

To prevent insect damage, install protective row covers over your squash as soon as you're done planting.

Summer squash produce male flowers on bare stems, while female flowers—usually preceded by the males—show a tiny squash at their base. You can improve yields in small plantings (fewer than five plants) by using a small paintbrush to spread pollen from male to female flowers, supplementing insect pollination.

HARVESTING AND STORING SUMMER SQUASH

Summer squash blossoms are edible, and you can harvest fruits from baby-sized up until they toughen with age. Harvest at least twice a week, using a sharp knife to cut fruits (leave a small stub of stem attached). Promptly wash fruits in cool water and store in the refrigerator. For long-term storage, freeze or dry blanched pieces of summer squash.

PROPAGATING SUMMER SQUASH

With the help of bees and other pollinators that fly long distances, summer squash plants readily cross with one another, which doesn't affect the current season's crop but will change the genetic code carried in the seeds. Summer squash also cross with several varieties of winter squash that are of the same species (*C. pepo*), such as acorn or delicata squash. To grow summer squash for seed saving purposes, set aside a hill where you can grow two plants of the same open-pollinated variety together. When the plants begin to bloom, cover them securely with a tent made of row cover or tulle to exclude pollinating insects. For a 2-week period, hand-pollinate female flowers during the morning hours and promptly replace the tent. When three perfect fruits have set on each plant, remove covers and pinch off new flower buds until the seed-bearing fruits are fully ripe (with hard rinds and brown stems). Save and dry the largest seeds from the insides of each fruit. In good storage conditions, summer squash seeds will remain viable up to 6 years.

PEST AND DISEASE PREVENTION TIPS

All types of summer squash face challenges from insects, including squash bugs, squash vine borers, and cucumber beetles. To defend your plants from all three pests, cover them with row covers held aloft with stakes or hoops until the plants begin to bloom. Big healthy plants will produce well despite pest challenges.

TIPS FOR GROWING SUMMER SQUASH

- Wait until the weather warms to grow summer squash, otherwise your plants will sulk in cold soil. Also, try growing summer squash around a compost pile located along the edge of your garden.

- Choose hybrid varieties if you need a space-saving bush plant or a special form of disease resistance. Open-pollinated varieties often grow long vines that produce for an extended period of time and may send out supplemental roots where the stems touch the soil.

- Grow at least two different colors of summer squash each season for more colorful pizzas and prettier casseroles.

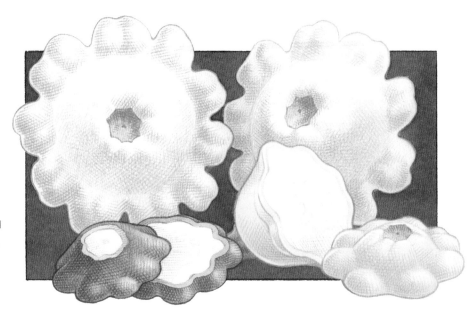

Colorful and low in calories, summer squash offer quiet flavors that blend beautifully with fresh herbs, mushrooms, and all sorts of cheeses.

Powdery mildew is a late-summer disease best prevented by growing resistant varieties, which often have the letters PMR (for "powdery mildew–resistant") after their variety name.

IN THE KITCHEN

Colorful and low in calories, summer squash offer quiet flavors that blend beautifully with fresh herbs, mushrooms, and all sorts of cheeses. When freezing blanched squash, include chopped herbs and fresh greens or cherry tomatoes for added color and flavor. Grilling enhances the flavor of both fresh and frozen summer squash. A bumper crop will fill a freezer; drying blanched squash pieces will save storage space and give you high-quality veggies for winter soups and stews. Grate slightly overripe zucchini and use it in baked breads and muffins. All summer squash provide vitamins A and C along with dietary fiber. Many of the nutrients are most abundant in the squash skins.

get the most from vegetable garden mulches

 by Barbara Pleasant

ONE OF THE hallmarks of any healthy organic garden is the effective use of mulches. Defined as materials used to cover the soil's surface, mulches help control weeds, prevent disease, conserve moisture, maintain consistent soil temperatures, enrich the soil with organic matter, and just make the garden look good. According to Texas A&M University, a well-mulched garden can yield 50 percent more vegetables than an unmulched garden space, thanks in part to mulches' ability to reduce foliage and fruit diseases.

Most gardeners prefer biodegradable mulches such as compost, grass clippings, leaves, or straw because they decompose into soil-building organic matter. In vegetable garden pathways or in orchards, sawdust and wood chips are hard to beat as perpetual mulches. Here we will focus on vegetable garden mulches used during the growing season, when their immediate purposes are to suppress weeds and diseases while moderating soil temperature and conserving moisture.

MULCHING TO CONTROL WEEDS

The longer a crop's growing season, the more likely it is to benefit from mulching. In terms of weed control, the timing of the application of the mulch can be crucial to its effectiveness. For example, you could get good weed control at the start by mulching with newspaper and grass clippings over the area where squash or melons will run. But by the end of the season, the plot will be knee-deep in weeds that can't be pulled without mangling the vines, so the best you could do at that point would be to cut back the weeds before they shed unwanted seeds. With peppers and tomatoes, however, it's better to mulch later to get more sustained weed control. Weeding by hand for the first month or so and mulching after weeds have been subdued will usually keep weeds down for the entire summer.

To enhance weed control provided by organic mulches, many gardeners place newspaper beneath other organic mulches. Overlapped sheets of newspaper—about six sheets thick—will block light that could pass through thin layers of grass clippings or weathered leaves, resulting in far fewer weeds.

The best vegetable garden mulches are those that your property produces itself, such as grass clippings, leaves, and compost made by combining kitchen and garden wastes.

HOMEGROWN MULCHES

The best vegetable garden mulches are those that your property produces itself, such as grass clippings, leaves, and compost made by combining kitchen and garden wastes. Grass clippings are particularly useful because they contain abundant nitrogen and other nutrients, which feed both soil life and plants. If used as mulch over fertile, organically enriched soil, a 2-inch blanket of fresh grass clippings can provide all the nutrients most crops need for the season.

I've begun developing the area over my septic field (where trees and other deep-rooted plants can't be grown) into a special patch for grass clipping production. By seeding in well-adapted grasses and clovers, I hope to have a lush plot that can be harvested four or five times a year using my walk-behind mower and bagger. This should satisfy about half of my mulch needs during the summer months. You can collect grass clippings from your neighbors, but if you do, make sure they haven't been contaminated by persistent herbicides.

Leaves gathered in the fall make fine mulch too, although black walnut leaves should be avoided because they leach chemicals that inhibit the growth of tomatoes and many other plants. All leaves are easier to handle and more likely to enhance plant growth if you run over them with a mower once or twice before gathering them up. If you don't have a bagger but do have a mower that will spew cuttings off to one side, you can quickly make piles of chopped leaves by mowing in concentric circles and directing the shredded leaves toward the center of the circle.

In my garden, I especially like the way long-vined squash behave if given a summer mulch of leaves over newspaper, so I go ahead and pile leaves on or near next year's squash row in the fall. Indeed, any vacant veggie bed makes a fine winter holding place for leaf mulch. The pile will suppress cool-season weeds and attract earthworms, which are always more numerous under mulch.

Still, I need more mulch! As the public mulch supply has become less trustworthy, I've stopped buying hay. Instead, I find myself growing more plants specifically to turn them into vegetable garden mulch. Twice a summer, I cut back waist-high comfrey plants that grow along a half-shaded fence. Persistent yet non-spreading, comfrey produces lots of big leaves that can be used to mulch beneath peppers, tomatoes, and even sweet corn. An added bonus: between cuttings, comfrey's blue blooms attract lots of pollinators.

Other options for growing mulchable vegetation include maintaining a plot of tall perennial clover that can be cut with a scythe or including dedicated, double-cropped mulch-producing plants in your garden rotation plans. Based on biomass crop-production research conducted in 2006 at Iowa State University, you could try growing a winter-hardy grain from fall to spring (rye, triticale, or wheat) followed by sorghum or a sorghum-sudangrass hybrid during the summer. (In climates with mild winters, you could use crimson clover or oats for the winter crop.)

Either way, you'll come away with a cool-season mulch crop to harvest in early summer—just when you need lots of fresh, clean mulch. Another mulch crop will come along during the growing season's second half, with another in time for mulching beds in fall and winter. (Sorghum regrows if cut back by half its size.)

Winter-killed sorghum plants will mulch the soil through winter. In spring, you can turn under or gather up and compost the remaining sorghum skeletons and rotate the bed back to vegetables.

Other parts of your landscape can be tweaked to produce more mulch too. As long as you avoid invasive species, large ornamental grasses can produce several armloads of straw when they are pruned back in late winter. Top choices include giant miscanthus (*Miscanthus × giganteus*) and 'Karl Foerster' feather reed grass. Growing seed-sterile varieties of giant miscanthus (maiden grass), researchers at the University of Illinois achieved double the straw yield typical of switchgrass, a popular native grass grown for hay. When I cut back my big clump of maiden grass in late winter (a pruning saw works well for this), I usually get enough "hay" to mulch a 2-by-20-foot row.

THE THICK AND THIN OF MULCHING

Organic mulches cool the soil, which is great if you live where summers are hot. In Texas, 4 inches of organic mulch is recommended for top performance from tomatoes, peppers, and other summer vegetables. But in climates with short, cool summers, a thick mulch can become a slug haven that keeps the soil cold and clammy.

The solution? Thin sheets of black plastic film mulch. Numerous studies have shown that black plastic film mulch improves the performance of many plants by warming the soil while also keeping it moist and free of weeds.

Other parts of your landscape can be tweaked to produce more mulch. As long as you avoid invasive species, large ornamental grasses can produce several armloads of straw when they are pruned back in late winter.

COLORED PLASTIC MULCHES: A RAINBOW OF BENEFITS

Colored plastic film mulches offer special benefits unique to their hues. If you don't have these needs, organic mulches may do a better job in the long run. Organic gardening standards allow the use of plastic films as long as they are gathered up at the end of the season.

- **Black.** Controls weeds and warms the soil beneath by up to 7°F. Black film mulches work best where summers are mild. While more expensive, black plastic landscape fabric allows water to pass through it and can be reused for several seasons.

- **Brown.** Works like black mulch but looks better in the garden and may also be available as reusable fabric.

- **Red.** Reflects far-red rays from sunlight back onto plants, which can improve production of tomatoes by 10 to 30 percent.

- **Green.** Can improve the performance of squash, melons, and watermelons in climates with cool summers.

- **Silver.** Confuses thrips and makes flea beetles nervous, so can be useful where either pest needs better management, especially in warm climates.

- **White.** Controls weeds without warming the soil, so it makes a good substitute for black plastic in climates with hot summers.

- **Clear.** Warms the soil for early spring planting more so than black plastic does, but it doesn't do as good a job at controlling weeds as the black plastic.

For several years, I've experimented with two alternatives to black plastic film mulch: roll-out paper mulches and cornstarch-based biodegradable plastic films. A double thickness of biodegradable black film gave decent weed control, but I didn't like seeing bits and pieces of it leftover in the soil the following season. Left bare or topped with organic mulch, I can't say that biodegradable plastic films or roll-out paper mulches showed noticeable advantages over old newspaper.

In some situations, the use of black or colored plastic mulch, which runs $12 or so for a 4-by-20-foot piece, may be worth the trouble and cost. Colored plastic film mulches are only as thick as lightweight garbage bags, so they usually can't be reused. The special single-season uses for colored plastic films are summarized in "Colored Plastic Mulches: A Rainbow of Benefits," above.

MULCH FIRST, DIG LATER

Many research studies have compared how crops respond to organic materials used as a surface mulch versus mixing the same materials into the soil. Vegetable crops vary in how they respond to the direct incorporation of leaves, wood chips, yard waste compost, and other organic materials into the soil, but yields are almost always better if organic materials have been applied as mulches rather than when the fresh materials have been mixed into the soil. So when in doubt about how to use any organic material to enhance plant growth while enriching soil, first try applying it as mulch.

wise watering

by Barbara Pleasant

IN A PERFECT growing season, 1 inch of gentle rain falls each week. Gardeners dream of such a season, but plants know better than to expect perfect weather. In response to dry conditions, they close their stomata (the thousands of "breathing" pores located on both sides of the leaves) to limit moisture loss, and they send roots deeper in search of water. Roots change their growth pattern to accommodate wet conditions too, often staying close to the surface where they have better access to oxygen.

These are admirable talents, but few plants are water-handling acrobats. Compared to your area's native plants, most food-garden plants are amateurs at adapting to your local rainfall patterns, so they need help. Delivering water wisely means minimizing wasted water and wasted time. In more practical terms, it means anticipating your garden's needs and setting priorities, having a conservation-based watering system in place, preserving water through mulching, and finding innovative ways to work out the kinks in your garden's water supply.

Newly planted seeds, transplants of any kind, and plants grown in containers almost always need supplemental water. Plan ahead to provide water in these situations, which can usually be done with hoses and watering cans. To help maintain continuous surface moisture in newly seeded beds, cover them with burlap or thrift store curtains on sunny days until the seeds start to sprout. Use overturned flowerpots or other shade covers to make sure the soil around newly planted seedlings stays moist, and to reduce overall transplanting trauma. Remove the covers after a few days.

The next priority plants are crops that can suffer permanent damage due to inconsistent soil moisture. Lettuce and other salad crops lose their flavor when the soil gets warm and dry, and tomatoes often split when dry conditions give way to a soaking rain. Mulches are the easiest way to avoid fluctuating soil-moisture levels when growing these and other sensitive plants. Biodegradable mulches (leaves, compost, clean grass clippings, etc.) block surface evaporation while suppressing weeds and making important contributions to the soil's supply of organic matter. You can even double-mulch by covering a sheet-type mulch of newspaper or cardboard with grass clippings or another biodegradable mulch.

DIFFERENT SOILS AND TYPES NEED DIFFERENT TECHNIQUES

Mulching cannot do it all. To enhance the flavor, nutrition, and productivity of your garden plants, sooner or later you will have to supply water. Your goal is to simulate drenching rain that replenishes moisture throughout your plants' root zones. Any soil will accept and retain water better if it contains plenty of organic matter, but when and how you water should be tailored to your soil's natural tendencies. For example, water percolates slowly through tight clay soil, so a slow, deep soaking once a week works well. Sandy soil has plenty of open spaces that help water move downward quickly, so concentrated drenches twice a week are a better strategy. Site is a factor too: high, sunny spots always dry out faster than low, shady ones.

Sprinklers are fun to use, but depending on weather conditions, half the water that runs through them can be lost to evaporation and runoff. Occasionally there are good reasons to use a garden sprinkler. If very dry weather hits just as corn shows its silks and tassels or when tomatoes are in full bloom, a late afternoon sprinkling session will increase overnight humidity levels and enhance pollination by making it easier for pollen grains to fuse with waiting ovaries. Sprinklers also are great for providing moisture for seeds planted in broad blocks, a cover crop of buckwheat, for example. Watering by hand is more efficient than sprinklers, but doing it right eats up hours of time.

You will need to have a standard garden hose at the ready for spot-watering, but your best bet for general watering chores is to use porous soaker hoses that slowly weep water into the soil or drip lines that emit water in tiny trickles. Either will efficiently distribute water exactly where it's supposed to go, with little or no waste. You can put a simple system together as you plant your garden and change the location of the soaker hoses or drip lines as crops come and go. For maximum versatility, limit the length of soaker or drip hoses to fewer than 50 feet and install pop-in connectors to the female (incoming) ends of each hose.

Soaker hoses and drip lines depend on pressure from a faucet to push water through them, but if you have a little elevation to work with, you may be able to set up a gravity-fed bucket drip system.

To supply water to plants outside your drip lines or soaker hose network, punch a few small holes into the sides of plastic milk jugs or kitty-litter jugs an inch from the bottom, fill them with water, and let them drip their moisture into the root zones of thirsty plants. The water that remains in the bottom of the jugs, below the holes, will keep them from blowing away.

USE WATER-SMART HARDWARE

Good watering hardware can save hours of time—and hundreds of gallons of water—in the course of a growing season:

- Replace washers as needed to make sure hoses and faucets connect tightly.

- Outfit your outdoor faucets with splitters so you can attach two hoses to each one.

- When using a sprinkler, soaker, or drip system, use a timer so you won't have to remember to turn the water off.

- Buy high-quality hoses that are not prone to kinking. If you keep numerous containers on your deck or patio, consider getting a springy coil hose that can be stashed in a corner between uses.

- Keep a supply of couplers on hand to repair cracks and leaks in hoses or to splice together pieces of soaker hose.

HARVEST THE RAIN

Harvesting rain for garden use can begin in the garden. As long as you're hoeing out weeds, use your hoe to create shallow furrows along planted rows to detain rain that would otherwise flow into pathways. In similar fashion, you can make raised rims around beds to create a basin effect. Should you get too much rain, one decisive swipe with a hoe or spade will open the earthen floodgates.

You also can collect rain in containers stationed in or near the garden. Last summer when my neighbors downsized their herd of cows, I gained use of an oval-shaped 50-gallon stock tank, which partially refills itself with each passing shower. The sun-warmed water is great for rinsing dirty hands or washing pots, or for dipping out to pour on parched plants. Maintenance is limited to dumping the tank often enough to interrupt the 7-day life cycle of mosquitoes, or adding mosquito-killing Bt (*Bacillus thuringiensis*, an organic pesticide) doughnuts to the water.

If your house has gutters and is located slightly higher than your garden, you may be able to connect the downspouts to a temporary plastic pipeline to distribute the roof runoff directly into your garden.

garden disease prevention basics

by Barbara Pleasant

IT HAPPENS IN the best of gardens. Your plants are growing beautifully, and then you notice some of them are being consumed by pathogenic (from the Greek *pathos*, meaning "suffering") microorganisms. The good news is you don't have to be a plant pathologist to prevent many of the diseases that threaten a food garden, because disease-resistant varieties that are grown in soil enriched with organic matter usually stay healthy when the going gets tough.

Cured compost helps plants prime themselves to better handle challenges from diseases while improving the soil's tilth. Providing enough water to avoid drought stress helps too. Many gardeners include seaweed sprays in their garden's preventive health care program, which provide nutrients for both plants and beneficial microorganisms.

Still, some leaves will shrivel and entire plants may sometimes suddenly collapse. To offer the best help to troubled plants, first you'll need to know how different types of diseases tick. Seeing is believing. In late summer, most gardens offer some examples of common garden diseases such as leaf blemishes and fruit rots, stem and root infections, and viral diseases spread by insects.

GARDEN FUNGAL FOLLIES

Let's start by looking at your tomatoes, especially the leaves closest to the ground. That area stays damp longer than the plant's high branches, and the leaves down there are getting old—two factors that make them prime victims for early blight (dark brown patches) or several other leaf-spot diseases, including gray leaf spot and *Septoria* leaf spot. All are caused by fungi that busily release millions of spores that spread to new leaves by the time the colonies become big enough to see. If those new leaves are damp and temperatures are right, the spores germinate and penetrate the leaf using enzymes to melt entryways into plant cells, and a new leaf spot is born.

Leaf blemishes come in a variety of colors. Among your squash, you may see some white patches of powdery mildew, which is caused by spore-producing fungi that weaken plants by robbing leaves of their ability to perform efficient photosynthesis. You might see streaks of cinnamon-like rust in your corn or

patches of orange rust powder on bramble fruits or beans—more examples of spore-producing parasitic fungi. If you grow fruits, the velvety brown patina on your shriveled peaches or plums is caused by brown rot and *Botrytis*. Other spore-producing fungi turn strawberries and grapes into moldy mummies.

Resistant varieties are available for many of these diseases—especially powdery mildew of squash family crops and various blemishers of beans. (There are no highly resistant varieties to help prevent tomato early blight, grape powdery mildew, or brown rot of peaches, plums, and cherries.) Once an outbreak is underway, you can slow its spread if you move in during a period of dry weather and clip off affected leaves, fruits, or branches, *but only if the foliage is dry*. Fungal spores usually arrive in the garden on the wind or on insects' feet, but nothing spreads spores faster than a gardener mucking around in damp, diseased foliage or fruits.

Judicious grooming followed by a cleansing drench with a fine spray of water will reduce the number of spores present on the plants, and should you catch an outbreak early, there are several sprays that make good follow-up treatments. Or, the sprays can be used as preventive measures, if past experience makes you think an outbreak is likely.

When exposed to sunlight, plain milk diluted in water (use a 1:6 ratio of milk to water) briefly changes into a disinfectant compound that's murder on fungal spores yet gentle to plant leaves. You should see results after two sprays applied 3 days apart.

Baking soda (1 teaspoon per quart of water, with a few drops of liquid soap added to help it stick) is an old and trusted intervention, but it's hard to get good coverage on plants with hairy leaves. A product called GreenCure (sold whole-sale as MilStop) is based on potassium bicarbonate, baking soda's first cousin, held in suspension through a unique process developed by Ken Horst, professor emeritus of plant pathology at Cornell University. New fungal colonies that are just beginning to grow (and are still too small to see) suffer shriveled hyphae (the fungal counterpart to roots) when exposed to bicarbonate sprays.

Some research indicates that compost tea sprays can reduce disease, but I don't recommend using compost tea as a foliar spray on food plants. The bacte-rial load in compost tea is unpredictable and may include *Salmonella*, *E. coli*, and other microorganisms that can make you extremely sick. If you want to stage a microbial war against leaf-spotting or fruit-rotting fungi, it is much safer to use Serenade or another packaged biofungicide based on *Bacillus subtilis*—an aggres-sive naturally occurring bacterium that destroys many types of fungi.

Various fungicides containing sulfur and copper are allowed for restricted use on organically grown food crops, but copper can wreak havoc on your soil's food web. Once it drips into the soil, copper does not break down or leach away, and even moderate copper levels are toxic to earthworms and many soil microor-ganisms. Sulfur is safer for soil life, but sulfur sprays often injure plant leaves, especially in hot weather, and prolonged use of sulfur could make soil too acidic.

GARDEN SOIL: TROUBLE DOWN BELOW

Fungi are essential components of any healthy soil food web, but some soilborne fungi such as *Fusarium* and *Phytopthora* species are on gardeners' most unwanted lists. Different *Fusarium* strains attack tomatoes, onions, basil, and many other plants, first by stripping off the roots' outer tissues (causing the plants to grow slowly and turn yellowish) and then by clogging up the plants' stems, at which point you see a steady wilting. *Verticillium* wilt often looks similar, only without the yellowing, and the same complex of fungi that cause "damping off" of seedlings (a fungal infection that occurs in excessively damp conditions) can emerge as the culprits behind plants that collapse due to sudden root rot.

Numerous plant varieties are available that offer good resistance to these and other soilborne diseases; the best way to find resistant varieties is to buy seeds from the better seed catalogs, which list specific disease resistances. You can further reduce problems by adding compost to your soil and rotating crops so they are not planted in the same place more often than once every 3 years. Promptly removing plants that exhibit symptoms of root problems (for example chronic thirst and little or no new growth) also will reduce the number of destructive fungi left behind in the soil.

Soil biologists have identified several microorganisms that can outcompete or even attack pathogenic fungi in the soil, and some have been developed into organic fungicides. These products are especially useful in greenhouses, where soil diseases spread like wildfire, or when starting seedlings. Here are four examples:

- SoilGard (*Gliocladium virens*), a product that inhibits fungal growth, emerged from research into ecological controls for damping off at the USDA's Agricultural Research Service in Beltsville, Maryland.
- Mycostop (*Streptomyces griseoviridis*) harnesses the ability of naturally occurring bacterium to maim and kill *Fusarium* and some other soilborne fungi.
- RootShield uses the fungus *Trichoderma harzianum* to outcompete fungi that cause roots to rot.
- Contans (*Coniothyrium minitans*) does a number on *Sclerotinia* fungi, reducing the numbers of fungi capable of causing stem and root rot of lettuce, cabbage family crops, and many other edible plants.

PLANT DISEASES ON THE WING

Plant pathogens can't fly on their own, but the tiniest of them all—viruses—often travel for miles inside the bodies of leaf-hoppers, aphids, flea beetles, whiteflies, and thrips. These insect carriers, or vectors, also provide entry holes for the viruses when they puncture leaves or stems with their mouthparts. Once inside a plant, viruses interfere with the plants' inner communication systems and instruct them to grow in odd ways that serve the virus rather than the plant. Squash family crops infected with cucumber mosaic virus show thick, brittle leaves mottled with patches of dark green and yellow, but when the same virus hits tomatoes or peppers, you see thin, stringy leaves. Beans stricken with curly top virus develop spirals of flowering stems that fail to set fruit. Some plants do outgrow viral infections, but most decline slowly and rarely produce a good crop. If you see plants that "don't look right," it's best to remove them to prevent viruses from spreading to neighboring plants.

Viruses can travel only as far as insects can carry them, so they tend to be local or regional phenomena. Once you learn that a certain virus is prevalent in your area—for example pea enation virus in the Northwest or maize (corn) dwarf mosaic virus in the South and East—growing resistant varieties is your best defense. In cases where genetic resistance is not available, you may be able to exclude insect vectors with row covers, though really tiny insects often find ways to breach even these barriers. Alternatively, you can deter them with aluminum-coated reflective mulch such as Brite'Nup or with sheets of cardboard covered with aluminum foil, shiny side out. Insects are confused by the light-mirroring effect of the mulch, so they stay away until the plants become so big and leafy that they cover the mulch. In numerous research trials from Florida to California, reflective mulches have proven their worth as viral deterrents, often resulting in huge increases in the productivity of cantaloupes, pumpkins, and tomatoes in areas where viruses are rampant.

Do not expect to emerge from battles with garden diseases without a few scars—and a new appreciation for the power of prevention. Wisdom comes with experience. After you have grown a food garden for a few seasons, you'll know which diseases are most likely to appear, and that puts you in a much better position to prevent them in the first place.

when to harvest garden-fresh produce

by Kris Weatherbee

THE SECRET TO enjoying garden-fresh produce at its prime is knowing when to harvest. If you've ever eaten a melon that lacked sweetness or green beans that were fibrous and tough, you know how crucial timing can be. Just as different vegetables have their own distinct needs for planting, fertilizing, and growing, each also will give certain clues when it is ready to pick.

A few vegetables are very accommodating and can stay in the ground for weeks until you're ready to eat them. Others need continual picking to ensure ongoing production of a crop, but most have a short window of time during which they can be gathered at peak flavor. After a vegetable passes its prime, it undergoes permanent changes that alter its taste, appearance, quality, and sometimes its future production. Sugars turn to starches, and the texture becomes mushy, like an overripe melon or chewy green beans.

On the other hand, if you pick too soon, you'll harvest a vegetable that has not had adequate time to develop peak flavor, substance, or nutrition.

The following is a guide to help you know precisely when your summer and fall fruits and vegetables have reached their peak of perfection and are ready to be picked and eaten.

- **Beans** should be checked daily for harvesting. Snap beans/green beans are ready when the pods have filled out but the seeds are still tiny, which, depending on weather conditions, is usually some 2 to 4 weeks after bloom. The pods should be firm and crisp, with pliable tips. Pick haricot (French filet) types when the pods are about ⅛ inch in diameter, while they're still young and very slender.

- **Beets** can be picked when the roots are from 1½ to 3 inches in diameter, and most taste best when they are about the size of a Ping-Pong ball or golf ball. White and golden varieties are tasty and tender until they reach baseball size, but storage (winter-keeping) varieties remain tender until they reach softball size or even slightly larger. When harvested past their prime, beets have a strong taste and a tough, pithy texture.

- **Broccoli** should be harvested when the buds are still tight and before the florets begin opening their yellow flowers. For the first harvest, cut the central stalk at a slant about 5 to 6 inches below the base of the head. This prevents rot and encourages production of new side shoots, which can be harvested at a later date.

- **Brussels sprouts** develop a sweet flavor after the plant has gone through a couple of mild frosts. The buds at the base are the first to mature, so pick from the bottom up when sprouts become firm and are about 1 inch in diameter. To encourage larger sprouts, which mature more uniformly, cut the top of the plant back by about 4 inches about 4 weeks before the harvest is to begin.

- **Cabbage** offers some leeway as to when it can be picked at perfection, though larger heads are more likely to split than smaller ones. If a head is threatening to split, twisting it a quarter turn will slow down the splitting. Cabbage heads that have split are still tasty and should be picked; they just won't store as well as solid heads. Begin harvesting cabbage anytime after developing heads have become solid and firm.

- **Carrots** usually hold well in the ground and can be harvested over a long period of time. Begin as soon as the roots color up and grow to from ½ to 1 inch in diameter. Continue harvesting until the last frost-sweetened carrots are dug before the ground freezes for winter. Careful digging—rather than pulling—is best as a harvest method; only pull the roots if your soil is extremely friable. The texture of a fresh carrot is at its finest in the young ones, but the sugar content heightens as they mature.

- **Cauliflower** is at its best when 6- to 8-inch fully formed heads are firm and the curds in them are solid. If you wait until after the curds have opened (they resemble rice grains), you have passed the window of opportunity for harvesting optimum-quality heads.

- **Corn** should be picked when the kernels have swollen to their maximum juiciness, usually about 20 days after the first silk strands appear. When the silks begin to turn dry and brown, partially peel back the husks and pierce a kernel with your thumbnail. If a milky juice squirts out, the corn is ready to eat. To harvest, snap off the ear by pulling it downward, then twist and pull again. If allowed to overripen, corn will lose its sweet flavor and become starchy.

- **Cucumbers** grow fast, so check them daily if you plan to keep up with the peak of harvest and ensure continued production. For fresh use, a cucumber should be filled out enough to be crisp and juicy, and should measure from 6 to 9 inches long. For sweet pickles, cucumbers are best harvested when they measure from 1½ to 2½ inches long; for dill pickles, the ideal length is from 3 to 4 inches.

- **Eggplant** has received a bad rap as a bitter-tasting vegetable because of the oversized fruits often sold in supermarkets. Eggplant past its prime is soft, pithy, and laden with seeds, which are what give it the bitter taste. Fruit harvested while still young and firm is actually rather sweet and very tender; that's when the vegetable measures from 4 to 8 inches in length, or about one-third of its mature size. Use strong scissors or pruning shears to harvest the fruit rather than pulling it, which will injure the plant.

- **Leeks** can be pulled from the ground anytime the stem is an inch in diameter or larger. Use them when they are still very small for the mildest, most delicate flavor. Cut off the roots and most of the top green portion before storing in the refrigerator. (Save the green part to use in soup stock.) Many varieties will overwinter in mild climates and remain harvestable into March. After that, they can develop a hard core in the center that will not soften even when cooked.

- **Lettuce** can be picked in stages: tiny leaves for a gourmet salad mix or larger leaves for a main dish. For loose-leaf varieties, pick outer leaves as needed, or cut the head an inch above the ground for a "cut-and-come-again" crop. Butterheads, romaines, and crispheads should be harvested when the head begins to form and—for peak perfection—before the center begins to elongate, which means that the plant is preparing to flower. After that point, the lettuce will taste bitter. For refrigerator storage, run washed leaves through a salad spinner, place in a sealable plastic bag with a paper towel or tea towel, and store in the crisper section of your refrigerator.

- **Melons** can be a challenge, but several telltale signs can help you decide when the fruit is perfectly ripe. On some cantaloupes, which may also be called muskmelons, netting (venation) that overlays the skin becomes more pronounced and the melon will separate easily from the vine when it has fully ripened.

  True cantaloupes and honeydew types soften and give slightly to pressure on the blossom end, and the background color will change. Cut these from the vine, as they will not slip from the stem. Pick for optimal quality after the tendril closest to the fruit has turned completely brown. On watermelons, the surface of the fruit loses its gloss, the belly side touching the ground changes from white to creamy yellow, and the tendril turns brown and begins to shrivel. Thumping as a measure of ripeness is a matter of luck; it works for some and not for others. Those who claim the gift say the thump should sound hollow and deep.

- **Okra** should never be allowed to get too big. Harvest short-pod varieties when they are from 2 to 3 inches in length, usually about 4 to 6 days after flowering. Long-pod types such as 'Cow Horn' are best picked at 6 to 8 inches in length. Tips of tender pods will snap, but those on older pods won't because pods mature from the tip down, which means the tip turns fibrous first. Check pods daily, because they can go from prime to pitiful in just 24 hours' time.

- **Onions** can be harvested in two stages: the green "scallion" stage or the bulb stage. Green onions are best when tops are 6 to 8 inches tall and stems are the thickness of a pencil. For maximum size and mature bulbs, wait until more than half of the tops have fallen down, then push over the remaining tops. A week later, harvest the bulbs and set them in the sun for a day or two (cover at night). Cure the bulbs with tops intact for about a week in a sheltered, dry area; during this time, the outer layers will form a dry skin. After that, cut the tops about an inch above the bulbs, trim off the roots, and store the onions in a well-ventilated, dry, cool, and dark location.

- **Peas** are best harvested in the early morning or early evening, but the stage at which to harvest the pods depends on the type. Snap peas and snow peas are both eaten pod and all. For best flavor, pick snap peas when plump and well colored but not as fully filled as garden peas. Pick snow peas before the pods fill out, when they are young, tender, and thin. In contrast, garden peas, often referred to as shell peas, are ready to harvest and shell when the pods are bright green and fully filled. Then the peas inside are sweet, plump, and tender—a true treat of the early summer garden.

- **Peppers** can be harvested anytime in the immature green stage—the more you pick, the more your plant will produce. However, for a fully flavored and sweet pepper, wait until it changes color. (Some varieties turn red, others gold, some yellow, and still others orange.) Hot peppers also usually take on more flavor when their color changes as they mature.

- **Potatoes** give an easy signal as to when they're ready to harvest: their tops die down. About 2 weeks after that happens, dig the potatoes; the delay gives them time to toughen their skins for long-term storage. You can leave potatoes in the ground longer—just be sure to dig them before rain or frost sets in. Carefully dig tubers with a spading fork, allow them to dry for a few hours in the sun, and then cure them for about 2 weeks at 50 to 60°F in a sheltered, well-ventilated, high-humidity area. After they have been cured, potatoes store best at 40 to 50°F.

- **Southern peas** such as black-eyed peas and crowder peas are not peas at all, but instead a type of bean that grows in warm locations. Pods are ready to harvest when well filled with fully developed seeds. Harvest purple pods after the hulls have turned mostly red and green pods after the hulls have turned a light yellow-green (but not too yellow).

- **Summer squash** is at its best if harvested on the small side, while skins are still tender. For zucchini, straightneck types, and crookneck types, harvest when fruits are 4 to 8 inches in length; for pattypan varieties, up to 3 inches in diameter. Don't let your squash get too big or the plant's production will falter.

- **Tomatoes** are tops if picked between the semifirm and semisoft stages, when the fruits are fully colored (whether gold, pink, orange, red, black, or white). Second best is to pick fruits a few days early and allow them to finish ripening indoors, a great option when temperatures are too hot or frost threatens. Tomatoes are best stored at temperatures higher than 50°F—never in the refrigerator, which will turn their texture to mush.

WORTH THE WAIT

When harvest time finally arrives, the fun really begins!

Scrutinize the fruits of your labor daily. Keep handy a sharp knife, pruning shears, and a bucket or basket. At the very moment your (now) discerning eye sees "ripe," whisk those prime morsels out of your garden and into your kitchen, and devour them with gusto—or preserve them for future gusto. Handle every piece like the delicate jewel that it is in order to avoid bruises or nicks that would invite decay and thus jeopardize your enjoyment.

8

FALL/
WINTER

Lacinato kale (left) and lettuces flourish in autumn's cooler temperatures. If covered, they can last into winter and sometimes come back in spring.

top tips for great fall gardens

by Vicki Mattern

WHEN TOMATOES, PEPPERS, and melons hit their late summer stride, it's easy to forget that autumn and early winter can be as abundant as spring and summer. Those who seize the opportunity for a second season of growth will find the planning and planting well worthwhile.

The steps to a bountiful fall garden are simple: Choose crops suited to fall growing conditions. Ensure your chosen site has organically enriched soil and adequate water. And start now.

You can replace spring-planted lettuces, peas, and brassicas (broccoli and its relatives) with new plantings that mature in fall. Seeds and transplants will take off quickly in the warm summer soil. They'll appreciate cooler nights too.

Look forward to peak flavor and performance for many crops that do not prosper in summer heat. Lower temperatures are ideal for producing crisp lettuces without the bitterness or bolting that can occur in hot weather. Frost-kissed kale, brussels sprouts, and cabbage have a special sweetness. Carrots, beets, and turnips also thrive in the fall garden and, after harvest, can be kept in a pantry or root cellar so you can enjoy their goodness well into winter. Collards, mustard, and other greens also like cool weather.

FAVORED CROPS FOR FALL

When deciding what to plant for fall harvest, gardeners throughout most of the country should think greens and root vegetables, advises John Navazio, a plant-breeding and seed specialist at Washington State University and senior scientist for the Organic Seed Alliance in Port Townsend, Washington, which conducts annual tests of crops and varieties to evaluate their cold hardiness.

Leafy greens (such as lettuces, spinach, arugula, chard, and mâche) and root veggies (such as beets, carrots, turnips, radishes, and rutabagas) as well as brassicas (including broccoli, cabbage, cauliflower, collards, kale, and Chinese cabbage) and peas will all thrive in the cooler weather and shorter days of fall. In many regions, some of these cold-hardy crops will even survive the winter to produce a second harvest in spring.

If you garden in the South or other areas with mild winters, you can grow all of those crops as well as heat-loving favorites. "Here, we can set out tomato transplants in late August," says David Pitre, owner of Tecolote Farm, a certified organic farm near Austin, Texas. Pitre also plants okra, eggplant, peppers, winter squash, cucumbers, and potatoes in August and September for winter harvest. Plant cool-season crops in the garden after temperatures cool—late September or later.

Fall is also prime garden season in the Pacific Northwest, where abundant rain and cool (but not frigid) temperatures are ideal for growing brassicas, root crops, and leafy greens planted in mid- to late summer. The hardiest of these crops often hang on well into winter if given protection such as row covers or cold frames.

HARDY FALL VARIETIES

After you've decided which crops to grow for fall harvest, zero in on specific varieties. "There are big differences in cold hardiness among varieties," Navazio says. "Some are better able to photosynthesize at cooler temperatures."

For the past several years, the Organic Seed Alliance has been conducting trials of as many as 170 varieties of eleven different crops for their quality and

Above left: Carrots make a sweet, crunchy addition to your fall garden crops.

Above right: Plant lettuces for fresh greens in your fall garden.

performance in fall and winter. Among them, kale, radicchio, and swiss chard have been tested extensively and confirmed cold hardy to 14°F with no protection. Several varieties stood out for the Alliance and market gardeners.

- **Broccoli:** Opt for varieties that produce plenty of side shoots rather than a single large head. "'Diplomat' and 'Marathon' can survive the heat of late summer and thrive when cool weather arrives in fall, producing a second cutting as late as Thanksgiving," says Elizabeth Keen, co-owner of Indian Line Farm, a 17-acre organic operation in Great Barrington, Massachusetts. In Austin, Texas, Carol Ann Sayle, co-owner of Boggy Creek Farm, grows 'Packman' and 'Diplomat' for harvest by Thanksgiving and cuts 'Marathon' by Christmas.

- **Carrots:** Consider storage ability when choosing carrots for your fall garden, says Thomas Case, owner of Arethusa Farm, a certified organic farm near Burlington, Vermont. Both Keen and Case like 'Bolero' for fall growing and winter storage.

- **Lettuces:** Whether you garden in the North or South, lettuces are a mainstay of the fall garden. Several European heirloom varieties are especially durable: 'Rouge d'Hiver' (a flavorful romaine whose leaves blush red in cool weather), 'Marvel of Four Seasons' (also called 'Merveille de Quatre Saisons', a sweet and tender butterhead with red-edged outer leaves), and 'Winter Density' (also called 'Craquerelle du Midi', a compact Bibb type with deep green leaves) are good bets. Even in Zone 5, these lettuces will hang on into December and, with the protection of heavy mulch or a cold frame, will often return with renewed vigor in early spring.

When the lettuces go dormant in winter, you can count on mâche to fill your salad bowl. Mâche (or corn salad) is delicious and will survive and continue to grow in colder weather longer than any other salad green, says Eliot Coleman in his classic book *Four-Season Harvest*. In his Zone 5 Maine garden, Coleman seeds mâche inside a cold frame from September through early November for harvest until April, when overwintered lettuce resumes its growth.

- **Kale:** Of the popular Lacinato-type kales, 'Black Tuscan' consistently rated best in the Alliance tests for cold hardiness, vigor, flavor, and stature. The Alliance also recommends 'Winterbor' (a tall Dutch kale), 'Red Russian', and 'White Russian' (two tasty Siberian kales). It's hard to go wrong with kale in fall, no matter the variety: all have superior flavor when temperatures drop into the 20s or below. "Sugar is the plant's natural antifreeze, so as the temperature drops, more starches are converted to sugar, sweetening the flavor of kale and other brassicas," Navazio says.

- **Radicchio:** Still considered a specialty vegetable by many, radicchio thrives in the cool conditions of fall and offers a wealth of possibilities in the kitchen. Of the more than twenty varieties tested by the Alliance in the past 2 years, a few Italian open-pollinated varieties proved most cold hardy. 'Variegata di Luisa Tardiva' and 'Variegata di Castlefranco' produce upright variegated heads similar to romaine lettuce, with beautiful hearts and radicchio's signature bitterness.

  "Grown in cool weather, they are delightful, with a mild spicy flavor," Navazio says. Although some of the plants' outer leaves were "toasted" at 14°F in the Alliance trials, you can strip off any damaged leaves and enjoy the tasty interior.

  Navazio suggests slicing the heads, then wilting the leaves in a pan with cipollini onions, as cooks do in Italy, or dressing the heads lightly with olive oil and roasting them on the grill or a campfire. For cold hardiness and flavor, Navazio also recommends 'Rossa di Verona' and 'Grumolo Rossa'.

- **Swiss chard:** The Alliance has found that chard hardiness generally corresponds to leaf color. Green varieties tend to be most cold hardy, followed by gold, then pink, magenta, and red varieties, which tend to be the least tolerant of cold. "Old-fashioned 'Fordhook Giant' is very cold hardy," Navazio says.

Based on their trials—which evaluated vigor, stature, and flavor—the Alliance staff also recommends the following varieties for fall.

- Arugula: 'Astro', 'Sputnik'
- Beets: 'Chioggia Guardmark', 'Red Ace', 'Shiraz', 'Touchstone Gold'
- Collards: 'Champion', 'Flash'
- Spinach: 'Olympia', 'Space', 'Tarpy'

Plant cover crops such as oats, winter wheat, or rye in any empty beds to over-winter. In spring, till them under or chop them in using a heavy hoe.

THE MATTER OF TIMING

Late summer is prime time for starting your fall garden. To determine starting dates for each variety you plan to grow, first check the "days to maturity" listed in the seed catalog or on the back of the seed packet. Add an extra week or two to factor in the shorter day lengths of fall, which delay plant maturity. Then count backward, subtracting that number of days from your average first fall frost date. Find your average frost date by visiting the National Centers for Environmental Information website's U.S. Climate Normals Freeze/Frost Data.

SOW AND GROW

Start seeds of broccoli and cabbage in flats or pots indoors (outdoor soil temps may be too high for good germination), then transplant the seedlings to the garden about 4 weeks later, when temperatures are cooler and seedlings are large enough to compete against weeds. Direct-seed carrots, beets, and other root crops, as well as greens, into prepared beds.

STRETCHING THE SEASON

Extend your fall harvest an extra month or more by shielding plants from hard freezes. Simple methods include blanketing low-growers with a thick layer of straw mulch or leaves (pull it aside during the day), a clear plastic tarp, or a floating row cover. Lightweight floating row covers protect crops down to about 28°F; heavier-weight covers will protect to 24°F. Go further with a simple cold frame.

Plastic-covered tunnels supported by hoops are also excellent for stretching the fall growing season into winter (and also for getting a jump-start in spring).

Master gardeners Eliot Coleman and Barbara Damrosch in Harborside, Maine, give greens, broccoli, carrots, beets, and other cool-weather crops a double layer of protection from the cold by growing them in a cold frame inside a high plastic-covered tunnel.

Coleman estimates that "each layer of covering is equivalent to growing your plants one and a half USDA zones to the south." Thus, for Coleman, in Zone 5, a single layer moderates the temperature to that of Zone 6-plus; a double layer moderates the climate to that of Zone 8.

These tips should help you see that your garden's useful time is only half over at summer's end. Don't miss one of your garden's most productive seasons!

Because you're likely planting your fall crops in soil that has already fed a spring planting, be sure to replenish the beds with a generous helping of organic fertilizer and/or compost before planting. "People often forget you need to prepare the soil, and you should do it a little earlier than you think," Pitre says. He mixes compost into fall garden beds a few weeks before he plants.

Sayle reshapes her farm's beds in fall using a hilling disc to move soil from pathways up onto the surface of the raised beds. "We hill the beds higher in fall to improve the drainage of our clay soil during the cooler, wetter fall and winter conditions," she says.

Before fall planting, incorporate soil amendments such as sulfur and gypsum (as needed) as well as compost.

Seeds and transplants take off quickly in the warm soil if they have adequate water. To help retain soil moisture, surround seedlings with a thick layer of mulch. Finely shredded leaves or straw will keep soil moist while slowly contributing organic matter to the soil as they decompose.

Keep plants growing strong as temperatures drop by giving them a midseason nutrient boost. Sayle makes her own foliar fertilizer by mixing 1 tablespoon each of fish emulsion, seaweed, and molasses in a gallon of water, then sprays it on using a backpack sprayer. A spray bottle works too.

Elizabeth Keen of Indian Line Farm simply side-dresses plants with compost. "With brassicas especially, the compost really helps," she says. "We've found the best time to apply it is when plants are in the teenager stage—about 4 weeks after transplanting. It's foolproof."

Another tip for your most bountiful fall garden: harvest early and often. Frequent cutting stimulates continual new growth and gives you plenty of chances to enjoy the fruits of your labor.

winter gardening tips for better gardening soil and harvests

by Barbara Pleasant

WHAT ARE YOU growing in your garden this winter? This is not a trick question. When you work an organic food garden in ways that bring out the best in your site, your soil, and your plants, winter is an interesting and useful stretch of time. In most regions, you can enjoy spinach, brussels sprouts, sunchokes, kale, carrots, parsnips, and other cold-hardy crops all through the winter.

To help you brush up on your cold-season gardening skills, let's tick through the simplest, most sustainable ways to address the three main winter gardening tasks:

- Growing cold-hardy edibles
- Using compost, cover crops, and mulch to radically improve soil quality
- Enhancing habitats for hard-working beneficial insects and wildlife

No matter where you live, you can make use of climate-appropriate techniques to bring spinach, kale, chicories, and other hardy vegetables through the winter. You will need an attached greenhouse in Zones 2 to 4, but in Zones 5 to 7 you can get by with a tunnel covered with one layer each of row cover and plastic (the plastic comes off easily for ventilation). Support the tunnel with an arch of heavy-gauge wire fencing to make sure it can stand up to accumulated ice and snow, like a green igloo (for more on constructing tunnels, see "Make an Inexpensive Mini-Greenhouse with Low Tunnels" on page 36) .

PROTECT FALL CROPS

If you have carrots in the ground, take this tip from Eliot Coleman, author of *Four-Season Harvest*. In early winter, enclose the carrots in a cold frame and sprinkle an inch of compost over the tops of the plants. Add enough straw to fill the frame and close the top. Pull carrots as you need them, and be prepared to be amazed at their sweet flavor—what Coleman calls "carrot nirvana." Parsnips need no protection to make it through winter, but a thick mulch (or a garbage bag stuffed with leaves) makes it easier to find them and keeps the

soil from freezing. In any climate, early winter is the best time to harvest brussels sprouts and sunchokes, both of which benefit from exposure to freezing temperatures.

Mulched soil doesn't wash away in heavy rain, but the biggest advantage of winter mulch is that it moderates soil temperatures, slowing the speed at which the soil freezes, thaws, and freezes again. Because water expands as it freezes, shallow roots are often torn and pushed upward—a natural phenomenon called heaving. Winter mulches reduce heaving around winter crops, decrease compaction from heavy rain or hail, and enrich the soil with organic matter as they decompose. They also look nice.

Fall-planted garlic, shallots, and perennial onions are priority crops for a 4-inch winter mulch of hay, straw, chopped leaves, or another locally abundant material. Mulch kale, too, but wait until after the first week of steady subfreezing weather to protect the latent flower buds of strawberries with a 4-inch mulch of hay, pine needles, or shredded leaves. Shroud the bases of marginally hardy herbs such as rosemary with a 12-inch-deep pyramid of mulch to protect the dormant buds closest to the ground. If you're really pushing your luck by growing figs or other plants that cannot tolerate frozen roots, surround them with a tomato cage and stuff it full of straw or chopped leaves. Use this technique to safeguard the graft union and basal buds of modern roses too.

Once you've done what you can to maximize the productivity of hardy plants, either gather up dead plants and surrounding mulch and compost them or turn the residue into the soil. This will reduce pests such as squash bugs and harlequin bugs, which over-winter as adults in plant debris, as do Mexican bean beetles and some other pests. Old mulches can harbor cabbageworm pupae, but these and other pests seldom survive winter in the wild world of a compost heap or when mixed into biologically active soil. To be on the safe side, you can create a special compost heap for plants that often harbor pests or diseases and seed-bearing weeds.

In spring, after the heap has shrunk to a manageable size, mix in a high-nitrogen material such as manure, grass clippings, alfalfa meal, or cheap dry dog food (mostly corn and soybean meal) to heat the heap to 130°F—the temperature needed to neutralize potential troublemakers.

With this housekeeping detail behind you, think about what next year's garden will demand of the soil. Sketch out a plan for where you will plant your favorite crops in spring and summer, and tailor your winter soil care practices to suit the needs of each plot's future residents.

In areas to be planted with peas, potatoes, salad greens, and other early spring crops, cultivate the soil, dig in some compost, and allow birds to peck through the soil to collect cutworms, tomato hornworm pupae, and other insects for a week or two. Then rake the bed or row into shape and mulch it with a material that will be easy to rake off in early spring: year-old leaves or weathered hay, for example. Spring planting delays due to soggy soil will be a thing of the past.

In the space you will use in early summer for sweet corn, tomatoes, and other demanding warm-weather crops, you may still have time to sow a winter cover crop, such as hairy vetch, Austrian winter peas, or crimson clover. Cover crops make use of winter solar energy, energize the soil food web as their roots release carbohydrates down below, and amass large amounts of organic matter. The deep roots of hardy grain cover crops, such as cereal rye, will spend the winter hammering their way into compacted subsoil, and nitrogen-fixing cover crops can jump-start soil improvement in new garden beds and save time in spring.

For example, if you get a good stand of hairy vetch growing in fall, simply cut the plants down in mid-spring (or pen your chickens on the bed), allow the foliage to dry into a mat, and plant tomatoes right into the mulch.

For all those "to be determined" spots, you can enrich the soil and prevent winter erosion by tucking beds in with compost, mulch, or a hybrid of the method I call "comforter composting." Piles of organic matter in any configuration will turn the soil's surface into a compost factory. Several 3-inch layers of dead plants, chopped leaves, spoiled hay, and other mulch materials will compost themselves when placed atop unemployed soil.

If you would rather make a mountain of compost from autumn's haul of yard and garden waste, why not locate the pile in a place where it will travel across cultivated soil as you turn it every few weeks? A "walking heap" leaves a trail of organic matter in its wake, and nutrients that leach from the pile at various stopping points go straight into the soil.

HOW TO PROTECT YOUR TREES

Mulches, compost piles, and beneficial bug-havens all have one drawback: they provide snug, diversified winter quarters for mice, voles, rabbits, and other small animals. As these animals run short of food in winter, they often girdle shrubs and trees as they dine on the nutrient-rich cambium just under the bark. If dogs, cats, owls, and other predators don't keep damaging critters in check, use wire cages to protect fruit trees and other high-value woody plants.

Use wire hardware cloth, at least 24 inches wide (go wider in areas with heavy snowfall), to make trunk cages. Just before positioning a cage, lay down a 3-inch-wide collar of pebbles or small stones around the base of the tree for an extra measure of deterrence. Shimmy the cage down into the soil. Place additional stones around the base of the cage to help hold it in place. Or, make ground staples for your cages from wire clothes hangers cut into 6-inch pieces and bent into a *U* shape.

all about growing kale and collards

by Barbara Pleasant

TWO OF THE easiest-to-grow cabbage family crops, kale and collards (*Brassica oleracea*), are closely related veggies with similar cultural requirements. You can grow quick crops of kale or collard greens in spring, when the weather is cool, and then plant them a second time in late summer for harvesting after the weather cools again in fall.

If you live where winter temperatures stay above 15°F, you can grow kale and collard greens right on through the winter months. As true biennials, kale or collard plants that survive winter will rush to produce flowers and seeds in spring.

TYPES OF KALE TO TRY

Kale varieties vary in leaf shape and color as well as overall vigor. 'Red Russian' kale produces heavy yields of green leaves with reddish-purple ribs.

Tuscan kales, such as 'Lacinato', produce long, narrow dark-green leaves with a waffle-like texture.

Numerous curly kale varieties including 'Winterbor' and 'Redbor' feature leaves with rumpled, curled edges.

TYPES OF COLLARD GREENS TO TRY

Collard varieties vary in leaf color and texture as well as regional adaptation. 'Georgia' collards grow well in the sandy soils of the Gulf Coast, while 'Champion' and other strains bred in Virginia perform better where winters are cold.

Try the 'Green Glaze' collard variety, which has bright green leaves and is slow to bolt, if you're looking for a plant that is both heat resistant and frost resistant.

HOW TO PLANT KALE AND COLLARD GREENS

You can grow kale or collards from seeds sown directly into prepared soil, but especially in spring it's best to start seeds indoors and set them out under protective cloches 4 to 6 weeks before your last spring frost. As long as they are protected from cold winds, kale or collards transplanted into cool soil will quickly establish themselves and start growing.

Kale and collard greens grown in spring often become magnets for pests in early summer, so most gardeners pull up the plants and compost them. Then, in July or August, new seedlings are started that will serve as the fall to winter crop.

Recommended seeding dates for growing kale and collards in fall include late June in New Hampshire, early July in Maryland, late July in Alabama, and late August in Arizona. Harden off the seedlings before setting them out in well-prepared soil, and plan to cover them with lightweight row cover or tulle to exclude insect pests and provide a little bit of shade.

Kale and collard plants are heavy feeders that grow best in moist, fertile soil with a pH between 6.0 and 7.5. Mix in a generous application of a balanced organic fertilizer before planting, and allow at least 12 inches between plants. Use a biodegradable mulch of grass clippings or coarse compost to insulate the roots from any warm weather.

Don't stop at lettuce and spinach in the greens department. Grow these nutrient-packed cabbage cousins to enjoy a wider depth of flavor and cooking versatility.

HARVESTING AND STORING KALE AND COLLARD GREENS

Begin harvesting when plants' leaves are larger than your hand, and just break off the older, bigger leaves as you need them for cooking. New leaves will continue to grow from the plants' centers. After the plants reach harvestable size, most varieties will yield three leaves per plant every 5 days.

Leaf quality is best in the fall, after the plants have been exposed to a few light frosts. These are the best leaves to blanch and freeze for long-term storage. Kale and collard greens also can be dried into snackable chips.

PROPAGATING KALE AND COLLARD GREENS

As biennials, kale and collard greens produce yellow flowers followed by elongated seedpods in their second year. When the seedpods dry to tan, gather them in a paper bag and allow them to dry indoors for a week. Shatter the dry pods and collect the largest seeds for replanting. Under good conditions, kale or collard seeds will store for up to 3 years. Be sure to work only with open-pollinated varieties when saving seeds because hybrid varieties may not breed true from seed.

PEST AND DISEASE PREVENTION TIPS

Featherweight row cover held aloft with hoops or stakes is the easiest way to protect actively growing kale and collard greens from cabbageworms, harlequin bugs, grasshoppers, and other summer insects. When the row covers are removed, monitor plants closely for pest problems and use either a *Bacillus thuringiensis* (also known as Bt) or spinosad-based organic pesticide to limit feeding by leaf-eating pests.

all about growing garlic

by Barbara Pleasant

THE LAST CROP to go into the garden, garlic is planted in fall and harvested the following summer. Flavorful, nutritious, and helpful for warding off vampires, garlic also is easy to grow as long as you plant varieties suited to your climate. Fertile, well-drained soils with a near-neutral pH between 6.5 and 7.0 are best for growing garlic.

Your reward for growing garlic is the world of flavors that await in every bulb! Garlic's taste has several dimensions that come alive depending on how the plant is cooked. Shown here, left to right, are braided softneck garlic, fresh elephant garlic, and purple stripe hardneck garlic.

TYPES OF GARLIC TO TRY

Softneck types grow best where winters are mild, though some tolerate cold to Zone 5. Most varieties do not produce scapes (edible curled flower stalks), but softnecks are great for braiding. Subtypes include Creole, artichoke, and many Asian varieties.

Hardneck types adapt to cold-winter climates, and all produce delicious curled scapes in early summer. Popular subtypes include porcelain, purple stripe, and rocambole varieties.

Elephant garlic produces a large, mild-flavored bulb comprised of four to six big cloves. Closely related to leeks, elephant garlic is hardy to Zone 5 if given deep winter mulch.

WHEN TO PLANT GARLIC

In fall, plant cloves in well-drained beds after the first frost has passed and the soil is cool. Cloves can also be planted in late winter as soon as the soil thaws, but fall-planted garlic produces bigger, better bulbs.

HOW TO PLANT GARLIC

Choose a sunny site, and loosen the planting bed to at least 12 inches deep. Thoroughly mix in a 1-inch layer of mature compost. In acidic soil, also mix in a light dusting of wood ashes. Wait until just before planting to break bulbs into cloves. Poke the cloves into the ground 4 inches deep and 6 to 8 inches apart, with their pointed ends up. Cover the planted area with 3 to 5 inches of organic mulch such as hay or shredded leaves.

GARLIC AT A GLANCE

TYPE	DESCRIPTION	VARIETIES
Softneck garlic (*Allium sativum sativum*)	Large bulbs comprised of twelve to twenty cloves, with the largest ones on the outside of the bulbs. Large, vigorous plants grow best in mild winter areas. Most grocery store garlic is softneck garlic. Flavor is generally mild, with more spiciness in some Asian strains. Will keep for 8 months under cool, dry conditions.	Creole types such as 'Burgundy' taste great and store well, even in the humid South. In the West, try late-maturing 'Susanville' or other California-bred varieties. 'Red Toch' is remarkably tasty and cold-hardy.
Hardneck garlic (*A. sativum ophioscorodon*)	Medium to large bulbs comprised of six to twelve symmetrical cloves around a hard central stalk. Cold-hardy plants produce delicious edible scapes. Plants that are allowed to flower may produce bulbils. Often sold in gourmet shops, hardneck garlic has a complex, spicy-sweet flavor. Storage time ranges from 3 to 8 months.	Often called porcelain or continental strains, 'German White' and 'Music' produce tender scapes and six or more big, juicy cloves. Big-flavor rocamboles such as 'Chesnok Red' and 'Spanish Roja' excel in cold winter climates.
Elephant or Buffalo garlic (*A. ampeloprasum*)	Large, upright plants with strappy leaves need wide, 12-inch spacing. Baseball-size bulbs comprised of four to six cloves have mild flavor, which makes them great for roasting. To increase bulb size, harvest the edible scapes or use blossom clusters as cut flowers.	Seed is sold simply as elephant garlic, or you can start with a store-bought bulb. In areas where elephant garlic grows wild, feral seedlings moved to the garden will form bulbs in 2 years.

Wait until just before planting to break your garlic bulbs into cloves. One pound of cured bulbs will split into about fifty individual cloves, which is enough to plant a 25-foot-long double row.

HARVESTING AND STORING GARLIC

From early summer to midsummer, watch plants closely and harvest when the soil is dry and about one-third of the leaves appear pale and withered. Use a digging fork to loosen the soil before pulling the plants. Handle the newly pulled bulbs delicately to avoid bruising them. Lay the whole plants out to dry in a warm, airy spot that is protected from rain and direct sun. After a week or so, brush off soil from the bulbs with your hands and use pruning shears to clip roots to ½ inch long. Wait another week before clipping off the stems of hardneck varieties or trimming and braiding softnecks into clusters. Do not remove the papery outer wrappers, as these inhibit sprouting and protect the cloves from rotting.

Storage life varies with variety and with growing and storage conditions. When kept at 50 to 60°F, rocamboles store for about 4 months, other hardneck garlic varieties usually last 6 months, and softneck and elephant garlic store for 8 months or more. Hang your cured crop in mesh bags or braid softneck types and suspend from rafters in a cool, dry basement or garage.

PROPAGATING GARLIC

Many garlic varieties fine-tune their growth patterns to the climate in which they are grown, so planting cloves from bulbs you grew yourself can save money and also result in a strain that is especially well suited to the conditions in your garden.

As you harvest and cure your crop, set aside the biggest and best bulbs as your "seed" stock. One pound of cured bulbs will break into about fifty individual cloves, which is enough to plant a 25-foot-long double row.

If allowed to flower, some varieties produce fleshy bulbils (little bulbs) atop the flower stalk. Elephant garlic often develops elliptical hard-shelled corms underground outside the main bulbs. Garlic bulbils and corms can both be replanted. The first year after planting, bulbils and corms will grow into small plants that can be harvested as scallion-like "green garlic" in late spring, just before the roots swell. If left unharvested, bulbils and corms develop into full-sized bulbs in 2 to 3 years.

PEST AND DISEASE PREVENTION TIPS

Tiny onion thrips rasp pale grooves into garlic leaves, but they have many natural predators. Keep areas near garlic and onions mowed to reduce the weedy habitat thrips prefer. Monitor populations with sticky traps, and use a spinosad-based biological pesticide to control serious infestations.

Onion root maggots seldom infect garlic planted in soil where onion family crops have not been planted for 2 years, but the mobile adults may still lay eggs around the base of young plants. Where pest pressure is severe, dust the area around plants with diatomaceous earth in late spring, which is when the egg-laying females are most active.

Prevent *Fusarium* and other soilborne root rot diseases by growing garlic in well-drained, fertile soil. Avoid injuring the roots when weeding, because diseases often enter plants through broken tissue.

IN THE KITCHEN

Without a doubt, garlic works culinary miracles when added to food. The pungency of raw garlic varies depending on the variety, and all types of garlic mellow when cooked. In addition to tossing chopped garlic into soups, stews, and stir-fries, try baking whole bulbs with a little salt and olive oil, and then spreading the soft, creamy flesh on warm bread. If you grow hardneck types of garlic, be sure to harvest the curled scapes that appear in early summer. Scapes can be eaten fresh or blanched and frozen.

TIPS FOR GROWING GARLIC

- Experiment with types and varieties, because each reacts differently to weather and rainfall patterns. A spring hot spell that bothers one variety may benefit another.

- To grow garlic greens for cooking, plant whole bulbs 12 inches apart in the fall. In spring, when the greens are 10 inches tall, grab them with one hand and use your other hand to lop them off with a knife. You should get two more cuttings before the plants give out.

- You can make garlic powder by drying thinly sliced garlic at 150°F until it's crisp. Grind to a powder in a food grinder or blender.

If you enjoy gardening, you'll enjoy growing winter squash in its many diverse types. Shown here, from left to right, are buttercup, delicata, 'Red Kuri' buttercup, butternut, and dumpling squash.

all about growing winter squash

by Barbara Pleasant

COLORFUL, CURVACEOUS, AND a cinch to store, winter squash is one of the most nutritious crops you can grow, and these spectacular fruits hold their nutrients—vitamins A and C and other healthful riches—throughout their long storage life. Growing winter squash is easy whatever the variety you choose, and butternuts, buttercups, and other types with dense flesh can stand in for carrots, pumpkins, and sweet potatoes in any recipe.

TYPES TO WINTER SQUASH TRY

Seed catalogs typically sort winter squash varieties into the following types, listed here in order of their popularity with the *MOTHER EARTH NEWS* Gardening Advisory Group:

- Butternut squash combine rich flavor and smooth texture with natural resistance to squash vine borers. These bottle-shaped fruits have buff-brown rinds and will store for 6 months or longer.
- Buttercup squash rival butternuts in flavor and productivity. The vigorous plants produce heavy crops of squat green fruits. Fruits will store for 4 to 6 months.
- Hubbard squash and kabocha squash range from medium-sized to huge and have drier flesh than other winter squash. Rind color varies with variety, and all varieties will store for 4 to 6 months. (Hubbard squash are so attractive to squash vine borers that some gardeners use this type as a trap crop for this insect pest.)
- Cylinder-shaped delicata squash and pumpkin-shaped dumpling squash produce single-serving-sized ivory fruits with green stripes that turn orange in storage. Fast to mature, these are among the easiest winter squash to grow in cool climates. Fruits will store for 3 to 5 months.
- Acorn squash are ribbed round fruits that have gold or green rinds. They mature quickly and will store for at least 3 months, making them popular in areas with short summers.
- Spaghetti squash are full of stringy fibers that resemble pasta. The oblong fruits have smooth rinds that range from tan to orange, and they will store for 3 to 6 months.
- Cushaw squash produce big bulb-shaped fruits with dense, sweet flesh. Plants need a long, warm growing season and will store for at least 4 months.

WHEN TO PLANT WINTER SQUASH

In spring, sow seeds in prepared beds or hills after your last frost has passed, or sow them indoors under bright fluorescent lights. Set out seedlings when they are about 3 weeks old. In Zone 6 and warmer, you can plant more winter squash in early summer using space vacated by fall-planted garlic or early spring lettuce. Stop planting winter squash 14 weeks before your expected first fall frost.

HOW TO PLANT WINTER SQUASH

Winter squash grow best in warm conditions and in fertile, well-drained soil with a pH between 6.0 and 6.5. Choose a sunny site and prepare 3-foot-wide planting hills within wide rows, or position them along your garden's edge. Leave 5 to 6 feet between hills. Loosen the soil in the planting sites to at least 12 inches deep. Thoroughly mix in a 2-inch layer of mature compost and a light application of balanced organic fertilizer. Water well. Plant six seeds per hill, poking them into the soil 1 inch deep. After seeds germinate (about 10 days after sowing), thin seedlings to three per hill. Set up protective row covers as soon as you're done planting.

WINTER SQUASH AT A GLANCE

The wide, wonderful world of winter squash includes hundreds of heirloom varieties. If you're not sure where to start, try the varieties in the right column below, which were rated best by our Gardening Advisory Group. Days to maturity are for fully ripe squash.

SPECIES	DESCRIPTION	VARIETIES
Cucurbita moschata (butternut squash, cheese pumpkins)	These squash are highly resistant to squash vine borers and aren't preferred by squash bugs. Fruits have dense flesh with excellent flavor and will store for 6 months or longer.	'Burpee's Butterbush' (75 days) 'Long Island Cheese' (105 days) 'Waltham Butternut' (105 days)
C. maxima (buttercup, hubbard, and kabocha squash)	Large, vigorous plants need room to run. These squash attract squash vine borers. Plants tend to develop supplemental roots where stems touch the ground. Quality of taste varies with variety and is usually best with buttercups. Fruits will store for 4 to 6 months.	'Baby Blue Hubbard' (105 days) 'Burgess Buttercup' (95 days) 'Sweet Meat' (95 days)
C. pepo (acorn, delicata, dumpling, and spaghetti squash)	Plants mature quickly but still need protection from insects. Delicata squash are prized for their excellent flavor. Fruits will store for 3 to 6 months.	'Delicata' (100 days) 'Spaghetti' (88 days) 'Table Queen' (100 days)
C. mixta (cushaw squash)	These huge fruits (up to 40 pounds) usually have hard rinds. Cooked flesh is firm and sweet. If grown in warm climates, plants' sheer vigor can offset pest problems. Fruits will store for 4 months or longer.	'Green Striped Cushaw' (115 days) 'Orange Cushaw' (115 days) 'White Cushaw' (115 days)

HARVESTING AND STORING WINTER SQUASH

Fruits are ripe if you cannot easily pierce the rind with your fingernail. Never rush to harvest winter squash, though, because immature fruits won't store well. Unless pests or freezing weather threaten them, allow fruits to ripen until the vines begin to die back. Expect to harvest three to five squash per plant. Use pruning shears to cut fruits from the vine, leaving 1 inch of stem attached. Clean away dirt with a soft, damp cloth, and allow fruits to cure for 2 weeks in a spot that's 70 to 80°F. Store cured squash in a cool, dry place such as your basement, a cool closet, or even under your bed. Check every 2 weeks for signs of spoilage.

PROPAGATING WINTER SQUASH

If you harvest your winter squash after the fruits have fully matured, saving seeds is simply a matter of rinsing, drying, and storing the biggest, plumpest seeds that come across your cutting board. If stored in a cool, dry place, winter squash seeds remain viable for up to 6 years. Be sure to isolate varieties of the same species by planting them at opposite ends of the garden or by growing one variety early in the season and another from midsummer to fall. Also keep in mind that acorn, delicata, dumpling, and spaghetti squash can cross with summer squash, which is of the same species (*Cucurbita pepo*).

Old-fashioned squash pies laced with cinnamon and ginger will never go out of style, but newer trends in winter squash cuisine favor savory risottos and creamy squash-stuffed ravioli—and don't forget to eat the tasty seeds!

TIPS FOR GROWING WINTER SQUASH

- Grow open-pollinated varieties so you can save your own seeds for eating and replanting. Only choose hybrids if you need a space-saving bush habit or a special form of disease resistance.

- Try growing winter squash in an old compost pile located along the edge of your garden. Small-fruited varieties do well if allowed to scramble up a fence.

PEST AND DISEASE PREVENTION TIPS

Winter squash face challenges from squash bugs, squash vine borers, and cucumber beetles. To defend your plants from all three insects, shield them with row covers held aloft with stakes or hoops until the plants begin to bloom. Big healthy plants will produce well despite pest pressure. Among diseases, powdery mildew is a common problem best prevented by growing resistant varieties, which often have PMR (for "powdery mildew–resistant") after their variety names. In addition, a spray made of 1 part milk and 6 parts water can suppress powdery mildew if applied every 2 weeks during the second half of summer.

IN THE KITCHEN

Old-fashioned squash pies laced with cinnamon and ginger will never go out of style, but newer trends in winter squash cuisine favor savory risottos and creamy squash-stuffed ravioli. Sage is a great accent herb for winter squash, and some cooks brush maple syrup or honey onto chunks of baked (or grilled) squash to create a caramel glaze. Make large fruits easier to cut by lopping off a slice from one side using a sharp, heavy knife, creating a flat surface. Cut large fruits into chunks before removing the rinds. Winter squash seeds are also edible and delicious! Roast the rinsed, dried seeds at 275°F until they just begin to pop, about 15 to 20 minutes. Season with sea salt and enjoy.

grow nutritious
spinach in the fall

by John Navazio

Sᴘɪɴᴀᴄʜ ʀᴀɴᴋs ᴀs one of the most delicious and tender of all the leafy greens, yet this delightful crop is conspicuously absent from many gardens. The reason? Frustration likely settled in for growers who had planted spinach in spring and reaped only a small harvest of undersized, parched leaves before the spindly central flower stalk appeared, signaling the plant was starting to bolt or run to seed.

What's the best remedy for the spring spinach blues? Plant a fall crop! By planting spinach at the end of summer, your crop will get off to a running start and mature to its luscious best during the cool, golden days of fall.

UNDERSTANDING SPINACH

To appreciate why spring-sown spinach misbehaves, one must be familiar with the plant's humble origins. Spinach is a cool-season vegetable originally grown in fall and winter in the fertile agricultural valleys of the Middle East. In spring, longer days and higher temperatures prompt spinach to finish its cycle and go to seed.

While many modern spinach growers deem early hot weather to be the villain behind spinach's bolting, the true culprit is actually the increasingly long days of spring, which signal to the plant that it's time to reproduce. Most present-day spinach varieties will initiate flowering when the daylight duration reaches 14 hours—as early as mid-May in the northern half of the United States.

The influence of hot weather, while more subtle, also has an adverse effect on the quality of spring-sown spinach. Even mildly hot days in the upper 70s can dramatically speed up the flowering of a spinach plant that has already been triggered to bolt by day length. Additionally, the tenderness and juiciness of spinach leaves diminish greatly after just a couple of days of hot spring weather.

Some gardeners can certainly boast success stories of spring-planted spinach, but any grower will be challenged by the one-two punch of longer daylight hours and early hot weather. Timing a fall crop properly can help you avoid the pitfalls of a spring one, resulting in a bumper harvest of huge, succulent, easy-to-pick spinach leaves.

YOUR FALL SPINACH TARGET PLANTING DATE

Seed catalogs and gardening guides often advise planting fall spinach crops 4 to 6 weeks before a hard frost. In my own experience in both coastal Washington State and southern Wisconsin, that means planting between September 1 and 10. Unfortunately, this strategy delivers plants that are only about the diameter of a teacup and develop leaves the size of silver dollars before the days become too cool for continued growth. This teacup size is perfect for overwintering spinach, but it doesn't produce the yield a fall crop should.

Taking a tip from commercial spinach farmers who plant their fall crop 8 to 10 weeks before the first hard frost, I tried planting a number of spinach varieties between the first and third weeks of August. That method has worked so well that I've been spreading the news to my spinach-growing friends in other parts of North America, and all of us have been amazed at our success.

PROLIFIC FALL VARIETIES

I've grown a wide range of spinach varieties—open pollinated and hybrid, smooth leaf and savoy (wrinkled or curly)—in my fall gardens. The first thing I discovered was that varieties I knew well from spring planting performed differently in fall. For example, in spring, 'Olympia' grows more quickly than the bolt-resistant standard 'Tyee', but in hot August weather, 'Tyee' outyields 'Olympia'. I've had similar success with the semi-savoy variety 'Indian Summer', which, like 'Tyee', quickly produces baby-leaf cuttings by the end of August and nice full-grown leaves by mid-September.

Other varieties that do well from early-August plantings (August 1 through 10) are the smooth-leaf varieties 'Olympia', 'Space', and 'Viroflay'. While these are not as fast growing in August as 'Tyee', they seem to come into their own with the cooler weather of September, sometimes producing leaves that are 5 to 6 inches in diameter. In several regions, 'Olympia' performs superbly from August plantings, offering the largest yields of all the varieties tested. 'Olympia' and 'Viroflay' have also proved to be especially tasty varieties if harvested in late September and October. 'Winter Bloomsdale' doesn't grow quickly but keeps turning out succulent savoy leaves into the cold days of October.

David Cavagnaro, a veteran vegetable gardener and photographer, has tried his hand at planting spinach in August in his gardens in Decorah, Iowa. Cavagnaro is enthusiastic about the tremendous yields he gets in late September from his early-August plantings. He says fall spinach is by far the best spinach he's ever grown. "Even the big leaves are still succulent and juicy," he says. Smooth-leaf 'Olympia' and 'Space' varieties are also the top yielders in my own garden in Bellingham, Washington. In late September, both grow to sizes most gardeners only dream about.

C. R. Lawn of Fedco Seeds in Waterville, Maine, had a similar experience, with 'Olympia' outperforming all other varieties in his fall garden. Lawn praises the whole concept of fall spinach. "There's nothing like the spinach you harvest on those crisp fall days," he says. "By the time it's ready, the weather is cool and there's plenty of moisture—that's what spinach really likes."

Steve Bellavia, a vegetable researcher at Johnny's Selected Seeds in Winslow, Maine, also grew August-planted fall spinach a couple of years ago. While many of the varieties he planted were impressive for their tenderness and yield, Bellavia says he was most struck by the performance of 'Spinner', which he says grew to a nice full size, was dark green and flavorful, and was the best variety in the trial.

Many people think savoy spinach varieties taste better than smooth-leaf types, but that assessment doesn't necessarily seem to hold true in the case of fall crops. In our trials, the smooth-leaf varieties 'Olympia' and 'Viroflay' both received rave reviews for flavor, while the standard savoy variety 'Bloomsdale Long Standing' and its modern semi-savoy cousin 'Tyee' both proved to be less flavorful.

SEEDS: KEEP YOUR COOL

Bellavia also reminded me of one of the drawbacks of planting fall spinach. When he planted a fall spinach plot in early August, the soil was somewhat dry and then received just ⅓ inch of rain, after which daytime temperatures hovered in the low 80s for a couple of weeks. Although the soil never became excessively dry, the spinach came up rather sparsely.

Of course, this can happen with any crop if you allow the seedbed to dry out after planting, but this is especially problematic for spinach when the weather is hot. Spinach seed doesn't germinate well at temperatures above 75°F, and it won't come up at all if soil temperatures are above 85°F. One way to get a good stand of spinach when planting in late summer is to water it lightly on hot days. This will cool the soil enough to get your crop established.

We also found that not all spinach varieties planted in early August fared as well as some of our big winners, such as 'Olympia' and 'Spinner'. Cavagnaro and I have had early-August plantings of savoy varieties 'Bloomsdale Long Standing' and 'Coho' bolt by early September. Why? Presumably because in our locations, the day length was long enough in mid-August to trigger flowering.

By trying a number of different planting dates throughout August, we've found that planting between August 15 and 20 seems to be the best time for northern gardeners. You'll bypass the hottest days of early August, which can be tough on spinach germination, and you'll avoid possible bolting problems if you're in the higher latitudes of the North. We've found that all of the best fall varieties did well when planted in mid-August.

PLANTING SPINACH IN THE SOUTH

Growing fall spinach has a long legacy in parts of the southern United States. A large amount of fresh-market spinach was at one time grown for fall consumption in coastal Virginia and Maryland, near the Chesapeake Bay. These crops were traditionally planted for the fall crop from mid-August until mid-September. Long, warm autumns in this and other mid-Atlantic areas ensure bountiful crops that may yield until the new year.

In Arkansas and Oklahoma, spinach can be planted in the second half of September for fall salads that easily last into December. In southern Texas and in much of the Deep South, spinach can be planted anytime from early October until the middle of November for a fall crop that will grow through winter. In the Desert Southwest, where there's a wide range of environments based on elevation, planting from late August until late November is possible, but you'll have to experiment to determine precisely what's best for your location.

When you plant spinach in these hotter regions, it's much like planting it in August in the North: keep the seedbed cool with some irrigation water (or some shade) until the seedlings have emerged.

OVERWINTERING SPINACH

Spinach is one of the hardiest winter vegetables, sometimes surviving temperatures far below freezing if grown to just the right size before the most frigid part of winter. 'Giant Winter' and 'Winter Bloomsdale' are the standards for over-wintering, and 'Melody' and 'Tyee' have been successfully over-wintered in upstate New York and New England. Savoy varieties generally endure cold better than smooth-leaf types.

The general rule for getting the right-sized spinach for over-wintering is to plant it 4 to 6 weeks before your average first hard frost date. This should produce a spinach plant about 3½ to 4 inches in diameter—the best size for over-wintering. As far as mulching the plants for protection, in my own experience in wet Maine and Washington winters, I've killed the plants, as they ended up rotting under my leaf mulch by the time I uncovered them in early spring. Perhaps porous row covers would work better.

grow winter tomatoes

by David Cavagnaro

JUST ONE ENCOUNTER with a tasteless, artificially ripened, imported winter supermarket tomato makes you want to grow your own tangy, sweet-tasting tomatoes in the off-season.

It sure did for me, and I met with enough initial success and continued refining my technique until now, in a good winter, at peak production, a single plant in my window produces a pint of cherry or pear tomatoes every day or two. Here's how to do this yourself.

Although many varieties of "compact" bush tomatoes are advertised as good for container production, they won't perform well over a long winter. These are determinate varieties—plants with branches that grow to a certain length and then stop. They produce a finite number of fruits over a limited period—certainly far less time than a long stretch of northern winter.

Better options for indoor winter tomatoes are indeterminate varieties—those that continue growing and producing indefinitely. Furthermore, I've found that cherry and plum types, bearing small fruits in abundance, are more productive than large slicing types.

FAVORITE VARIETIES

Because indeterminate vines bear a blossom cluster at each node and the stems between nodes grow longer indoors in the dimmer light of winter than they would outdoors in summer, I recommend you choose from among the less-vigorous indeterminate varieties on the market lest the vine take over the house without bearing much fruit. My favorite choice is old-fashioned 'Yellow Pear', but the red 'Tommy Toe', an Ozark heirloom and frequent winner of taste tests, and 'Pink Ping Pong', called "very sweet, smooth, and juicy" by heirloom tomato expert Carolyn Male, are worth growing this way too.

Sufficient light is paramount for successful indoor cherry tomato production. Choose a window as nearly floor-to-ceiling in height and as south facing as possible. Large picture windows or sunroom exposures are ideal.

A large-enough container will be needed at the outset too. Choose a 5-gallon container at a minimum—and 10-gallon is even better—to support the rather massive winter-long growth that will accumulate.

To get a head start, you can start your indoor plants from cuttings at the end of the summer. If grown from seed, indeterminate varieties must reach several feet in height before the first blooms appear, so the cuttings save precious time.

To start your own, cut a branch from a favorite variety in your garden in late summer and section it into several cuttings, each with two sets of leaves. Clip off all but one leaf at the top and place the whole bundle in a jar of water in a sunny indoor window.

READY TO ROOT AND BLOOM

The lower sections of long vines are already covered with bumps that are roots just waiting to grow, so rooting will take place very quickly using these lower, older parts of stems. After cuttings root, pot them up and keep them outdoors, in full sun, until frost threatens. They should be well in bloom when you move them indoors, and these mature stems will produce blossoms immediately on new growth.

Train the plant, which will grow like a climbing vine, on a sturdy string trellis tied from and between small nails solidly hammered into a window frame, or build an independent trellis. Just be sure to accommodate the considerable weight of a huge vine amply loaded with many quarts of ripening fruit.

Regular fertilization is a must to support the vigorous growth of an indeterminate tomato vine. Fish emulsion or any other liquid nutrient mix will do. Just follow the instructions on the product label.

Also, be sure to consider pollination and potential pests. Tomato blossoms are internally pollinated, an act aided outdoors by the vibratory action of wind and visiting bees. To mimic such vibration indoors, lightly tap or shake the vines each time you water, or turn a fan on them.

Insect pests can be a much more difficult problem to solve. Whiteflies, once established on an indoor tomato plant, eventually will defoliate and kill it. The best solution is to be extremely careful not to introduce these insects indoors in the first place. Also, install yellow sticky traps (widely available online) before you notice any whiteflies, to catch any that sneak inside.

The same can be said for spider mites. Both of these pests also attack a variety of houseplants and are extremely difficult to control, especially on an edible crop where only nontoxic controls would be acceptable.

One final advantage to growing a tomato vine indoors in winter becomes clear in spring: you have a ready source of plant material from which to take blossoming cuttings for a jump-start on the outdoor tomato season of summer.

Simply repeat the procedure used in the fall by rooting cuttings well enough in advance of the growing season that you have potted vines already in bloom in time to set out as soon as any danger of frost has passed. These plants will bear a good month or more in advance of even the earliest varieties you could start from seed in the spring, offering once again, at their natural time, the delicious sweet-sharp taste of vine-ripened, sun-warmed tomatoes.

resources

GARDEN ADVICE

MOTHER EARTH NEWS

www.MotherEarthNews.com/Better-Garden-Soil
Tons of information about healthy soil, compost, and organic fertilizer.

www.MotherEarthNews.com/Crops-at-a-Glance
This guide walks you through the specifics of growing fifty-one garden favorites, including recommended varieties.

www.MotherEarthNews.com/Garden-Know-How
A collection of organic gardening advice that covers everything from the basics to advanced techniques.

www.MotherEarthNews.com/Garden-Planner
Design your best garden ever with the help of our easy-to-use, interactive Vegetable Garden Planner. Try it free for 30 days!

www.MotherEarthNews.com/Organic-Gardening
Learn how to use natural methods to grow fresh food and productive crops, sans toxic chemicals. Find featured Organic Gardening articles, Ask Our Experts entries and the Organic Gardening Archive.

www.MotherEarthNews.com/Organic-Gardening-Products. A custom search tool to help you find advice about organic methods of pest control and locate the products you need.

www.MotherEarthNews.com/Pest-Control-Series
Resources for pest identification and organic control methods.

www.MotherEarthNews.com/Season-Extension
Our best plans for greenhouses, hoop houses, cold frames, and more season-stretching gear.

www.MotherEarthNews.com/What-To-Plant
Get precise planting dates for thirty garden crops based on the average last spring frost date in your region.

AMPLE HARVEST

www.ampleharvest.org
Extra produce? This site helps home gardeners donate extra food to a local food pantry.

LOCAL HARVEST

www.localharvest.org
An excellent directory to help you locate local food and farmers.

RECOMMENDED BOOKS

All-New Square Foot Gardening
by Mel Bartholomew

Back to Basics: Traditional Kitchen Wisdom
by Andrea Chesman

Backyard Bounty by Linda Gilkeson

Edible Landscaping by Rosalind Creasy

The Four Season Farm Gardener's Cookbook
by Barbara Damrosch and Eliot Coleman

Four-Season Harvest by Eliot Coleman

The Garden Primer by Barbara Damrosch

The Gardener's Weed Book: Earth Safe Controls
by Barbara Damrosch

Greenhouse Vegetable Gardening by Inger Palstierna

Heirloom Vegetable Gardening by William Woys Weaver

The Polytunnel Book by Joyce Russell

The Resilient Gardener by Carol Deppe

Starter Vegetable Gardens by Barbara Pleasant

The Tao of Vegetable Gardening by Carol Deppe

The Winter Harvest Handbook by Eliot Coleman

The Year-Round Vegetable Gardener by Niki Jabbour

SEED SOURCES

www.MotherEarthNews.com/Custom-Seed-Search
A custom search tool to help you locate sources for the fruit and veggie varieties you want to grow.

www.MotherEarthNews.com/High-Quality-Seeds
Experts explain seed genetics and the seed industry, and give recommendations for locally adapted seed companies.

SEED COMPANIES

The following companies have at least 25 percent organic offerings, and many have signed the Safe Seed Pledge:

Adaptive Seeds
 seed@adaptiveseeds.com
 www.adaptiveseeds.com
Baker Creek Heirloom Seed
 Company, 417-924-8917
 www.rareseeds.com
Botanical Interests, 877-821-4340
 www.botanicalinterests.com
Fedco Seeds, 207-426-9900
 www.fedcoseeds.com
Filaree Garlic Farm
 509-422-6940
 www.filareefarm.com
The Growers Exchange
 888-829-6201
 www.thegrowers-exchange.com
High Mowing Organic Seeds
 866-735-4454
 www.highmowingseeds.com
Irish Eyes Garden Seeds
 www.irisheyesgardenseeds.com
Johnny's Selected Seeds
 877-564-6697
 www.johnnyseeds.com

Mountain Valley Growers
 559-338-2775
 www.mountainvalley
 growers.com
Natural Gardening Company
 707-766-9303
 www.naturalgardening.com
Nexus Gardens
 www.nexusgardens.com
Nichols Garden Nursery
 800-422-3985
 www.nicholsgarden
 nursery.com
Renee's Garden Online Catalog
 888-880-7228
 www.reneesgarden.com
Restoration Seeds
 support@restorationseeds.com
 www.restorationseeds.com
Strictly Medicinal Seeds
 (formerly Horizon Herbs)
 541-846-6704
 www.strictlymedicinal
 seeds.com

Seed Savers Exchange
 563-382-5990
 www.seedsavers.org
Seed Treasures
 www.seedtreasures.com
Seeds of Change
 888-762-7333
 www.seedsofchange.com
Seeds Trust, 720-335-3436
 www.seedstrust.com
Select Seeds, 800-684-0395
 www.selectseeds.com
Southern Exposure Seed
 Exchange, 540-894-9480
 www.southernexposure.com
Sow True Seed, 828-254-0708
 www.sowtrueseed.com
Star Seed, 800-782-7311
 www.gostarseed.com
Terroir Seeds, 888-878-5247
 www.underwoodgardens.com
TomatoFest, www.tomatofest.com
Turtle Tree Seed, 800-930-7009
 www.turtletreeseed.org

GARDENING TOOLS AND SUPPLIES

American Garden Tool Company
 www.americangardentools.com
ARBICO Organics, 800-827-2847
 www.arbico-organics.com
BCS America, 800-543-1040
 www.bcsamerica.com
ChickenFuel/DankoDirt
 541-313-6455
 www.dankodirt.com
CobraHead, 866-962-6272
 www.cobrahead.com
Earth Tools, 502-484-3988
 www.earthtoolsBCS.com
Florian Tools, 800-275-3618
 www.floriantools.com

Gardener's Supply Company
 888-833-1412
 www.gardeners.com
Green Heron Tools, 610-844-5232
 www.greenherontools.com
Homestead Iron, 417-543-9182
 www.homesteadiron.com
Hoss Tools, 888-672-5536
 www.hosstools.com
Lee Valley & Veritas Tools
 800-871-8158 (US)
 800-267-8767 (Canada)
 613-596-0350
 www.leevalley.com
Meadow Creature, 360-329-2250
 www.meadowcreature.com

Peaceful Valley Farm
 & Garden Supply
 888-784-1722
 www.groworganic.com
Red Pig Garden Tools
 503-663-9404
 www.redpigtools.com
Rogue Hoe, 417-962-5091
 www.roguehoe.com
Srills Products
 844-477-4557
 www.srills.com
Valley Oak Tool Company
 530-342-6188
 www.valleyoaktool.com

index

Special thanks
to Barbara Pleasant
and all of the authors
who have shared their
gardening expertise
with our readers
over the years.

The articles in this book appeared in their original form in *MOTHER EARTH NEWS* magazine, published by Ogden Publications Inc. *MOTHER EARTH NEWS* is America's leading magazine about sustainable and self-reliant living. Founded by John and Jane Shuttleworth in 1970, it is owned today by Ogden Publications of Topeka, Kansas, and boasts a growing circulation of over half a million. Since the magazine's founding, *MOTHER EARTH NEWS* has been a pioneer in the promotion of renewable energy, recycling, family farms, sustainable agricultural practices, better eating habits, medical self-care, more meaningful education, and affordable housing. The magazine's mission is extended by six annual *MOTHER EARTH NEWS* fairs and a vibrant website.

Publisher: Bill Uhler
Editorial Director: Oscar H. Will III
Merchandise and Event Director: Andrew Perkins
Premium Content Editor: Christian Williams
Premium Content Senior Associate Editor: Jean Teller
Marketing Coordinator: Bret Harshbarger

Acquiring Editor
Thom O'Hearn

Project Manager
Caitlin Fultz

Art Director
Cindy Samargia Laun

Design and Layout
Diana Boger

Illustrations
Keith Ward

Quarto is the authority on a wide range of topics.
Quarto educates, entertains and enriches the lives of
our readers—enthusiasts and lovers of hands-on living.
www.quartoknows.com

First published in 2017 by Voyageur Press, an imprint of Quarto Publishing
Group USA Inc., 400 First Avenue North, Suite 400, Minneapolis, MN 55401 USA.
Telephone: (612) 344-8100 Fax: (612) 344-8692

quartoknows.com
Visit our blogs at quartoknows.com

Voyageur Press titles are also available at discounts in bulk quantity for industrial or
sales-promotional use. For details contact the Special Sales Manager at Quarto Publishing
Group USA Inc., 400 First Avenue North, Suite 400, Minneapolis, MN 55401 USA.

10 9 8 7 6 5 4 3 2 1

ISBN: 978-0-7603-5187-1

Library of Congress Cataloging-in-Publication Data

Title: The Mother earth news guide to vegetable gardening : building and
maintaining healthy soil, wise watering, pest control strategies, home composting,
dozens of growing guides for fruits and vegetables / Mother Earth News.
Other titles: Guide to vegetable gardening | Mother earth news.
Description: Minneapolis, MN : Voyageur Press, 2017.
Identifiers: LCCN 2016038467 | ISBN 9780760351871 (sc)
Subjects: LCSH: Vegetable gardening--United States.
Classification: LCC SB321 .M883 2017 | DDC 635--dc23
LC record available at https://lccn.loc.gov/2016038467

Printed in China